Phillis Wheatley's
Poetics of
Liberation

Phillis Wheatley's Poetics of Liberation

Backgrounds and Contexts

John C. Shields

THE UNIVERSITY OF TENNESSEE PRESS / Knoxville

Copyright © 2008 by The University of Tennessee Press / Knoxville.
All Rights Reserved. Manufactured in the United States of America.
First Edition.

This book is printed on acid-free paper.

Shields, John C., 1944–
Phillis Wheatley's poetics of liberation : backgrounds and
contexts / John C. Shields. —1st ed.
    p. cm.
ISBN-13: 978-1-57233-499-1 (acid-free paper)
ISBN-10: 1-57233-499-1 (acid-free paper)
1. Wheatley, Phillis, 1753–1784—Criticism and interpretation.
2. American literature—African American authors—History and criticism.
3. American literature—African influences.
I. Title.
PS866.W5Z697 2008
811'.1—dc22   2007037805

*For his superior example,
this book is dedicated to*

Henry Louis Gates, Jr.

Contents

PREFACE
ix

ACKNOWLEDGMENTS
xi

INTRODUCTION
Prejudices
1

CHAPTER ONE
A Poetics of Liberation
15

CHAPTER TWO
Wheatley Considered Intellectually Impoverished:
The First 190 Years
43

CHAPTER THREE
Wheatley Intellectually Gifted—Maybe:
The Last 25 Years
71

CHAPTER FOUR
African Origins
97

CHAPTER FIVE
Post-African Religious Development
125

CHAPTER SIX
Intellectual Development
149

CONCLUDING REMARKS
The Dignity of Wheatley's Poems Restored
185

NOTES
193

WORKS CITED AND CONSULTED
209

INDEX
231

Preface

In this text, I have certainly not, in any sense whatsoever, attempted to give what some persons may wish to call a definitive treatment of the complex artist Phillis Wheatley. My effort has been directed only toward provoking a better informed approach to the fascinating problem of trying to "read" the wonderful, but complicated texts produced by our worthy poet and cultivator of the epistolary style. In other words my desideratum has been to facilitate our understanding of Wheatley, that is, to provide a broader, more instructive context within which to attempt to grasp Wheatley's accomplishment.

Who then is Phillis Wheatley? While I believe the work of this accomplished genius defies concrete definition, we can assuredly declare what this artist is not. She is not a derivative imitator. She is not one who wrote white. And she is not a religious dogmatist—although I want to make it clear that I, for one, have never thought of her as anything less than a sincere believer in her idea of the Deity.

If it helps to release her work from the shackles of a heretofore destructive and detested conventional wisdom, then this book, a labor of love, will have been worth the effort. Conventional wisdom be damned! The time has arrived for the genius known as Phillis Wheatley Peters to reclaim her dignity.

As a declared Native American of Oklahoma Cherokee descent, I have, for some thirty years of teaching, always referred to Black Folks and white folks in order to distance myself from each group. Ask any of my students who have sat in my classes over the period named, and they will affirm this practice. After so long a time, I am not going to alter this habit of mind, or practice just to affect the illusion that I subscribe to any present-day fashion of political correctness.

Acknowledgments

As this project has evolved over some twenty to thirty years, I have many to thank. My deepest gratitude goes to my friends and colleagues, Russell Rutter and Eric D. Lamore, whose encouragement and support have sustained me.

To Scot Danforth, acquisitions editor of the University of Tennessee Press, goes my heartfelt gratitude for putting up with me through still another project. Tom Post, publicity editor, has also given me generous treatment. As well, I thank Stan Ivester, managing editor, for his counsel and Robert Land, field editor, for his patience and his thoughtfulness. Many thanks to Thomas Wells.

I would be remiss if I failed to thank the director of my dissertation, "Phillis Wheatley's Poetics of Ascent," R. Baxter Miller. Other colleagues who have exercised a reinforcing effect upon me include the members of my dissertation committee, Percy G. Adams, Bain Tate Stewart, and the late John A. Hansen. James A. Levernier has long supported all my efforts on this project, on *The American Aeneas,* and on many others. Special thanks to Jim. I owe a significant debt of gratitude to several members of my department at the Illinois State University: the late Marna Winters (a favorite friend), Carol Eagan (another favorite friend), Sue Martin, Diane L. Smith, and Irene Taylor. I would also like to take this opportunity to express thanks to Al Bowman (who causes me to believe I matter), our university president; Gary Olson, dean of Arts and Sciences; and John W. Presley, provost and vice president. All these gentlemen have made my tenure at Illinois State comfortable. I should also like to thank Kenneth Earl who helped to prepare the index.

As well there are several repositories across the country, each of which has contributed mightily toward my research efforts regarding Wheatley. On the occasions of having been awarded three National Endowment for the Humanities Summer Seminar grants, I have been fortunate to tap the resources of the University of California at Berkeley (the Bancroft library), Yale University (the Beinecke and Sterling libraries), and Princeton University (the Firestone library). While at

Yale, I also visited Harvard's Houghton Rare Book Library and the Widener repository. But perhaps the best, most accommodating library for my needs was much closer to home; only fifty miles away from ISU are the wonderful collection and staff of the University of Illinois Libraries. Special thanks go to Frederick Nash, formerly head librarian of U of I's Rare Book Room, and Vera Mitchell, librarian of their Afro-American and African Studies Collection. Also at U of I is Diane Pye, who helped me solve problems and made me feel welcome.

At my own Illinois State University Milner Library, many have through the years made me think my research has been important. I shall always be in considerable debt to Cheryl A. Elzy, dean of University Libraries; Patricia Ann Meckstroff, associate professor, Milner Library; Vanetta Mae Schwartz, professor, Milner Library; Elizabeth M. Schobernd, associate dean; and Joan Winters, administrative associate, Milner Library.

In addition to the Summer Seminars listed above, the NEH has generously awarded me a Summer Stipend for the Proposal, "Phillis Wheatley's Poetics of Liberation" in 1983 and a Conference Grant in 1984 for the scholarly celebration of Phillis Wheatley on the bicentennial of her death. Cornell University's Society for the Humanities, under the directorship of Max Black, was kind enough to award me a yearlong fellowship in its Society for the Humanities (1984–85); during this most productive year, I made ample use of Cornell's Olin Library and had the time to develop in detail the early derivation of Wheatley's liberation poetics.

Others who have had a hand in shaping my career and interest in Phillis Wheatley are Frances Ferguson, now of Johns Hopkins University, and Paul H. Fry of Yale University. Paul has ever been a faithful supporter and listener of me and my "weird" ideas.

But the most indefatigable supporter of my interest in Phillis Wheatley has always been Henry Louis Gates, Jr. Words fail me as I endeavor to suggest his constant and positive influence on my career. Perhaps the fact that I have dedicated this volume to him in some measure addresses my indebtedness.

Introduction

Prejudices

PHILLIS WHEATLEY, THE FIRST AFRICAN AMERICAN TO PUBLISH A BOOK ON ANY SUBJECT AND AMERICA'S SECOND WOMAN TO DO SO, IS PERHAPS THE LEAST UNDERSTOOD AMERICAN AUTHOR. Wheatley's life and career are now and always have been filled with controversy. That controversy has largely, but not entirely, been promulgated by the remarks of a single man, Thomas Jefferson. This man was, it must be underscored, not just any man, but one of our nation's central founding fathers, one who many think was the most important (my choice goes to George Washington). The weight of his observations regarding Wheatley and other African Americans, extended in his famous 1785 *Notes on the State of Virginia*, were and have remained incalculably deleterious to our African American citizenry. While I shall leave it to others to assess the enormity of his influence upon African Americans as a whole, I shall endeavor in this book to estimate his negative effect, along with that of other factors, on the life and work of Wheatley. I do so to attempt to allay this prejudice, and others, always with the objective of freeing this brilliant poet's texts from the shackles of opinion which obfuscate fair and balanced analysis of her extant oeuvre.

"Among the blacks is misery enough, God knows, but no poetry. . . . Religion indeed has produced a Phyllis Whately [sic], but it could not produce a poet. The compositions published under her name are below the dignity of criticism" (189). So wrote Thomas Jefferson in his Notes. William H. Robinson, indefatigable scholar and apologist of Wheatley, points out in *Phillis Wheatley: A Bio-Bibliography* that "Jefferson owned a copy of [her] 1773 volume of poems [as did Washington], where her name is spelled correctly."[1] Just prior to making these calculated remarks, Jefferson asserted that "in imagination they [black people] are dull, tasteless, and anomalous" (188). Jefferson's pronouncement here is particularly ironic, given that Wheatley had placed her "On Imagination," perhaps her most intricate poem, squarely in the center of her 1773 *Poems on Various Subjects,*

Religious and Moral. By calling her poems "compositions," Jefferson underhandedly refuses to grant Wheatley the dignity of having created poetry. But this assault is hardly the only indignity this powerful man levies upon this highly vulnerable and wholly innocent artist. For in the phrase, "published under her name," Jefferson dispossesses Wheatley of her intellectual property. Not satisfied that he has done enough damage, Jefferson then wields yet another blow, one we may call his *coup de grâce*, when he declares her "compositions" are "below the dignity of criticism." Jefferson's uncharitable, accusatory "reading" of Wheatley can be explained, at least partially, by the fact that he himself held slaves throughout his long life, and that, despite his caveats against prolonged praxis of the hateful institution, it was, during his lifetime, in his best interests to support slavery.

To have acknowledged Wheatley's capacity to create poetry would have been tantamount to declaring the black race unsuited to serve white folks! In his article on Jefferson in the *American National Biography,* Merill D. Peterson, perhaps the most prolific living Jefferson scholar, observes of *Notes* that "some of its passages—on slavery, on the virtues of husbandry, on religious freedom, on the errors of the Virginia constitution—became so well known that they were said to be 'stereotyped in the public voice'" (11:912). I find arresting Peterson's almost glib listing of slavery among the other subjects named. The temper of Jefferson's racist remarks typifies, nevertheless, the majority of Wheatley criticism from the date of their utterance until very recent times. For that matter, Henry Louis Gates, Jr. has cogently observed that this sort of demeaning attitude shown toward Wheatley exposes the cast of mind adopted by most critics throughout the general history of African American letters. In his words, "The peculiar history of Wheatley's reception by critics has, ironically enough, largely determined the theory of criticism of creative writings of Afro-Americans from the eighteenth century to the present time" (*Figures* 79). The utter contempt in which the principal author of the Declaration of Independence and the soon-to-be third president of the United States held Wheatley's race, her Congregational faith, her authenticity, and subsequently the products of her pen suggests major prejudices that continue to this day to prevent balanced, fair assessment of one of Early America's best poets.

As I have good reason to believe that additional aspersions Jefferson casts on displaced Africans in his infamous chapter 14, "Laws," from the only book he published in his lifetime, *Notes on the State of Virginia,* are not widely known, I shall enumerate several. For example, he claims that Blacks "secrete less by the kidneys, and more by the glands of the skin, which gives them a very disagreeable odour" (187). I submit that, if one of any race were forced to labor daily for stretches of sixteen hours in the cotton or tobacco fields and she or he were not usually given the time or the opportunity to bathe, she or he may very well emit a "disagreeable odour." He continues by asserting "their griefs are transient" (187). "In general, their existence appears to participate more of sensation than reflection" (188); these two observations are then followed by the particularly damning one that, "comparing them by their faculties of memory, reason, and imagination, it happens to be, that in memory they are the equal to the whites; in reason much inferior, as I think one could scarcely be found capable of tracing and comprehending investigations of Euclid" (188). This last remark provoked the Black astronomer and writer of almanacs Benjamin Banneker's skilled defense, made to Jefferson, of his own expertise.

Jefferson next levies an attack on the African American creative imagination, seemingly aimed directly at Wheatley, whose "On Imagination" forms the center piece of her *Poems* and perhaps may be considered the central poem of her entire oeuvre. As Wheatley's theoretics of imagination dynamically impacts her poetics of liberation, it is worth repeating Jefferson's damning assertion that, " . . . in imagination, they [Blacks] are dull, tasteless, and anomalous" (188). Then Jefferson insists, "But never yet could I find that a Black had uttered a thought above the level of plain narration; never see even an elementary trait of painting, or sculpture" (188–89).

Yet a brief glance through Wheatley's *Poems* would have led Jefferson to the poem, "To S.M. a Young African Painter, on Seeing His Works," which clearly identifies a Black painter who had completed several notable canvasses; as well he would surely have discovered "On Imagination." Given Jefferson's allegations, however, that the poems of this volume were "published under her name," he appears to be disposed not to believe her capable of the office of poet, at least as pertained to those works in *Poems*.

Jefferson's discussion here, approaching diatribe ("Perhaps the man doth protest too much"), contrasts remarkably with George Washington's known attitude toward slavery, and especially with his appreciation for at least one poem by Wheatley, her "To His Excellency General Washington" (*Collected Works* 145–46). His letter of appreciation (304–5), has become well known; Wheatley accepted the general's invitation to visit him while he was stationed in Cambridge, at which meeting they spent at least thirty minutes uninterruptedly.

According to Thomas Flexner, one of Washington's recent biographers, the slavery question caused our first president considerable angst in his final years. Unlike Jefferson, who sold his slaves "down the river," locating them more deeply within the slave-holding South in order to pay his large debts incurred largely because of his elaborate lifestyle, Washington planned to free all his slaves. He even went so far as to project in his will provisions not only freeing his slaves, upon the death of Martha Custis, but even to teach them how "to read and write, and [to be] brought up to some useful occupation" (Flexner 4:446). I will venture a guess that Washington's meeting with Wheatley contributed mightily to both his angst and to his decision to free his slaves, as well as to provide them with literacy and skills training. Indeed the encounter with Wheatley put forever to rest the claim that Black peoples were "made for servitude."

Other factors which militate that negative assessment include the perennial, implacable one, her sex; the romantic prejudice against her neoclassical style; the accusation that she was a derivative imitator of Alexander Pope; the totally unfounded notion that she never addressed her Africanness; and the misguided insistence that her alleged piety toward New England Congregationalism did not allow her to grasp the duplicitous position of white folks, whereby the promise of equality for all believers in the next life somehow mitigated the practice of slavery in the present.

Yet another factor prejudicing a fair evaluation of this fine poet, one which work on an earlier book has taught me, surfaces in the realization that, even at our allegedly enlightened multicultural moment, all writers whose works appeared before the "grand transubstantiation" of July 4, 1776—this event eternally dividing all that preceded this date, believed to be only derivative of British culture, from all that came after, construed to be absolutely American—can only be viewed as unoriginal or at best predictive of some greater author or literary movement in the American Renaissance. While one would hope such attitudes have become obsolete, just a glance at "current" critical opinion of the period into which the majority of Wheatley's extant literary production falls indicates that old prejudices are slow to be unlearned.

I offer three of the most respected sources of general critical opinion as touchstones of this persistent and intensely negative appraisal. In the current edition of the *Reader's Encyclopedia of American Literature* (2002), Hayden Carruth and George Perkins (one of this popular work's editors) in their essay "Poetry: Before 1960," characterize Colonial American poetry in this condescending manner: "all of it copied English models, and almost all of it was bad." Early Americans were, according to these two, "rarely knowledgeable in the technical aspects of literary theory" (818). After naming Wheatley and her 1773 *Poems on Various Subjects, Religious and Moral,* they move on to observe that "classicism was never more than a password to the *haut ton,* sincerely as it may have been imitated" (819). Where Wheatley is concerned, I have in numerous fora demonstrated how original and sophisticated a classicist Wheatley truly was. And in *The American Aeneas: Classical Origins of the American Self* I have proved that Early American poets were, for the most part, anything but derivative of any other literary sources.

William Harmon and C. Hugh Holman, in their now famous *A Handbook to Literature,* declare American poetry from 1765 to 1790 was "largely neoclassical, with the influence of Pope dominating" (441); while naming such male poets as Trumbull, Freneau, Hopkinson, Dwight, and Barlow, they make no mention of Wheatley or of any other woman poet. In his magnum opus, *From Dawn to Decadence: 500 Years of Western Cultural Life, 1500 to the Present,* Jacques Barzun, regarded as America's master historian and cultural critic, quips that "In original literary works, the colonies in the 18C were plainly deficient." Although he does call Anne Bradstreet and Edward Taylor "poets of merit," he lists no other Colonial American poets, nor does he pause to recognize Wheatley or her achievement (406).

Just so, Barzun polishes off Colonial American poetry, in less than three lines of text. From this brief, but telling survey and despite cries from several of my Early American Studies colleagues that the status of the field is "doing just fine, thank you very much," Early American literature, at least the poetry of that literature, is anything but "fine." This demonstrable prejudice toward Early American poetry which calls into doubt that poetry's originality seriously complicates any judicious attempt to evaluate Wheatley's achievement in this genre. One of the central objectives of this investigation is assuredly, as I have remarked, to explode these several prejudices and thereby reveal the substantial worth of this significant poet's work. Lifting of these prejudices allows Wheatley's readers to understand her to be a committed poet who constructs in her work an entirely original theory of poetry—a poetics of liberation—which looks directly toward British Romanticism. Now, however, we must begin to unpack the 220 or so years of almost universal misreadings and misunderstandings which encumber the life and particularly the work of this vast creative artist.

While the days when authors were dismissed out of hand because of their color are receding into the past (though they have regrettably failed to disappear), an entirely opposite attitude obtained in

Wheatley's Boston of the pre–Revolutionary War era. As Robinson and Mukhtar Ali Isani instruct us, Wheatley's first proposal for a volume of her poems, made in Boston a year and a half before the publication in London of her *Poems on Various Subjects Religious and Moral*, was rejected by the citizens of her "adoptive" New England hometown, for racist reasons.[2] Immediately upon publication of *Poems* in 1773, the nine known reviews appearing in London all express surprise, even amazement, at the poet's color but none addresses the content of the poems.[3] In short, imposed on Wheatley is the dubious distinction of being considered a mere curiosity. Commentators of the past, nevertheless, have no monopoly on failure to examine the content of Wheatley's verse; Cheryl Walker, for example, in *The Nightingale's Burden: Women Poets and American Culture before 1900*, can assert, without quoting even a phrase from her work, "Her poetry seems distracted both from black and from female experience."[4] Walker's strategy, as is the practice of so many of Wheatley's commentators, is to rely on the opinion of other Wheatley commentators, thereby confirming this limited and ill-informed view to be categorical.

Quite the contrary, Wheatley's poetry articulates poignantly the Black experience of her day as subsequent pages will demonstrate, and her predicament as a struggling author is certainly representative of the plights of other female authors of her time. Regrettable to relate, however, is an incidence of racial prejudice leveled at Wheatley by one of her fellow Boston women authors, Jane Dunlap. In her 1771 *Poems upon Several Sermons*, these homilies delivered by the voice of the Great Awakening, the Reverend George Whitefield, Dunlap notes in her "Introduction" that, "Several there are, who has [sic], in a public manner, both from the Pulpit, and Press, testified their esteem of, and regard for that most worthy Man."[5] One of these testimonials was Wheatley's most famous, often reprinted, elegy, "On the Death of The Rev. Mr. George Whitefield." Dunlap specifically cites Wheatley and her elegy in the first poem of the nineteen-page pamphlet: "Shall his due praises be so loudly sung / By a young Afric damsels virgin tongue: / And I be silent and no mention make / Of his blest name, who did so often speak."[6] Not only is there resentment here for Wheatley's race, but at least envy, in the phrase, "so loudly sung," of the apparent success of Wheatley's poem. It is to Wheatley's credit that she never, in her poetry, addresses such personal affronts (though she does often speak of the predicament of her race), whether originating from women or men. Instead, she chooses to manipulate the facts of her sex and race for her advantage.

Indeed, the two factors which advanced her international success in the 1770s more than any others were first that she was a black author and second that she was female. Rather than disguise or deny either of these facts, she allowed a vivid and, we are told, accurate engraving of her likeness[7] to serve as frontispiece to her 1773 *Poems*. Hence she not only announced to the world her color but her sex, and in as bold a manner as was then possible. Wheatley, as did Martha Brewster before her, even had to bear the indignity and embarrassment of having her credibility as a female writer, as well as a Black slave, challenged in public. While Brewster was forced, in Boston of 1757, to attest her capacity to write "by publicly paraphrasing a psalm into verse,"[8] Wheatley had to submit to having her poems "read by the best judges" who in their infinite wisdom found "the declared Author was capable of writing them" (7). A document was drawn up to mark this event, which apparently took place in Boston on October 28, 1772. Because, according to John Andrews, a signatory of Wheatley's letter of attestation and one of the coterie of merchants which included John Wheatley, Phillis's master, the earlier attempt to publish a volume based on the "Proposals" of February 29, 1772, was unsuccessful "by reason of their [the Boston white folks] not crediting the performances to be by a Negro." Including some sort of attestation became a necessary condition toward securing a London publisher, hence leading to the poet's humiliation before the "Wheatley Court," this phrase recently applied by Nellie McKay. In the article in which McKay uses this phrase, she argues, with much cogency, that the "Wheatley Court" remains in session. Indeed, this authenticating exercise endured by Wheatley set the precedent for some two hundred years of similar exercises endured by both sexes, designed to ascertain that African Americans are capable of creating not only literary texts equal to those of any by white folks, but to establish superlative achievements within the other arts. Jefferson's damning of Wheatley of course declared that even a group of white, supposedly well-educated males did not and could not, to his satisfaction, provide sufficient evidence for asserting the equality of Black people within the arts.

In *The Black Atlantic: Modernity and Double-Consciousness*, Paul Gilroy, in ostensible attitudinal agreement with McKay, asserts that the occasion of the Wheatley court must have caused quite a shock to "Phyllis [sic] Wheatley's startled inquisitors that fateful day in Boston when the power of imaginative writing was first enlisted in order to demonstrate and validate the humanity of black authors" (152). Note the spelling, "Phyllis," which recalls Jefferson's scorn.

Gilroy gives as his source several pages in Henry Louis Gates's *Loose Canons: Notes on the Culture Wars*; yet a quick check into Gates's text ascertains that Gates never spells Wheatley's given name with a "y." For that matter, Gates never, in any of his writings about our poet, gives Phillis a "y." Gilroy, nevertheless, consistently spells Phillis with a "y" in *The Black Atlantic*, both in the text and in the index. Phillis Wheatley herself *never* spelled her name with a "y." So I am left to wonder why Gilroy adopted this spurious spelling. Why did not the readers of his manuscript for Harvard University Press, the house of publication, or indeed the editors of that press, correct this misspelling?

Copyrighted in 1993, this book's misspelling is well nigh inexplicable, given the plethora of sites where her name appears correctly spelled. I am forced to conclude that Gilroy and his associates simply do not hold our black poet in enough regard even to attend to a proper spelling of her name and that, when her name or example proves useful to them, they use her merely as a tool in their socio-anthropological undertaking. The relegation usage she subsequently undergoes in Gilroy's presentation bears an unfortunate resemblance to that regrettable humiliation she surely felt when she found herself "examined by some of the best Judges" (vii). This sort of relegation usage of Wheatley characterizes a major portion of the commentary about this poet from her death until quite recent times.

However unintentional Gilroy's initial humiliation of Wheatley surely must have been (one may be tempted to explain this "y" spelling as a sort of modernization), certainly the humiliation imposed on her because of her gender has *never* been unintentional. Concerning the issue of Wheatley's gender, as Paul Lauter put it so well some twenty years ago in the centennial number of *PMLA*, this statement still resonating with considerable validity, "most of my colleagues are as yet unmoved by, even somewhat antagonistic toward, the enormous energy generated by women's studies (and black and ethnic studies) practitioners" (Lauter 420). Prejudice provoked by Wheatley's sex alone remains a formidable obstacle to any attempt to judge her work objectively. Wheatley herself, despite preceding years of opposition to her assumption (some would doubtless advance "presumption") of the role of poet, and not to mention the centuries of hostility which followed her, never apologized for her sex or for her color. In "On Recollection" the poet asks the mother of the muses to inspire "Your vent'rous Afric in her great design,"[9] once again identifying here, as at many other points in her writings, both her race and her sex. In her 1784 elegy on the Reverend Samuel Cooper, she writes these intensely personal lines, "The hapless Muse, her loss in Cooper mourns, / And as she sits, she writes, and weeps, by turns" (153); this minister baptized her in 1771. Wheatley seems to me to be proud of her womanhood, and especially of her Black womanhood. The story she tells in her poetry is that of a struggling but undaunted young Black woman who creates works that will be read almost exclusively by a white audience; in short, her work speaks of a Black woman determined to survive, with dignity, as an author in a white world.

Once again Jefferson is hardly alone in challenging Wheatley's struggle to speak with a dignified, authentic voice. When not accusing her of derivative, slavish imitation, hence denying her the possibility of embodying an authentic, sincere voice, many of her commentators allege she "writes white." On the one hand, for example, undergraduate anthologies of American literature continue to claim that her work is derivative of Alexander Pope and other British authors, while on the other hand, S. E. Ogude, in "Slavery and the African Imagination: A Critical Perspective," asserts that Wheatley and some of her contemporary Black writers, Francis Williams, Ignatius Sancho, and Olaudah Equiano, "were unable to transcend the ideological chains clamped on their imagination by the European societies in which they lived" (22). Although I will not here attempt a defense of Williams, Sancho, or Equiano, all of whom have recently received much positive critical attention, I certainly do intend to demonstrate not merely that Wheatley does, in fact, transcend in her work all barriers her white oppressors would have imposed on her had they the intellectual acumen, but that Wheatley's poetic imagination was very probably the most liberated of her time.

Another old saw that challenges her authenticity comes from those who censure her for not writing in accord with some particular interpretation of the Black Aesthetic, whose primary emphasis in literature by Black authors resides in the common bond shared by all displaced and/or oppressed Black people—the brotherhood of a people oppressed. This predicament in Wheatley studies was partially justifiable back in the days when the Wheatley canon was much reduced, that is, when few of her extant works appeared to address the issue of slavery. At the present time, however, such a charge is quite simply no longer tenable. Even twenty-five years ago, no substantial declaration of Wheatley's liberation poetics would have been possible; today it is. And one final word about prejudice against this poet's authenticity is in order, though it appears to me so obvious it should not require the saying. In "Slavery and the African Imagination," Ogude remarks of Wheatley, "When she wrote of Africa and of the African, she totally, completely ignored her feelings and went to the Bible and the Puritan imagination of New England for her models" (22). What this investigation accomplishes makes groundless just this sort of immoderate claim. So intense and so personal is Wheatley's construction in her poetry of a liberation poetics that it has been overlooked. Wheatley wrote out of no African tradition of displacement and oppression, though of course she was herself both displaced and oppressed. The only other African writer of merit of whom she was aware was the Roman playwright Terence, whom she names in "To Maecenas." To fault her, ever, for not writing in such a tradition, which is Ogude's point—that her imagination is the slave imagination and not the African—is quite simply illogical. Rather than following any such tradition, Wheatley is in the process of forging one. As for the charges that Wheatley's faith is strictly derived from the Bible and thereby limited by Christian dogma, and that her imagination follows the limits of New England Puritanism, subsequent examination proves both changes to be unfounded.

In what may be considered the first essay in which Wheatley's poetry is treated as poetry rather than as some tool in a socio-anthropological argument concerning racial issues, "Personal Elements in the Poetry of Phillis Wheatley" (1953) emphasizes the poet's sincerity in her attempts to record her authentic voice. The author of this perceptive and penetrating essay, Arthur P. Davis, one of the editors of the now "classic" collection, *The Negro Caravan*, points out that Wheatley sometimes inserts in her poems identification of her race for "no obvious reason" and is "Far from being shy about her race and native land" (A. Davis 193). In addition, Davis examines her determination to achieve excellence as a poet and her sincere religious commitment to her idea of God. Later critics have seldom been prompted by her religious consciousness so to respond. Consistently misspelling her name "Phyllis" in his entry "Literature: Poetry," prepared for the 1981 *Encyclopedia of Black America*, Donald B. Gibson finds her "so devoutly religious that she probably felt that the poetic expression of faith was far more significant than writing about personal concerns" (519). Yet in a fine essay on her elegies, Mukhtar Ali Isani has correctly called Wheatley's productions in this potentially artificial genre the "genuine effusions of a feeling heart" ("Phillis Wheatley and the Elegiac Mode," 208).

Though I will assuredly not take issue with Isani's assertion of Wheatley's sincerity of feeling, I must with the position taken by Gibson and others.[10] I will begin by asking the question, "How more personal can one be than to pursue in one's poetry the poetic expression of faith?" I am certain Gibson's oversight in logic here is not at all caused by any lack of intellect; rather, I find myself once again observing that few have been willing, so it seems, to take seriously this committed poet's works. We see several elegies addressed to New England clergy and assume Wheatley was, must have been, a pious, practicing Christian evangel. Do we ask in what context such allusions, paraphrases, and clergy are placed?

One case in point: one of the elegies is addressed to Samuel Cooper, who baptized Wheatley (as noted) and whom she vividly recalls in one of her poetry's most personal passages. Yet who was this man Cooper who apparently became Wheatley's spiritual advisor following the death of the orthodox Congregational minister, Joseph Sewall? Samuel Cooper was one of the most liberal, even latitudinarian, ministers of his day. Probably only his great personal charm and gifts for sterling conversation prevented him from being accused of heresy. After the death of her first spiritual advisor, Wheatley inculcates within her poetry and prose a gradual relaxation of early orthodoxy and subsequently evolves a humanistic perspective. I do not at all mean to suggest she became one wit less committed in her private religious consciousness, rather that she became much more tolerant and enlightened, in the best sense of this word. Seeing Wheatley's poetry not as the product of an absolutely orthodox Christian but as the psychomachic creation of a soul in pursuit of her own idea of God suggests this poet was hardly a parrot of white man's theology as has heretofore been thought; in fact, this view frees her poetry from the chains of dogma.

Another "dogma" that too often puts off readers of Wheatley's poetry is a literary one, associated with the term "neoclassicism," the style in which she casts many of her poems, but not all. While trying to make a case for her derivative status as a poet, one commentator maintains that her poems "relied on a repeated store of classical allusions," as if the use of classical elements is somehow indicative of a stylistic weakness. To be sure, this commentator does not demonstrate how this weakness manifests itself, only that it is surely there and the accusation alone is enough to prove guilt. Donald Gibson sounds the voice of the majority when he asserts:

> Her poetry is neither original nor highly imaginative, yet it reveals a thorough grasp of the diction and form of conventional neoclassic verse. As were so many of her contemporaries, she was content to follow the practice of the master of the heroic couplet, Alexander Pope. (519)

To Gibson and to such others as Larry Neal and Baraka, early promulgators of the Black Aesthetic, even to look like a product of the Western tradition, in which tradition Wheatley's neoclassicism would, on the surface, appear firmly to situate her, is to commit an unpardonable sin—conviction by mere appearance; and Gibson's use of the word "master" in association with the white Pope casts an unmistakable pall over all of Wheatley's work! The truth of this poet's reliance on elements taken from the ancient cultures of Greece and Rome is that such borrowings, or better in her case adaptations, first attest Wheatley's sophistication as a writer and second advance the case for the gradual relaxation of her religious orthodoxy. Third, and of crucial importance to assessment of her value as an artist, is the irrefutable case these adaptations make, as we shall see, for the establishment of her originality.

In her attempts to utilize literary elements of classical culture, Wheatley was subscribing to and forwarding the most pervasive tenet of American classicism, which was to manifest a return to the classical authors to seek close guidance in matters of form and content. While this practice was by Wheatley's time on the wane in Britain, in America it was in the full blush of expression—though after the American Revolution, American classicism would undergo a rapid decline as Americans determined to reject all things European and especially those British. Unfortunately for American classicism, this hostility extended to the institution of the Latin grammar school. Such major shapers of post–Revolutionary War culture as Noah Webster and Benjamin Rush determined to recast the former "British" colonial culture into what they argued would quickly become exclusively and identifiably *American*. The Latin grammar school was targeted most immediately because it was the most visible manifestation of the now-detested British colonialism and therefore had to go. What happened was not to be as severe as what these "soldiers" of the new culture attempted to accomplish. Indeed, Latin did not entirely disappear from the scene; it merely receded from the public view, becoming the province of the intellectual elite—a condition which, in the final analysis, was not much altered from the pre–Revolutionary War days. As all citizens were now to have access to public education, what changed radically was that classicism became, in the American public arena, forever denigrated (see chap. 7, "The Radical Shift in Discourse," in *The American Aeneas* for a full explanation of this phenomenon). As Wheatley died in December 1784, she did not live long enough to witness this "war" against classicism.

Wheatley's Boston of the 1770s did indeed celebrate Pope, great zion of the Augustan achievement in literature; many writers such as Mather Byles, probably the best-known Colonial poet prior to 1770, strove to emulate Pope and his Age. Wheatley made her own unique contribution to these efforts. Contrary to the popularly held position that her poems embody little more than exercises in slavish imitation of Pope and British literary virtues, Wheatley's poetry demonstrates her unique capacity first to grasp with amazing speed and agility the literary mode of American classicism but then to reshape this mode in such a way that it becomes the vehicle for expression of her liberation poetics.

This book proposes, then, to facilitate a fair and balanced reading of Phillis Wheatley's life and work by providing a more thorough account than has heretofore been attempted of the backgrounds and contexts out of which her oeuvre evolved. Such an account must delineate the stages of her career, explicate her liberation poetics, investigate her African origins, explore her practice of the elegy (her most frequently recurring poetic subgenre), reclaim her religious consciousness (i.e., her idea of God), establish her intellectual ambience, and describe her political world. While individual chapters are devoted to Wheatley's liberation poetics, to her African origins, to her religious consciousness and to her intellectual ambience, the tenets of her political world, of her elegiac praxis, and of the stages of her career so integrally interface with the other three areas named that they may be best taken up within the subsequent treatment where and when necessity dictates.

As the above discourse has pointed out, moreover, the commentary surrounding Wheatley's life and work has, for the most part, proven so deleterious to any just evaluation of this sensitive artist that detailed investigation of the tenor of this commentary, an investigation which ferrets out this commentary's numerous missteps, is quite simply required. Accordingly, I examine in two separate chapters what are perhaps the most consequential among these commentaries, wherein the first chapter treats the first 190 years and the second analyzes the last 30 or so years. I make no effort to be comprehensive; rather I select that commentary which, in my judgment, has most centrally problematized a balanced reading of our worthy subject. I should like to note that, recently, commentary we may identify as criticism has begun to appear, though some of this "criticism" demands serious scrutiny, if only because of its abuse of Wheatley's texts.

CHAPTER ONE

A Poetics of Liberation

To be sure, Wheatley was unique in her Boston of the early 1770s in her sheer capacity as a literary artist. To recognize her as such, however, is merely to begin constructing a list of the several ways in which she was unique. She was a literate slave who wrote poetry, many examples of which found their way into print. She was an American female author, only the fifth one, after Anne Bradstreet, Jane Turell, Martha Brewster, and Jane Dunlap, whose works were "allowed" to appear in print. When she arrived in Boston in 1761 to be "sold on the block," she had relentlessly thrust upon her New England Congregational Christianity and was summarily informed by her white captors that whatever faith she brought with her from West Africa was grievously erroneous, false, and absolutely intolerable. So much for an inaccurate perception that Early Americans were universally tolerant of non-Christian religious consciousnesses! Even so, she discovered in her early adulthood that these same white folks, who taught her that freedom was obtainable by all in the next world, were determined to keep her in chains in the present. The contradiction was not lost on one so intelligent and so sensitive. Politically, she sought equality with much courage and boldness yet never quite achieved it. One explanation for this displaced poet's great fondness for the highly structured and rigid balance of the heroic couplet may well be the simple suggestion that such structure and balance gave Wheatley in her poetry a semblance of the order she so ardently sought in the real world. Finally, however, not even American classical poetics, with its staunch, much desired command of order, could serve Wheatley adequately in her poetry.

The poetry itself, nevertheless, promised the most realizable opportunity for expression, for space, for freedom. For in her poems, Wheatley could be herself, even though at times she had to do so subversively. She could criticize her fellow Bostonian "Christians" at the age of only fourteen for giving lip service to one point of view, yet practicing another; in other words, she admonished, "Remember, *Christians, Negros,* black as *Cain,* / May be refin'd and join th'angelic train" (18). At a later time, she could as well query of her fellows in power whether the American victory of independence would include the gift of freedom for her much-oppressed race; in an elegy on the death of the patriot Major General David Wooster, who died on May 2, 1777, from wounds received in combat against the British, Wheatley celebrates the armed revolt against Britain by the emerging nation's citizens and then exclaims in the voice of her dying subject:

> But how, presumptuous shall we [mortals] hope to find
> Divine acceptance with th' Almighty mind—
> While yet, O deed ungenerous! They [the citizens] disgrace
> And hold in bondage Afric's blameless race?
> Let virtue reign—And thou accord our prayers
> Be victory our's, and generous freedom theirs.
>
> (149–50)

Having already been manumitted by the eighteenth of October, 1773, Wheatley unabashedly here pleads that those white folks who have formerly been "ungenerous" will find in their victory over their own oppression the generosity to free even their own slaves. Fair assessment of such a writer, writing against apparently insurmountable odds, demands other than an exclusively formalist approach.

To begin to understand the work of this complex artist, one must attempt to reclaim as much of that complicated world which could, and did, promise this poet freedom certainly in the next world, and sometimes cruelly titivated her and her enslaved Black brothers and sisters with the remote possibility of political equality and freedom even in the present, at least while such titivation could bring into the Revolutionary War new hands which could carry and fire a musket. Both the British and the Americans, of course, offered such a promise to Black men. My strategy, therefore, is to attempt to recapture as much of the intellectual, political, and social world which touched Wheatley and is indicated in her work as is in my poor power to accomplish. I do not, in any sense, propose to rehearse an elaborate history of ideas during this period; Henry May's *The Enlightenment in America* and Robert A. Ferguson's "The American Enlightenment: 1750–1820" admirably accomplish just this task. Although I do depend especially on May's book and the work of many others whenever it proves instructive to do so, I on some occasions, simply because of her condition as a female slave, strike out into forays of my own in order to establish my understanding of the literary and artistic milieu peculiar to Wheatley. This attempt I carry out by exploring Wheatley's sources at appropriate points when examination of specific threads of Wheatley's thought or analysis of a particular poem or poems demands such expansion, or when Wheatley's handling of an idea or poetic form may be better understood and appreciated when compared to the approach taken by one of her contemporaries.

To be more specific, my approach to Wheatley's work, both her poems and her letters, but especially her poems, demands interdisciplinary pluralism. Close reading of this artist must address the issues that recur in her work, those of historical moment, personal biography, the literary aesthetics of her day, psychology, politics, sociology, and philosophy as well as of the history of ideas and on some occasions the principles of classical art and music. The focal point is always, nevertheless, the products of her pen, the poems and letters. A principal thesis of this investigation is to demonstrate that the work of this Black female poet is throughout permeated by the dialectic of slavery versus freedom. A variety of tensions characterize this dialectic, including the conflict between things as they are (wholly unethical) and things as they should be (preferably ethical); the real world and the world in Wheatley's verse; the horizontal rhythm of her almost stubborn heroic couplets and the vertical aspirations of the content of Wheatley's verse (toward realization of her idea of freedom and of her God); her life as it is lived and the life of her imagination as recorded in her poetry; the objective as opposed to the subjective; the dispassion of the heroic couplet's repetitive rhythm versus the enthusiastic passions of sublimity, one of her major subjects; the mass of society, composed of freemen, and the New England minority of Wheatley's enslaved Black brothers and sisters; the relatively inflexible dogma of New England Congregationalism tempered by the so-called Enlightenment (now understood as deceptive—i.e., tolerance for some but hardly for all); and finally but most crucial to this intelligent and perceptive slave is the dialectic of disorder versus order, manifested by the chaotic society of Boston, which preached universal salvation for all but which held its Black minority in bondage, set over and against the implacable and certain arrangement of Wheatley's regular line and the secure world of her poems. This dialectic of freedom and slavery achieves resolution for Wheatley in the act of writing itself—in her energic capacity to create a satisfactory, free world in her poems.

Definitions and Methods

What results from her efforts is a poetics of liberation. As identification and definition of this unique theory of poetry should precede any attempt of readers reading Wheatley—that is, of readers trying properly to situate this poet's texts—an extended investigation of Wheatley's liberation poetics follows this section devoted to methods and definitions. I do use several terms, however, which if not delineated at the outset could be misleading. And I ardently wish to avoid the charge brought not so long ago by the president of the Andrew W. Mellon Foundation, John E. Sawyer, against what he perceived as the narrow aridity of much contemporary scholarship which he deplores as all too often characterized by "hyper-specialization and self-isolating vocabularies."[1] Because of their sometimes controversial applications, therefore, such terms as "classicism," "neoclassicism," "preromanticism," "elegiac mode," "sublime," "imagination," and even "moderate enlightenment" and "secularization" require explanation.

Particularly problematic for serious readers of literature are the terms "classicism" and "neoclassicism." So as not to exacerbate the problem, by general "classicism" I understand the contribution to Wheatley's poetics made from her knowledge and use of the mythologies, literatures, and histories of ancient Rome and Greece; and by "neoclassicism" I refer to a literary preference for such conventions as adoption of the relatively closed grammatical structure of the heroic couplet, for delight in the sense of design and symmetry, for restraint and distrust of imagination, for close attention to prescribed and generally accepted rules of composition, and above all for a resolute preference for order, each of which may be said to have characterized in Britain the Augustan Age or the Age of Dryden and Pope.[2] Particularly pertinent to consideration of Wheatley is a trenchant observation made by Rene Wellek that "English classicism [what I am here calling neoclassicism] seems most closely related to the Enlightenment, to realism, though on occasion it has affinities with what could be called rococo in its artistic style."[3]

As practiced by Early Americans, however, classicism takes on striking characteristics which we may identify as peculiarly American. The characteristics of this American classicism I have detailed in the fourth chapter of *The American Aeneas: Classical Origins of the American Self*. While Wheatley and all other Early American authors were certainly influenced by British neoclassicism, she was clearly more indebted to American classicism. Those tenets of American classicism that impact her poetics include a palpable determination to consult classical sources, usually bypassing British ones, in order to construct her own versions, for example, of pastoral, pastoral elegy, and epic; a steady practice of displaying an affinity for American authors, in Wheatley's case, particularly for the prolific American poet Mather Byles, nephew of Cotton Mather, who inherited his famous uncle's extensive library and who lived across the street from the Wheatleys; a healthy, energetic commitment to experimentation in matters of form and handling of subject; a conscious construction and appropriation of literary forms for her own individual needs; a candid resolve to discover to herself an identity, this undertaking proving to be problematic for Wheatley but nevertheless defining to the personal poetics she builds; and an obvious adaptation of the Vergilian virtue of pietas, devotion to the gods/God, to family and friends, and to country. As well, I should add that, as is so often the case in African American letters, music plays a vital role in this young poet's productions; at times she even suggests, in such poems as her hymns to the morning and evening, and in "Thoughts on the Works of Providence," the call-and-response motif, so characteristic a quality among African American artists. Wheatley's peculiar handling of the delicate details of prosody—for example, her use of syncope—moreover, bears resemblance to Wellek's rococo stylistics.

Another often misunderstood, perhaps abused term, is "preromantic." To be sure, any thought, author, or work appearing prior to the historical period in English letters commonly framed by the years 1798 to 1832—the period for the continent is considerably broader—and known by the name the Romantic Period, must be considered preromantic. My concern with Wheatley's writings, however, is hardly one restricted by chronology. The center of interest herein is always the manner by which this young American poet manipulates and arranges the subjects of nature, the individual, and human freedom; the genres of the lyric, the ode, the elegy, the pastoral, the pastoral elegy, and the epic; the aesthetic ideas of imagination and sublime; and the urgencies of discovering the possibilities of the self through inward meditation, of aspiring to grand achievement, and of establishing her identity in a world which labeled her pariah. I concur with Marshall Brown who, in his most helpful study *Preromanticism*, has counseled that we should avoid thinking of preromanticism as a predisposition toward Romanticism, but rather we may find it more useful to think of the preromantic as "that which designate[s] styles [both of form and of thought] different from yet dialectically related to" Romanticism (2).

In the case of Wheatley I am going to argue that certain of her poems and letters display not a preromanticism per se, but a romantic demeanor. While on occasion, in her emphasis on nature, on the lyric and on the horizontal/vertical pattern (tension) of her poetic lines, Wheatley's work gives evidence that she does set up a dialectical relationship with her successors which we may identify as a preromantic pattern, I am much more concerned to establish that at certain moments in her work, Wheatley demonstrated that she is decidedly a romantic. The most dramatic and dynamic manifestation of her romantic behavior occurs in her "On Imagination." As the nineteenth century draws to a close, that is, as the sensibility of this period approaches expression of the romantic temperament, we should not be surprised that such authors as Gilbert Imlay, John Stedman, Thomas Clarkson, and Johann Blumenbach in their published writing quote from this poem. As many intellectuals from Voltaire and Mary Wollstonecraft to the named Blumenbach and even to Samuel Taylor Coleridge were actually attending to this poem and others by Wheatley, I will argue that Wheatley's romantic demeanor intersected with the evolving thought which led to various European Romanticisms.

Those German romantic novelists, such as Goethe, Schlegel, and Hoffman, for example, who, as Gerhart Hoffmeister observes, "depict the constant struggle of the emerging artist versus the constraints of an alienating society that suffocates his desire for freedom" (14), had much in common with Wheatley as maker of heterocosms in "On Imagination" in reaction to her Boston's "alienating society." In other words I submit that Wheatley, at least in a few of her poems, became more than a mere curiosity or freak sideshow and that some of her texts participated in striking ways in the intellectual phenomena we call the several romanticisms of Europe, specifically those of Britain, Germany, and France.

In her praxis within the elegiac mode, Wheatley's sphere of influence was decidedly close to home, where home may be defined first as her native Gambia and second as her adoptive New England. In the "Prologue" to her now-classic *The Elegiac Mode*, Abbie Findlay Potts observes, "the eye of the elegist was first caught by . . . , the sun, and thus duly oriented to a life of discovery on earth."[4] Certainly the sun, the most frequently recurring image in Wheatley's poetry, has captured the eye of this young Black poet, and the prevailing sense of discovery or *anagnorisis* which characterizes all her poetry constitutes one of the most provocative reasons for pursuing this investigation. The elegiac mode—the quest for understanding of life's transience and its evanescence, the expression of anger because of loss, the tension between a vertical thrust toward explanation and a horizontal pull downward to a world "Oppressed with woes, a painful endless train" (152)—permeates Wheatley's prose and verse. Always and usually despite seemingly overwhelming obstacles, Wheatley consistently, determinedly, and heroically clings to the much more satisfactory world she creates in her poetry.

Another characteristic of elegiac praxis, as Peter Sacks has ably pointed out, is the elegists' aspiration to seize a moment of public power. Wheatley's recurrent publication in the elegiac mode precedes a virtual flood of elegiac performances by women in Revolutionary War America, strongly suggesting that Wheatley's example encouraged such female performances, thereby ascribing to Wheatley the distinction of serving as a progenetrix of productions in this genre. Contrary to stubbornly held critical perspective, then, she does not merely construct elegies upon demand and as external circumstances dictate; she composes her eighteen or so elegies, indeed most of her extant, mature poems, as self-conscious exercises or speculative meditations aimed toward discovering to herself, and to her serious readers, the meaning of life's vicissitudes and contradictions, both of which she received in disproportionately large sums.

Two of the most powerful aesthetic ideas at her disposal for expressing her poetic world of sun and earthly discovery were the imagination and the feeling of the sublime. Given the counsels of Pope and Henry Home, Lord Kames, among many others, to employ this allegedly lowest mental faculty, the imagination, always with caution and moderation, along with the admonitions of Locke and, closer to home, those of Jonathan Edwards, that imagination or fancy could lead the unwary to hell, it is indeed surprising to find that in one of her finest poems, "On Imagination," Wheatley, alleged voice of Congregational orthodoxy, has subversively elevated this faculty to "leader of the mental train" (67). According to her conception, imagination is no longer relegated to the function of mere image-maker. In this same poem which she has placed in the center of her 1773 *Poems,* she rebels against accepted tradition first by raising this power of the mind, at least insofar as poetry is concerned, to the level of Wordsworth's "reason in her most exalted mood," that is, to the level of the poet's reason or poet's power of creativity, and second by consciously subordinating fancy as agent of imagination. In this single poem, Wheatley has thereby enacted a pivotal moment in the history certainly of American aesthetics, but even of Western aesthetics as well. The question arises inexorably, and especially in the midst of so many injunctions to the contrary, whence has she derived this revolutionary posture? One may suspect such British poets as Young, Collins, Thomson, and Akenside to have well played their roles here—and in fact each has. Beyond this British influence, however, is a heretofore unacknowledged American revolt in literary aesthetics, including many soldiers, often paralleling and even aligning itself with America's evolving political revolution, about which much more is to follow.

Virtually inseparable from her grasp of the function of imagination in her poetics is the action of the sublime or of the enthusiastic passions. As was the case with imagination, Charles Chauncy, Jonathan Edwards, and others among the Colonial American establishment (not to mention Pope and Kames in the British) persistently recommended the tempering restriction of judgment over the potentially boundless and hence inevitably erroneous (so it was held) force of the passions. At one point in her poetry, Wheatley forcefully describes the action of imagination in sleep as a time when " . . . ideas range / Licentious and unbounded o'er the plains, / Where *Fancy*'s queen [i.e., imagination] in giddy triumph reigns" (47). It is clear that this poet does not subscribe to the conservative attitudes of Edwards, Chauncy, Pope, and other supporters of the traditional disdain toward imagination and the feeling of the sublime. In her pursuit of what David Morris has justifiably identified as the religious sublime, Wheatley most candidly reveals the object of her quest, freedom. Liberation for her fellow Americans, for her Black brothers and sisters and finally for herself is the subject of her poetry and prose. And it is in her expression of the acts of imagination and the sublime that she most fully realizes that liberation.

Finding white man's religion inadequate as practiced by those who continued to hold her in bondage and by the New England society which supported that bondage, Wheatley recognizes the advantages to her of a relaxed orthodoxy, eased somewhat by the moderate enlightenment and by the sort of secularization which Meyer H. Abrams has termed "natural supernaturalism." Generally, the Enlightenment refers to that Western intellectual and philosophical movement beginning in the seventeenth century but culminating in the eighteenth and characterized by celebration of the apparently limitless capacity of reason to explain the complexities of the universe and man's existence within that universe, by the ostensible infallibility of deduction and observation, and by the prevailing notion, actually an inevitable deduction if one fails to question the validity of the first two premises, that human beings possess the ability to attain individual and even cultural perfection. Of course this alleged perfection did indeed not lead those of the mid-eighteenth century on either side of the Atlantic summarily to condemn the hated institution of slavery, a reality assuredly not lost on our poet.

Henry F. May further qualifies what he calls the moderate enlightenment as that which "preached balance, order and religious compromise" and occupied a prominent place in the minds of literate Colonial Americans from 1688 (marking the introduction into British government of constitutional monarchy) to 1787 (the year the loosely constructed Articles of Confederation were rejected as a fit mode of government for the United States).[5] Whereas this moderate enlightenment helped to make possible Wheatley's turn away from absolute orthodoxy, at the same time observation of the white man's conduct toward her as a Black female, first, and then as a Black woman author quickly taught her that the juncture of man's perfectibility must surely reside in some far-distant, presently unrealized though glorious future and that balance, order, and religious compromise had best be pursued within her poetics of liberation. In other words, this tension between the way the white world in America perceived itself and the way things really were *for her* presented to this resourceful but grievously injured writer one of her most poignant challenges. From another perspective, then, one may conclude that, regarding failure of the Enlightenment's "reason" to realize that enslaving one's fellows was inherently horrific, Wheatley can readily be observed to reject this pretension to "balance." That is, while the moderate enlightenment, on the one hand, did encourage Wheatley to exceed traditional boundaries *in thinking,* on the other, this same so-called balanced attitude refused to release her body from bondage.

The central means by which Wheatley came to resolve this dilemma was through her syncretization of the religious consciousness she recalled from her African origins with the Christianity and the classicism she absorbed from her New England captors. In his *Revolutionary Writers: Literature and Authority in the New Republic, 1725–1810,* Emory Elliott proposes that, along with the restrictions of Puritanism, of survival in a new wilderness, and of a stifling attitude toward imagination, "it was the moral burden of the Enlightenment" which prevented late-eighteenth-century American writers from leading "the Western literary world into the Romantic era."[6] I submit these very restrictions are those against which Wheatley revolts in her creation of a liberation poetics. I further submit that Phillis Wheatley was the most revolutionary writer of her day and that her confrontation with dogma, with the issue of slavery, and with traditional literary theory constitutes not a retreat, but an offensive.

How Wheatley executed these issues in her poetry is quite simply more complex than few if any have heretofore been willing to consider. When I have maintained in conferences and in published articles that only now, after over two hundred years of commentary, are we beginning to recognize this phenomenon of complexity in Wheatley, I have received reactions of disbelief, masking implacable judgments (conventional wisdom) that, if nothing indicating a serious mind capable of working on many levels has turned up by now, surely nothing can be found. Perhaps, goes the implication, like Wheatley, Shields has fallen victim to an overactive imagination. Taking recent instruction from Linda Kerber, nevertheless, we find that, regarding past artistic productions *by women*, the creators of these products "were rarely evaluated for complexity, either in their thoughts, deeds or relationships" (Molho and Wood 42). The current climate is, then, despite sentiment to the contrary, friendly toward the sort of investigation I am pursuing. And it is precisely in this climate, wherein women artists must now be recognized as possessing intellectual and artistic capacities equal to those of any man, that I offer this revaluation of Wheatley's life and work.

One indication of Wheatley's complex artistry emerges when we acknowledge that, like male poets, her writing career should be granted stages of development. As in the case of her male counterparts, the poet examined undergoes an early development whose products are called juvenilia, then moves into a period of maturity, and finally falls into what is often referred to as a season of decline. While Wheatley's career does fall into three stages, they do not conform precisely to the pattern described, if only because dying at the age of thirty-one, she did not live long enough to experience a decline of her powers. Wheatley's career does, nevertheless, manifest a period of juvenilia, during which she constructs poems that are largely occasional, commemorating sundry events significant to her such as the Boston Massacre of March 5, 1770, and the repeal of the Stamp Act, or elegies celebrating the deaths of persons she knew, or panegyrics, or meditative poems on such subjects as atheism, deism, virtue, and friendship. The tone and temper of these pieces appear to suggest one of conciliation to Boston's white audience. The poems on atheism (1767) and deism (1767), for example, strike me as attempts to convince Congregationalists, especially someone like Joseph Sewall, principal minister of Old South Church and son of Samuel Sewall, the diarist, that she was fit to be baptized in the church and perhaps even to become a communicant and member. In an attitude of bitterness which anticipates Boston's rejection of her February 29, 1772,

"Proposals" and which denies her former conciliatory pose, Wheatley composed in December 1771 the first version of "On Recollection," perhaps her most accusatory and acrimonious poem. This poem signals a palpable turn inward toward probing contemplation and self-absorption. That is, the poetry of her mature period was pressed upon her by an unsympathetic and finally unresponsive public consisting almost entirely of white folks.

The poems composed between the end of 1771 and her manumission shortly before October 18, 1773—including "Thoughts on the Works of Providence," "To Maecenas," the hymns to the morning and evening, "Isaiah LXIII. 1–8," "On Recollection," "On Imagination," "Ode to Neptune," "A Hymn to Humanity," "Niobe in Distress . . . ," "To S.M a Young African Painter," "A Farewell to America," and "Ocean"—all display a clear, self-conscious preoccupation with aesthetics. And it is largely in these poems that she explicates her subtle and subversive liberation poetics, perhaps as a means toward survival. For those who may wish to hold that this turn inward toward aesthetics may well serve as yet another refusal to deal with the issue of slavery, I will argue that this interior emphasis constitutes Wheatley's strategy for dealing with her own enslavement *and* with that of her Black brothers and sisters. As well, it is perhaps no accident that during this year and seven months Wheatley becomes most emphatically Romantic.

After her freedom was granted, Wheatley's poetry becomes characterized by a candid and open aggressiveness, a now blatantly public stance. Heretofore critics of Wheatley have treated her poems as if they were written in some sort of continuum without demarcations of discriminate mental and aesthetic perspectives. For example, one critic, writing in 2001, perhaps thinking he is exploding the theoretics of what he calls recent "exercises in advanced hermeneutics" (Carretta and Gould 178), asserts that Wheatley's "To a Gentleman of the Navy" "is less subversive" when we contextualize its content; I would argue that, by late October 1774 (over a year after Wheatley's manumission), this poet no longer feels many of the constraints slavery had imposed on her and therefore has little or no motivation to write in her earlier subversive mode. The point here is that recognizing that this poet's career may constructively be divided into the three stages, those of juvenilia, interior maturity, and post-manumission, moves Wheatley's serious readers a long way toward clarifying explication of her sometimes difficult texts.

This Black woman writer refuses after her manumission to retreat behind a mask. She confronts the issues head on. In doing so she continues even today to alienate many of her readers, of which Thomas Jefferson was merely one of the first. I suspect the fact that she eventually does not wear the mask of subversion may be one of the factors which confounded and confounds many of her readers. Her early readers could and did simply dismiss her rebellious writing, both that which is subversive and that which is candid, as "below the dignity of criticism," but significantly even Jefferson was forced to deal with her, as readers have always been so forced from her 1773 *Poems* until today. Albeit dismissal manifests the consensus of critical temper regarding Wheatley, this dismissal now more and more frequently yielding to a grudging acceptance, ironically, she *must* at the very least *be* dismissed. Perhaps we have not yet forgiven her for stating the obvious as did Melville after her—that slavery is man's foulest crime; it is a fact that we have seldom taken her voice seriously.

The Derivation of a Poetics of Liberation

Before we begin to examine how Phillis Wheatley's poetry and letters display a poetics or theory of liberation, we must state as clearly as possible the tenets that constitute this liberation poetics. Since no less an authority of Black American history than John Hope Franklin asserts of Wheatley without qualification that "She was not concerned with the problems of Negroes or the country" (106) and since this sort of summary dismissal typifies the general disdain in which her life and work are currently held, by many, if not by most, the mere suggestion that this author could have formulated any theory of freedom, much less the notion that the central subject of all her work is, emphatically, liberation, must seem at the very least improbable if not quite simply preposterous. It is in the heat of such a pervading attitude that I propose we proceed deliberately and with caution. In direct contradiction to apparently overwhelming wisdom to the contrary, Wheatley has consciously constructed in her works both a poetics and a praxis of liberation in which she boldly and directly addresses the problem of freedom as a possibility, not only for the human race at large, but for those suffering the indignity of oppression at the hands of others and most particularly for those Black men and women serving their equals in the most wretched, most cruel condition as slaves, among whom for a significant time numbered the poet herself. This poetics evolves rapidly from 1770 until it reaches mature expression in such poems as "Thoughts on the Works of Providence," "To Maecenas," "On Recollection," and "On Imagination." In other words, this theory of liberation becomes recognizable upon the appearance of her 1773 *Poems* and before her manumission prior to the October 18, 1773.

One means toward accomplishing cautious procedure in enumerating the tenets of this poetics is to adapt four of Mortimer Adler's five kinds of Freedom, upon which he extensively elaborates in his monumental two-volume *The Idea of Freedom,* a project that has never been superseded,[8] to the conditions out of which the author has constructed her liberation theory and praxis. Such an approach should prove profitable and appropriate toward giving solid instruction on how to discover within her writings Wheatley's pervasive treatment of this most vitally human principle. Indeed, this approach illuminates Wheatley's choice of vocation as poet, her motivation for choosing that vocation, her discovery of the intense moral responsibility which she determined must characterize her role as poet, and finally her focusing on deliverance as the primary subject of her poems and letters. Although Adler treats five categories of freedom, Wheatley participates only in four; these categories define her vocation, motivation, role, and subject. Adler's fifth category, collective freedom, refers to that sort of freedom which such political theorists as Marx, Engles, Comte, and Bakunin maintain describes the social evolution of the entire human race toward a potentially inviolable, necessary societal construct presently, though inchoately manifest, so these theorists hold, in some of the planet's recently failed communist nations.[9] The idea of collective freedom does not address the predicament of an individual's need to be free (in fact, it denies such a need) and is, therefore, not applicable to Wheatley.

The other four, however, are in varying degrees applicable to her predicament and are subsequently considered. Also considered from time to time in the ensuing discussion are several of the remarks of Charles Secondat, the Baron de Montesquieu, on the subject of slavery, for three reasons: first, because in his *The Spirit of the Laws* published in 1748 he shows himself at least to be in topical agreement with each of these four categories of freedom; second, because Montesquieu was, among Americans, "The most often praised and cited of the major French figures" prior to the outbreak of the American Revolution;[10] and third, because in *White over Black: American Attitudes toward the Negro, 1550–1812* Winthrop Jordan identifies him as a frequently cited authority among antislavery advocates during Wheatley's time[11]— hence Montesquieu's *Spirit of the Laws* was probably known to this young Black intellectual.

Adler identifies the four applicable types of freedom as circumstantial self-realization, acquired self-perfection, natural self-determination, and last the freedom of political liberty. These four categories he elucidates in the following manner: the circumstantial freedom of self-realization "is possessed by any individual who, under favorable circumstances, is able to act as he [or she] wishes for [her or] his own good as he [or she] sees it"; acquired self-perfection "is possessed only by those men [and women] who, through acquired virtue or wisdom, are able to will or live as they ought in conformity to the moral law or an ideal befitting human nature"; the freedom of natural self-determination" is possessed by all [persons], in virtue of a power inherent in human nature, whereby [one] is able to change [her or] his own character creatively by deciding for [himself or herself] what [she or] he shall do or shall become"; and finally political liberty, which is actually a variant of circumstantial freedom, "is possessed only by citizens who, through the right of suffrage and the right of juridical appeal against the abuses of government, are able to participate in making the positive law under which they live and to alter the political institutions of their society."[12]

Since Wheatley was first a slave and second a woman, many readers may decide, too quickly, that this author does not viably participate in any of these types of freedom and subsequently may well think the exercise of dragging her through denial after denial fruitless, unnecessary, and perhaps the dramatization of some grotesque cruelty. It is easy to forget that imaginative artists enjoy license not available to the rest of us, as well as to lose sight of the fact that the New England attitude toward slavery just prior to and during the Revolution was considerably more tolerant than that characterizing the South, not even coming close to the sort of restrictive atmosphere that dominated South Carolina, for example, where atrocities toward Blacks were open and thought necessary to enforce order. In *American Odyssey, 1607–1789*, a history of Colonial America, Paul Lucas generalizes that "The institutions of northern slavery never took on the edge of cruelty and ruthlessness that developed elsewhere, simply because blacks and whites lived too closely together."[13] At the other extreme, I mean never even to suggest that Wheatley relished being a slave; no one was any more aware of slavery's assault on the very nature of humanness than this Black writer. I challenge the skeptical, then, to allow themselves to be dissuaded from their initial position and to be convinced that this talented, sensitive, and intelligent writer knew full well the power of the pen and that she often wielded that pen as a sword.

If the circumstantial freedom of self-realization allows "any individual . . . under favorable circumstances . . . to act as he [or she] wishes for his [or her] own good as he [or she] sees it," then certainly Wheatley, for whom circumstances were sometimes favorable, exerted a measure of this category of freedom. It is true that at least until mid-October of 1773 she functioned under the restraint of slavery, yet she was permitted, because of her capacity to compose apparently pleasing verses, certain privileges, such as the power to comment on the events—deaths, weddings (as, e.g., in her nonextant "Epithalamium to Mrs. H—"), personalities, ideas, and most significantly the politics—of her times. Even while her readers were aware of her race and her sex, the Boston public countenanced the appearance of some of her poems, especially her elegies. The elegy on the death of George Whitefield, for example, was printed on both sides of the Atlantic and brought her to the attention of Selina Hastings, Countess of Huntingdon, whose chaplain Whitefield had been and whose patronage eventually made possible the publication of Wheatley's *Poems on Various Subjects, Religious and Moral* in 1773. If one considers these privileges to have been granted even on the grounds that this young Black woman poet was merely a curiosity, it still remains that words from her pen did appear in print, that she did address an audience, and that she did receive responses from this audience, some favorable and some not so favorable.

One of the least positive responses she received to the publication of several of her poems was the rejection of her 1772 "Proposals" for a volume. This rejection, so it has been demonstrated, was made on racist grounds.[14] But this enterprising young author overcame this seemingly formidable obstacle by seeking and securing another environment of approval, the less racist (though perhaps no less curious) environment of the Countess of Huntingdon's England. So we see then that, even though no book was possible in 1772 Boston, or for that matter in 1779 when the author published another "Proposal" for a second volume of poems and on this occasion including a few of her letters, a book was possible in London of 1773; in other words, she was able, under more favorable circumstances, to translate her wish into action—but with this restriction, she must modify or soften some of her poems for the London audience. The fact that she did make such changes, ones that toned down, for example, her charges of British tyranny over the American colonies, should alert her present-day readers to the realization that this poet's work moved in accord with the revolutionary philosophy.

Wheatley's predicament surrounding the delayed publication of her first volume must have brought about conditions that were extremely disconcerting to her. Discovering that the Boston public's hostile attitude would not permit her the realization of her own good, to paraphrase Adler's circumstantial freedom of self-realization—we must note that she had written poems in celebration of this environment's building revolutionary philosophy, which her London editors saw as potentially unacceptable to that city's readers—she did find her objective advanced in London but only with decided restraints, the first already pointed out above. Second, her color and sex could be attested but then both required immediate defense—this appearing as the now well-known letter of attestation signed by the leading citizens of Boston, among whom were Governor Thomas Hutchinson, Charles Chauncy, Mather Byles, James Bowdoin, and John Hancock, in which its signers verify the authenticity of Wheatley's authorship. This circumstance is now usually referred to as the Wheatley court. This letter of attestation is preceded by a brief portrait of Wheatley's life written by her master, John Wheatley, in which much, too much (as such ability appeared somewhat miraculous), is made of this young slave's ability to master the English language. It was doubtless thought these forms of verification were necessary to the sales of the book, and William H. Robinson has pointed out that her credibility as an author had been challenged earlier by several of those among the Boston citizenry who had rejected her first, 1772 "Proposals."[15]

As a consequence of so much "to-do," Wheatley was viewed by most from the first as more of a curiosity than as a serious artist; hence her most ardent desideratum was then and has continued to be uncharitably thwarted. At the early age of thirteen or fourteen, she could begin a poem with this arresting pronouncement, "While an intrinsic ardor prompts to write" (5). Few critics of the past or of the present have been willing to grant this poet the right to her "intrinsic ardor." For over two hundred years, Wheatley's right to the circumstantial freedom of her acceptance as a serious artist has been almost constantly violated. Perhaps she has finally earned her day of fair, unbiased judgment. We may well be advised to pursue whence came to Wheatley this "intrinsic ardor." How can we explain such intensely declared motivation to compose? Indeed, how could one so young know so definitively her vocation? Such critics as June Jordan and Donna Landry claim that the phenomenon of a Black woman poet in late-eighteenth-century Boston "was," according to Jordan, "not natural" (97). Landry states with greater conviction: "It was certainly not 'natural' that a female slave wrote and published 'verse' in colonial Boston" (252). Not "natural" to or for whom?

The spectacle of a literate Black woman who could create impromptu poetry was assuredly for the time and place a phenomenal occurrence. But to this adolescent girl, just six or seven years deracinated from her native land, the composition of poetry, particularly elegies, was no phenomenon and was emphatically natural. Both Jordan and Landry comply with those who hold with Margaretta Oddell, perhaps Wheatley's oldest and most thorough biographer (to date), that *all* Wheatley recalled of "the place of her nativity" was the memory "that her mother *poured out water to the sun at his rising*" (Oddell 12) and that her mother then "prostrat[ed] herself before the first golden beam [of the sun] that glanced across her native plains" (Oddell 13). These remarks came from the recollections of white folks. We have no record of what memories Wheatley may have shared with her Black compatriots, such as her husband John Peters or with her "black soul mate" (a la Bill Robinson), Obour Tanner. The connection to Tanner, several years Wheatley's senior, was so close that I will hazard a guess that Tanner may have crossed the Atlantic with our poet and may have served the young girl as her protector on the horrific Middle Passage.

At any rate, the point here is simply that the only memory of her homeland Wheatley *cared to tell her white captors* was that related by Oddell. Arriving at Boston at about the age of seven or eight (judged so by the circumstance of her having begun to cut her adult teeth) and carrying with her the mind of a genius, this brilliant girl surely brought with her a virtual flood of memories about her native Gambia, including the most salient one that, as we shall learn in the chapter on Wheatley's "African Origins," in Gambia the delivery of elegies was the office of women. As Paul Gilroy puts it in *The Black Atlantic*, what some may construe to be an unnatural preoccupation with death in Wheatley's *oeuvre* is hardly surprising, for a defining "rapport with death emerges continually in the literature and expressive cultures of the black Atlantic" (198). Could it not then be that, for this sensitive manipulator of elegiac expression, the vocation of poet came as leaves to a tree? Not to allow Wheatley the benefit of her African origins is to rob her of the agency which, perhaps more than any other, led her to choose her vocation as poet.[16]

Having found her vocation, possibly as Houston Baker has suggested as early as the publication of her first poem in 1767,[17] she would now settle upon parameters which would define her role and function within that vocation. One of those parameters that confronted her was whether or not she would address the central issue of her day—the American struggle for independence; the solution to this problem would determine irreversibly first the primary motivation for her role as poet and second the principal content of her poems. Since she quickly came to terms with her role as poet amidst the developing revolutionary philosophy and since she did often compose poems which specifically celebrated that revolutionary mode of thought, it is appropriate to break the order of Adler's four freedoms and to treat now the effect on Wheatley's liberation poetics of political liberty. One would expect that, since Wheatley did not enjoy the status of citizen, if not by virtue of her color then because of her sex, and could not, therefore, exercise any "right of suffrage and . . . of judicial appeal against the abuses of government," surely her contribution here would remain severely limited. Such is hardly the case. This poet writes poems which amply show not only that she is politically aware but that she is politically and diplomatically active. And it is this political activism which helps to direct her toward discovery of her role as poet.

When we recall a few of the events of the times, we can better understand why Wheatley became caught up in the marvelous expectations and promises of the American adventure in freedom. John Hope Franklin informs us that "Negro patriots [among whom numbered Phillis Wheatley] saw clearly the implications for their own future in their fight against England." In fact, it was as early as 1766 that many "were seeking their freedom in the courts and legislatures." For example, in January 1773, "a group of 'many slaves' asked the General Court of Massachusetts to liberate them 'from a State of Slavery.'"[18] Other such petitions followed during the next several years, culminating in the famous *Walker v. Jennison* case. In *The Negro in Colonial New England*, Lorenzo J. Greene tells us that Walker's victory over his master Jennison in 1783 at Worcester, Massachusetts (less than fifty miles from Wheatley's Boston), "finally resulted in the emancipation of slaves in Massachusetts"[19] *in that same year.* Greene also notes that not only was a slave allowed to sue before the New England courts but he could even make a contract with his master "and, once the agreement was formally made, the master was as firmly bound as if he had contracted with a freeman."[20]

And of course, as alluded to earlier, it must not be forgotten that Black American men made a substantial military contribution to the American Revolution: "in all it is recorded," writes Greene, "that some 3,000 Negroes [from New England] fought in the American ranks during The Revolution."[21] Not all of these men subsequently were freed, but many did, in fact, become free men in New England. So even though Wheatley did not herself serve the revolutionary cause in a military capacity, she did witness that members of her race were so allowed and even urged to do so, and were able to exercise the capacity of bringing suits to the courts and of making contracts.

Although political liberty for blacks carried with it severe restrictions, such freedom was by no means absolutely denied them, as was indeed the case for less fortunate Blacks in the Colonial South.

Concerning the freedom issue for her sex, the period from about 1770 to the ratification of the U.S. Constitution in 1789 (went into effect in March of that year) was one of no little ambiguity. Recall that Abigail Adams, three months before the signing of the Declaration of Independence, importuned John Adams, her husband and our second president, to "Remember the Ladies" "in the new Code of Laws which I suppose it will be necessary for you to make" and thereby "be more generous and favorable to them than your ancestors." Adams continues in these emphatic words:

> Do not put such unlimited power into the hands of the Husbands. Remember all Men would be tyrants if they could. If perticular [sic] care and attention is not paid to the Ladies we are determined to foment a Rebelion [sic], and will not hold ourselves bound by any Laws in which we have no Voice, or Representation. (A Adams 1035)

As we may readily observe, Abigail's attitude here bespeaks one who has given the matter of suffrage for women considerable thought; the assertion, "we are determined to foment a Rebelion," indicates that this forceful woman has engaged in written and perhaps verbal discourse with others of her sex, those such as Mercy Otis Warren (we know, for example, that Abigail did write Mercy about this very letter to her husband) and Judith Sargent Murray, regarding women's participation in government.

The point here is that, in those fluid times, the promise of freedom held out substantial hope for women, as well as for those persons enslaved. Therefore, when Wheatley speaks of political liberty in such poems as "America," "On the Death of Mr. Snider Murder'd by Richardson," "To the King's Most Excellent Majesty," "To the Rt. Hon. William, Earl of Dartmouth," and later after the publication of *Poems*, "To His Excellency General Washington," "On the Death of General Wooster," and "Liberty and Peace," she is not addressing some remote, even vacuous and unrealizable improbability; she is, according to the female intelligentsia of the time, describing a thoroughly plausible and fully realizable probability, the dignity of political liberty for *all* human beings.

Deciding that she must pursue the calling of poet and responding to her personal predicament as slave and to the shared predicament of her fellow Black brothers and sisters along with those of her sex,

Wheatley strikes out boldly in her writings as a political activist who was more than merely eager to assist the promises of freedom for all which she believed attended the American revolutionary cause. Wheatley now faced the dilemma of defining to herself and to her audience the boundaries of her role as poet. This role she determined along the lines of self-imposed restrictions in accord with the moral law promulgated by the American revolutionary philosophy—that is, the often preached but seldom practiced principle that all human beings are created equal. Wheatley acquired this "moral law" or "an ideal befitting human nature" in her lifelong quest for wisdom, and here I speak of wisdom in the broadest, most humanistic terms as that mode of behavior practiced by those who refuse to be constrained by the limits of any dogma, whether religious or political, but live their lives by the moral imperative which teaches that *all* humans, not just a select few, ought to be allowed to lead their lives by that same adogmatic imperative.

In Wheatley's first published poem, "On Messrs. Hussey and Coffin" (1767), she describes God as "the Great Supreme, the Wise," in terms not strictly Christian but which seem to call up the most exalted classical ideas of God. In the later "Thoughts on the Works of Providence," she writes, "That *Wisdom*, which attends *Jehovah's* ways, / Shines most conspicuous in solar rays" (20). And in a letter to John Thornton of October 30, 1774, she concedes to the renowned philanthropic London merchant," . . . it is a difficult task to keep in the path of Wisdom" (183). It is out of this intense commitment to the pursuit of humanistic wisdom, as well as from her highly developed religious consciousness, that Wheatley derives her equally intense commitment to the moral law that all persons should be free. This quest for wisdom recurs with such frequency that it requires careful contextualization and therefore demands a large portion of a subsequent chapter.

In his *The Spirit of the Laws*, Montesquieu had earlier written, "In democracies, where they are all upon equality . . . slavery is contrary to the spirit of the constitution: it only contributes to give a power and luxury to the citizens which they ought not to have."[22] In a discussion of Crispus Attucks, the Black leader of the rebels in the Boston Massacre of March 5, 1770, John Hope Franklin observes, "It was a remarkable thing" to the white citizens of Boston "to have their fight for freedom waged by one who was not as free as they."[23] More specifically, then, Wheatley's dilemma was how to be an honest poet amidst so much contradictory idealistic theory and hypocritical behavior. She summarizes her predicament best in a letter of February 11, 1774, to Samson Occom, the celebrated Mohegan Indian minister, where she passionately declares, "How well the Cry for Liberty, and the reverse Disposition for the exercise of oppressive power over others agree I humbly think it does not require the penetration of a Philosopher to determine" (177). She decides to adopt the role of uncompromising, though not necessarily didactic, moralist. As we have already seen, she lashes out directly at alleged Christians who refuse to grant Black folks souls. And in the same letter to Occom, after invoking a harsh judgment from God "upon all those whose Avarice impels them to countenance and help forward the Calamities of their *fellow* [emphasis mine] Creatures," she asserts, "This I desire not for their Hurt, but to convince them of the strange Absurdity of their conduct whose Words and Actions are so diametrically opposite" (177).

Her moral role as poet, however, does not originate exclusively from her observation of contradictory behavior and from her experience of Boston Congregationalism. As the political arena not only promised her no formal office but also gave her no instruction (at least no immediate instruction) in poetics, and since eighteenth-century New England Christianity offered her little advice toward a poetics—though it did provide her several examples of poet-ministers who would play crucial roles in the development of her poetics—this young poet appears to have turned to classical sources for valuable counsel in constructing the boundaries of her role as poet. Before we outline Wheatley's debt to classical thought for certain aspects of her role as poet, in fairness to a consideration of Adler's four categories of freedom and indeed in order to provide a just perspective of Wheatley, we must examine how her acquired skills as poet—her knowledge of English and Latin, of many of the best authors of each language, and of English prosody—indicate an interdependence of the categories of circumstantial and acquired freedoms. To be sure, Adler acknowledges at many points in his two-volume treatise the inevitable overlapping and interplay at certain moments of particular categories.

In Wheatley's case, this interplay is particularly notable in the skills she acquired that were essential to the practice of her craft. It was these acquired skills, after all, which along with her own innate talent and strength of character, empowered her to participate in the American struggle for independence. Considering the South's enforcement of the death penalty upon anyone caught teaching Blacks to read, one may well ask how it was that this poet came by these skills. Lorenzo Greene describes the opportunity for education among Blacks in New England as extremely liberal. For that matter, many owners considered it necessary to educate their slaves, if only to make them more valuable assets. "As a result," Greene observes, "many of the New England Negroes received elementary instruction in writing, reading, and arithmetic as well as industrial training."[24] Even so, it is prudent to observe that, as William D. Piersen cautions in *Black Yankees: The Development of an Afro-American Subculture in Eighteenth-Century New England,* not all New Englanders were as generous or liberal. Indeed, says Piersen, one Chloe Spears's master, for example, "forbade her instruction; for as she reports, if she should learn to read she would find herself 'under penalty of being suspended by thumbs, and severely whipped; he said it made Negroes saucy to know how to read'" (45). Earlier in the century, Montesquieu had reasoned, insensitively, that if it should be argued that slavery has been beneficial to the slave as "his master has provided for his subsistence, slavery, at this rate, should be limited to those who are incapable of earning their livelihood. But who will take up with such slaves?"[25] Obviously, then, Wheatley took the fullest advantage of this liberal attitude.

One of the avenues that the advantage of education opened for her was acquaintance with classical thought and literature. Classicism's contribution to the establishment of her role as poet was determinative. Wheatley gives more specific attention to the Muses and their sovereignty over poetic afflatus or inspiration than any other author writing in English during or before her time that I can recall. For in her poetry, it is no exaggeration to observe that she summons their authority more frequently than she does that of the Christian Deity. In other words, what may be rightly construed as mere convention, certainly in most of the English and American authors of the seventeenth and eighteenth centuries, becomes for her a necessity toward the carrying out of her perceived responsibility as poet. In her two epyllia or short epics, "Goliath of Gath" and "Niobe in Distress . . . ," for example, the invocations alone run to 8 and 10 lines. When we remember that Milton's invocation in *Paradise Lost* and Pope's for *The Rape of the Lock* (a mock heroic form which works largely through exaggeration) are markedly shorter and that Wheatley's two epyllia comprise only 222 and 212 lines, the young Black American poet, whom countless critics among her celebrants as well as among her detractors would never accuse of not knowing the neoclassical conventions, clearly attaches more than simply conventional importance, at least in these two poems, to invocation to the Muse or Muses.

The readily observable fact is that this practice pervades her poetry. "On Recollection" is a 50-line poem dedicated to Mnemosyne, Mother of the Muses, in which Wheatley analyzes the function of memory, especially to the poet in the act of poésis, while "On Imagination," another poem of similar length in which she treats the act of poésis per se, contains a 4-line invocation, and even several of her elegies call upon classical muses. To assemble the numerous other illustrations of this practice would hardly further the point here. What is essential to Wheatley's aspiration to polish and perfect her role as poet, however, is her understanding of the function of the Muses. In *The Oxford Classical Dictionary,* George M. Hanfmann and John R. Pollard delineate that function as giving the poet "scepter, voice, and knowledge," or to put it another way, the Muses bring "to humanity [through the artist] the purifying power of music, the inspiration of poetry, and divine wisdom."[26] That Wheatley was not only aware of these functions but fully subscribed to them is evident in the following lines which open "Goliath of Gath":

> Ye martial pow'rs and all ye tuneful nine,
> Inspire my song, and aid my high design.
> The dreadful scenes and toils of war I write,
> The ardent warriors, and the fields of fight:
> You best remember, and you best can sing
> The acts of heroes to the vocal string:
> Resume the lays with which your sacred lyre,
> Did then the poet and the sage inspire.
>
> (31)

To this young poet the function of the Muses is eternal; that is, the same force which instilled the ancient Hebrew prophet Samuel with the inspiration to sing the saga of David and the giant now comes to her to assist in her reshaping of the biblical narrative. Wheatley has here brought about a unique syncretization of classicism and Judeo-Christianity. But more to the point, she has learned her role as poet not from the ancient Hebrew prophet, but from the classical example. This example has taught her that the poet can and must infuse her poems with the practice of good prosody, but that she must also interweave her lines with "the purifying power of music"; that the same poet must compose only from the honest source of sincere inspiration; and finally, though most crucially, that the poet is obligated, by the responsibility of this role given her from the Deity and made known to her by means of her natural and acquired capacity to represent in verse music's purifying power and inspiration's honesty, to convey to her readers whatever insight she receives concerning the workings of divine wisdom. As well it should not be lost on Wheatley's readers that these powerful muses are of the feminine gender. It is principally from this perspective that Wheatley defines her role as moral teacher;

contrary to Emory Elliott's insistence, then, that the moral burden of the Enlightenment stifled American creativity and imagination, at least in the case of this woman poet, acceptance of that burden freed her to discover the noble subject of her poetry—liberation.

The seat of Wheatley's insightful though inexorable discovery of her poetry's subject matter resides firmly within her own determination to be free. As she phrases it simply yet eloquently, "... in every human breast, God has implanted a Principle, which we call Love of Freedom; it is impatient of Oppression, and pants for Deliverance" (177). How can any feeling, human soul fail to be moved by the unadorned power of this definition of natural, human dignity? Montesquieu had at midcentury recognized the institution of slavery as a wholly artificial one that perverts and does violence to the natural freedom and equality of all humanity. In his words, he wrote:

> The state of slavery is in its own nature bad. It is neither useful to the master nor to the slave; not to the slave, because he can do nothing through a motive of virtue; nor to the master because by having an unlimited authority over his slaves he insensibly accustoms himself to the want of all moral virtues, and thence becomes fierce, hasty, severe, choleric, voluptuous, and cruel.[27]

Although Montesquieu's observations of the slave master, every painful and disgusting one of them sounding much like the pointed analysis Frederick Douglass would make in the middle of the nineteenth century, did indeed obtain in the Colonial South (a condition that King Cotton was soon only to exacerbate), we have seen that masters in New England were enjoined by certain restrictions. Montesquieu's insistence that masters exercised "an unlimited authority" over their slaves implies a right to life over death; Greene tells us, however, that New England masters had no such right. "As a person," so Greene writes, "the New England slave had a right to life; in short ... the slave had the same right to life as had the apprentice." To put it bluntly, "if a master killed his slave he was answerable as if he had killed a freeman."[28]

With the just noted right to life and the previously observed rights to redress wrongs (the condition of slavery itself, for example) in the courts, to draw up contracts, and to receive at least a modicum of education, Wheatley experienced a life, which allowed her to receive more than a modicum of education, wherein the attitude toward slavery was a mitigating one—not the harsh severity Montesquieu describes which was gathering force in the South. And yet, it would indeed be a mistake, even given the gentle treatment she allegedly received at the hands of the Wheatley family, ever to conclude of this black woman what Montesquieu does of well-treated slaves: "Men grow reconciled to everything, and even to servitude, if not aggravated by the severity of the master."[29] In her recognition of freedom as a natural right of all persons, Wheatley forever denies any such acquiescence! Quite the contrary, she sees herself and all other human beings as products of nature; but most of her Black brothers and sisters are at present constrained to function under the artificial and perverse institution of slavery. This acknowledgment once left her frustrated for her own freedom and still, after October 1773, leaves her longing to see *all* persons free; so she determinedly and heroically turns her pen toward securing realization of liberation for all, not just for white Americans. In other words, she enthusiastically embraces liberation as the subject of her writing.

To paraphrase Adler's freedom of natural self-determination, Wheatley, having discovered the right to be free as intrinsic to human nature, embarks upon a creative struggle to become free. By creative struggle I refer specifically to her use of her capacity as a writer to determine her poetics and praxis of liberation. In her poetry in particular, she presents to her readers the example of one who has decided white man's religion, his politics, and even his poetics do not suffice. I think Houston Baker is absolutely correct when he asserts, "I feel that the poet remained both outside and above the general culture of her age."[30] Her poetics of liberation proves the validity of Baker's assessment. Indeed the discovery of a satisfactory mode of writing—that is, of a compelling motive for the creation of poetry—is not to make jolly entertainments for her white captors, but to enable this highly moral, gifted, but frustrated artist to be free and consequently, by her example, to enable her readers to participate in that liberation.

In the sheer process of writing a poem, Wheatley doubtless experienced the dynamic, autonomous power inherent in the act of creation. This creative power is observable in "On Imagination," a poem central to her poetics and the one in which she identifies imagination as the poet's reason. "Thy various works," so the poem opens, "imperial queen [i.e., imagination], we see, / How bright their forms! . . . / Thy wondrous acts in beauteous order stand" (65). So, in the hands of the poet, imagination selects the forms and breathes life into them through "wondrous acts" of creativity. In other words, Wheatley appears to be highly exhilarated here because of her power over words and their arrangement; for as a creator she was almost always in absolute control of her materials. When she was not, as was the case in her catechistic poems, in the last twelve lines of "Niobe in

Distress . . . ," whose composition was "the Work of another Hand" (112), and in certain of her revisions in the 1773 *Poems* made in preparation for a London audience, her efforts bear identifiable restrictions in the areas of immediate (though not ultimate) subject matter: in catechistic pieces the case for her Christian stewardship must be strong, for example, and in the volume British tyranny must be muted.

Nevertheless, it is in such poems as "On Imagination," "To Maecenas," "On Recollection," and "Thoughts on the Works of Providence" that she achieves the condition of uncaused causer (Adler's phrase) or self-conscious initiator and controller. She chooses the subject matter of these poems, the tools for expressing that subject, the form in which to cast it, and most crucially she chooses the poetics, for all her poems, by which she allows them to become enactments of her poetic process. It is in the last named poems, the poems of her maturity, that this poet identifies the most exalted expression of her liberation poetics; for it is in the representation of the imagination and its concomitant the sublime that she achieves poetic representation of absolute freedom. The power of her imagination enables her, along with her readers, to discover, even if only temporarily and in the moment of philosophic/aesthetic contemplation, "Th' empyreal palace of the thund'ring God": "*We* [emphasis mine] on thy pinions can surpass the wind, / And leave the rolling universe behind" (66). The most effective tool, the most powerful means, toward accomplishing realization of her idea of God—and significantly her idea of God in this poem appears to be a syncretized version of Zeus and Christian Jehovah—is imagination blended with the feeling of the sublime.

It must not be forgotten that, in the England or in the America of 1773, neither imagination nor the sublime was accepted as yet by the literary establishment as legitimate means toward expression. Nor must it be forgotten that identification of imagination as reason, not merely the playful faculty of poets but reason as ordering principle, was tantamount to literary heresy and at the very least an act of rebellion. Yet these tools, imagination and the sublime, are Wheatley's most emphatic means toward representation of her poetics of liberation. The present-day reader may well be confounded that she was not prevented from committing such heresy. A Black woman slave, she was allowed to follow the profession of poetry, strongly suggested to her by her memory of her African heritage, and thereby to act as she wished for her own good and for the good of others; she was permitted to embrace the love of freedom as her principal motive for composition, having been compelled to this motive by her own predicament as slave, by the plight of her Black brothers and sisters, and by the promise of the American adventure in freedom; she was able to develop her role as poet along lines that exceeded the bounds of tradition, hence allowing a slave and a woman to seek wisdom which consequently empowered that woman to prescribe justly and accurately to an unreceptive, predominantly white audience the virtues and the realities of the moral law; and she was granted (or she seized) the opportunities to determine liberation as the primary subject of her compositions, subsequently giving noble expression to the inherent right of all persons to be free and providing specific representation, as free and unrestrained creator in certain of her most complex poems and in certain moments throughout most of her poems, of achieving momentary participation in the idealized realization of absolute freedom.

The wonder is that an artist so completely dedicated to deliverance of the oppressed was encouraged to write at all; it is, in a way, fortunate for her that she was not taken seriously. Without the opportunity for expression, I think it reasonable to conclude that Wheatley would not have survived even her brief thirty-one years. Finally, then, her liberation poetics—her struggle to achieve freedom through her poetry, which she freely offered to public scrutiny and/or for vicarious participation—is this young woman's instrument of survival in an oppressive world which, perhaps taking the lead from Jefferson, failed to hear her message and seemed determined not to appreciate her efforts.

Wheatley's liberation poetics takes shape, of course, within the body of her oeuvre—that is, in her poems and prose. Wheatley's life and career demonstrate that she participated in what Paul Gilroy has referred to as the Black Atlantic phenomenon. Despite his avowed concentration on the postslavery experience of Black peoples, Wheatley's quest for freedom, which is punctuated by episodes of limited achievement, closely predicts what Gilroy describes as "the turbulent patterns of modern social life that have taken blacks from Africa via slavery into an incompletely realized democracy that racialises and thus frequently withholds the loudly proclaimed benefits of modern citizenship" (192). As well, Wheatley's obvious trans-Atlantic, triangular peregrinations from Africa to Boston to London and back to Boston, when conjoined with her polyglot capacity (her knowledge of her native Fula [possibly attended by some familiarity with Arabic], English, and Latin) align her with the extensive culture Ira Berlin has identified as that of Atlantic Creoles, that is, displaced Africans, whose intellectual and linguistic talents enabled them to negotiate successfully the mixture of white cultures and languages which encircled the Atlantic from about the 1620s through the early 1800s.

Because the 220-plus years of commentary since Wheatley's death inexorably impact any attempt to read her oeuvre at the present time, and because most of that commentary, until very recent years, continues to plague Wheatley Studies with a lack of tolerance and understanding regarding her race and her sex and with a palpable hostility growing out of the facts that she composed the majority of her works before the divine transubstantiation of July 4, 1776, and that she wrote in the often-detested neoclassic idiom, it becomes necessary to give some time to an evaluation of that commentary. In the next two chapters, we will finally discover, with some relief no doubt, that the criticism of the last thirty or so years is, for the most part, surprisingly and pleasantly bereft of those earlier racist, sexist, anti-colonial, and anti-neoclassic (or pro-Romantic) biases. But we will be mistaken if we expect to find that even this most recent commentary is completely free of these all-too-persistent biases.

CHAPTER TWO

Wheatley Considered Intellectually Impoverished: The First 190 Years

I DO NOT CALL THIS SELECTIVE HISTORY OF THE COMMENTARY ABOUT PHILLIS WHEATLEY A SELECTIVE HISTORY OF *CRITICISM*, SIMPLY BECAUSE SO MUCH OF THIS COMMENTARY ASSUMES NOT A CRITICAL perspective per se, but a socio-anthropological character. That is, until very recent times, the temper of writings about this worthy American poet has participated, overwhelmingly, in arguments for or against slavery and/or for or against some misguided dispute over the alleged superiority of one race above another.

We must, therefore, search diligently for that commentary which attends to her texts and which has the purpose of bringing illumination to those texts; these tracts alone fall into what I shall herein refer to as criticism. For surely when racial and gender issues are set aside, we are left with this poet's texts; and it is, finally, only upon these texts that judgment concerning Wheatley's reputation *qua* poet can be registered. Given these circumstances, then, the following critical history of writings about Wheatley traces a pattern of commentary that is often, if not almost always, bipolar, resulting in commentaries strongly for or against this poet's life and career; notice that this bipolar pattern focuses on Wheatley's life and career—not on her texts. Curiously enough, this duality of attitude toward our subject ostensibly predicts what W. E. B. DuBois, at a later cultural moment, identified as the African American double-consciousness. For DuBois this double-consciousness confounded his sense of citizenship as he came to realize that white males intended him to have only partial citizenship; hence he was a citizen and he was not a citizen—he was a man but was not a man. And of course women, white and Black, were still left out of the picture.

In making this observation, I draw not upon what we will discover defines Wheatley's own experience as revealed in her texts, but on that exterior, insidious sense of self imposed upon African Americans by those among white folks who wish to oppress their Black brothers and sisters. As we shall see, Wheatley struggled in her texts, while a Black woman denied citizenship, to discover a means—a power, a favorite word with her—that would overcome this oppression.

Her poetry and prose reveal a consciousness fully aware of the oppressive nature of the so-called enlightened collect of white folks along the Atlantic strand. But, it can not be overemphasized, Wheatley struggled against this acknowledged oppression at a moment in our country's history when the issues of slavery, of the oppression of women, and of the oppression of free Blacks had not been codified, either by the U.S. Constitution or by the post–Civil War enforcement of Jim Crow as practiced by individual states' legislatures, both cultural imperatives that defined DuBois's most regrettable sense of self, his double-consciousness.

Wheatley could, in other words, reasonably, if overoptimistically, afford to be hopeful; or, for that matter, she could expect to be victorious in her quest for freedom for all. I hazard to consider what a devastating effect ratification of the Constitution of 1789 would have had on this sensitive and rational artist.

Certainly writings about Wheatley articulate this disappointing dual perspective. But space here does not allow me to explore all possible ramifications or avenues of pursuit suggested by the complexity of that reception which quantifies these writings, for ultimately such an investigation becomes coterminus with the predicament of Black people in the United States. It is my intention, therefore, not to be comprehensive but only to be representative. Indeed I dare say another book would be required to give this chapter's subject full coverage. In other words, the following discussion does not attempt a detailed or inclusive examination but takes a selective approach, capturing themes or trends of thought which characterize the years of writings about Wheatley, and thereby illustrates how readers attempting to read this complex artist have often misstepped. As Houston Baker has put it, once again, so well, " . . . the surface sentiments of black literary texts can obscure their more substantive meanings for the unwary observer" (*The Journey Back* 88).

I first became acquainted with the life and work of Phillis Wheatley while I was pursuing a doctorate at the University of Tennessee, Knoxville. In the winter quarter of 1977 (UT now has moved to the semester system), I was unexpectedly given an opportunity to teach the then recently instituted and soon popular undergraduate survey of African American literature, and I discovered that Wheatley was the first subject on the course syllabus, prepared by the gentleman whom I would later count myself fortunate to have as the director of my dissertation, the distinguished R. Baxter Miller. As I was given the class one day and had to meet it for the first time the next, I picked up the course's texts and scurried home to peruse this Wheatley person, never even having heard of her. Although I did not realize it at the time, what I experienced changed my life forever. Upon my very first reading, I found Wheatley's poems, reprinted in the Mnemosyne Press facsimile of G. Herbert Renfro's fine 1916 edition, *Life and Works of Phillis Wheatley,* to be thoroughly charming, hardly yet guessing the subtlety of their subversion. But then, almost immediately, I felt a sense of theft, as I began to ask myself, "Why had I never before seen this certainly competent and obviously wonderfully prepared practitioner of the neoclassic idiom?"—a poetic practice toward which, by the way, I have *never* been hostile. Had the pages of American literature been somehow surreptitiously and underhandedly robbed of this fine artist? And if so, why and how? I shared my enthusiasm with my class, which met that next day.

Not coming close to exhausting my interest in her intricate poems (I have never from that moment to the present been able to conclude any in-class investigation of Wheatley in a single period), I resolved to do some research about her and then try to understand how this sophisticated classicist had come to be dismissed—stolen from the anthologies of American literature. Perhaps it was the fact that, by that time, I had acquired the equivalent of an undergraduate Latin major that I so quickly recognized that Wheatley was not only manipulating classical allusions but classical forms, such as the Horatian ode, pastoral, and epic.

What research I recovered has gone a long way toward provoking my unflagging preoccupation with this worthy poet. To be sure, it is now and always has been the value and challenge of Wheatley's texts that have principally sustained my interest. The commentary I found for that second class meeting, nevertheless, appalled me. Rather than treat Wheatley's texts, all commentators I located during this first attempt to uncover criticism spoke of Wheatley as though she, her life and works, were pawns in some socio-anthropological argument aimed at constructing a defensive or offensive front for or against racism. At that point in the late 1970s, I would have to dig much further to discover a tract that I could call real criticism.

What more digging soon taught me was that I was behind the times. Indeed, in 1966 three of her poems were included in the Odyssey Survey's *Colonial and Federalist American Writing: 1607–1830*, her first appearance that I have come across in a twentieth-century anthology of American literature. This daring inclusion was not duplicated for almost ten years, when in 1974 George McMichael (et al., eds.) gave a few pages to her in his first venture into the field of American literary collections, *Anthology of American Literature* (2 vols.). During this period selections from Wheatley's poetry were even included in some high school texts, such as *The American Experience: Poetry* (1974) of the Literary Heritage Series and *The United States in Literature* (1973). Now, after the beginning of the twenty-first century, I have not encountered an anthology of American literature that does not include her; and lately the selections from her work have become more and more generous, including as many as eight to ten of her poems and the relatively recent addition of several of her letters.

One may suppose the predicament of Wheatley's texts would be more favorable in collections of African American literature. But such proves not necessarily to be the case. James Weldon Johnson in *The Book of American Negro Poetry* opens its selections with nine poems by Paul Lawrence Dunbar; he does, however, give several pages in his "Preface" to the 1922 first edition to treatment of Wheatley, wherein he makes this trenchant observation: "Phillis Wheatley has never been given her rightful place in American literature. By some sort of conspiracy she is kept out of most of the books, especially the textbooks on literature used in the schools" (23). Although Johnson's remark about Wheatley's exclusion from texts is thankfully no longer true, what he says regarding "her rightful place" is on target. It is my desideratum that this book will contribute significantly toward securing for Wheatley "her rightful place in American literature" and in the literature of the world.

Johnson continues by declaring, "Of course, she is not a *great* American poet" (23). In my 1988 *Collected Works of Phillis Wheatley* I make a similar statement: "Phillis Wheatley is not a great poet, but she is a good one" (267). When I wrote those words, two factors were on my mind. The first was the perception that to claim more for Wheatley, at that particular moment, would only have been construed as overstatement. As for the second factor, I was not at that time completely convinced that Wheatley merited the distinction of greatness. Now I think she does. That is, I have now become convinced, for reasons this book makes clear, that *Phillis Wheatley* is not just a great American poet; she *is a great poet!*

The road to greatness for Wheatley has truly been a long and precarious one, marred by blatant racism and gross gender bias. While we cannot claim racism in Johnson's judgment, perhaps a modicum of gender bias operates in the ecphonesis, "Of course ... ," as Johnson intones, "Of course, she is not a *great* American poet." Wheatley and Johnson, nevertheless, interconnect when Johnson comments that "because this [his anthology] is the first collection of its kind, I realized the absence of a starting-point" (40), so Johnson attempts to fill in the "gap" "with historical data," which the example of Wheatley provides. Here Johnson's situation parallels that of Wheatley in "To Maecenas," wherein she laments the nineteen or so centuries between Terence, the African playwright of sophisticated comedy, and herself, which she believes to be bereft of another Black artist. She too, lacking a sufficient starting point, must construct one out of her own ingenuity.

To be sure, both writers more forward in their respective projects without knowledge, through no fault of their own. Lucy Terry and Jupiter Hammon had both composed poems earlier than Wheatley (not to mention the several African poets writing in Arabic), and Johnson remained unaware of such African American poets as George Moses Horton, Ann Plato, and Francis Harper, who preceded Dunbar. The conditions here, that both writers are led to make sweeping judgments about their similar situations based upon a lack of knowledge, regrettably typify the conditions which have for too long characterized the field of African American Studies. Only the dedicated work of dedicated scholars has restored this debilitating lack of knowledge.

I make much of this lamentable state of knowledge within the early days of African American scholarship, overwhelmingly caused by racist devaluation and denigration of African American cultural history, because so much of the commentary about Wheatley can be demonstrated to have resulted from the same ignorance. In other words the intellectual impoverishment here cannot be ascribed either to Wheatley or to Johnson. In all honesty, I find myself asking, why did Johnson not find her to be a great poet? Why did I not do so in 1988? Could it be that we were both influenced by the racist and gender-biased efforts to deny Wheatley even the possibility to be considered one of the greats? In my case I can say candidly that what I have learned about gender bias in the last eighteen or so years has definitely taught me new ways of examining, of "reading," texts by women, especially texts by this special, talented person, Phillis Wheatley. As for the possible racism involved, reclamation during this same period of my own biological origins in the Native Peoples of this continent has profoundly enriched my approach to texts by those of any racial and/or ethnic identity.

As we journey through the history of Wheatley's readers, we will, for the most part, require little prompting toward ferreting out obvious episodes of racism and patriarchalism. More recently, however, manifestations of racism and gender bias have become remarkably more subtle; accordingly we must be on our guard to recognize them. Just as deafening as Jefferson's racism, her first reviewers sound a similar timbre. Of the nine reviews of the 1773 *Poems*, all were, for their time, favorable. Appearing from September to December, all express wonder and amazement that an African could have produced such a volume. One observed, for example, that "We are the more surprised too, as we find her verses interspersed with the poetical names of the ancients, which she has in every instance used with strict propriety" (Isani, "British Reception" 147).

Another reviewer, sounding a much more harsh judgment, spoke of her native Africa as "remarkable for nothing but the sloth and languor of their inhabitants, their lascivious disposition, and their deadness to invention," these sentiments echoing those of David Hume expressed at mid-century but predicting those Jefferson stated twelve years later. As for her poems, so this strident racist continues, they "bear no endemial marks of solar fire or spirit"—this last remark especially ironic given the fact that solar imagery is her most recurring pattern and that inspiration is one of her central concerns. Not yet finished with his racist diatribe, he declares, "indeed, most of those people have a turn for imitation, though they have little or none for invention" (Isani, "British Reception" 147). This otherwise unsympathetic reviewer nonetheless concludes his tract by expressing discontent that "this ingenious young woman [whose work appears to deny the accuracy of the stated perceptions] is yet a slave" (148).

One October reviewer asserted that "we were so far from expecting her to write better, that we were astonished to find her write so well"; then he strikes an unwittingly comic position as he ends his review by quoting "from a poem addressed to some person whom she calls Maecenas" (149). Despite his unintentional humor in not recognizing Maecenas as a classical symbol of patronage (were not white folks, British reviewers of this time, supposed to know their ancient authors?), he does at least quote from her poetry. Jefferson would later fire his penetrating critical acumen at Wheatley without quoting a syllable from her opus.

Setting aside our present-day condemnation of these racist reviewers, in her own time Wheatley's publication of *Poems on Various*

Subjects, Religious and Moral created nothing less than a sensation on both sides of the Atlantic. While Wheatley was in London in the summer of 1773, during which time she saw her poems through the press, Benjamin Franklin, then serving as Colonial American representative to Parliament, called upon "the black Poetess and offer'd her any Services I could do her" (Franklin).[1] During the same period, Voltaire declared, in a letter to the Baron Constant de Rebecq (in 1774), that Fontenelle was mistaken to have insisted there would never be black poets, for "il y a actuellement une Négresse qui fait de très-bons vers anglais" (Seeber 57; "there is at the present day a black woman [Phillis] who makes very good English verse"). This uncharacteristic position, one that acknowledged Black literary achievement, was probably forced upon Voltaire because he was himself in England, having fled yet another hostile ministry, at the time Wheatley published her *Poems*,[2] and was therefore a witness to this celebrated event.

In a letter to a fellow officer of the *Ranger*, probably his first mate, John Paul Jones praised Wheatley as "the Celebrated Phillis the African Favorite of the Nine and of Apollo." Jones's request in this missive to "put the Inclosed into the hands" of Wheatley suggests he may have composed a laudatory set of verses to the poet (Kaplan 184–85). When Wheatley sent her now famous poem on Washington, "To His Excellency General Washington," to the general on October 26, 1775, he replied in an almost as famous letter of February 28, 1776 that, since her letter and poem did not come into his hands "till the middle of December," he must now apologize for his delay in getting back to her. Of the poem Washington calls her lines "elegant" and finds "the style and manner ... a striking proof of your poetical talents" (in Wheatley, *Collected Works* 304). He then issues Wheatley an invitation to visit him at his Cambridge headquarters, for as he states, "I shall be happy to see a person so favored by the Muses, and to whom nature has been so liberal and beneficent in her dispensations" (305). A stark contrast to Jefferson's later denunciation!

Subsequently Washington almost assures publication of this encomium by passing the poem along to a former secretary, Colonel Joseph Reed (with connections to Tom Paine) accompanied by a tract which hints at possible publication. Reed took the prompt, and Tom Paine published the poem and Wheatley's introductory letter to Washington in the *Pennsylvania Museum* in the April number of 1776. Wheatley accepted the general's invitation and visited him "a few days before the British evacuated Boston," probably between March 4 and March 14, 1776, where "she passed half an hour with the commander-in-chief, from whom and his officers she received marked attention" (Lossing 556n.).

Even before Jefferson, one of the first in a long line of Wheatley's detractors, had written his denial of her power as a poet, an opposing group of celebrants challenged his position. Benjamin Rush, an untiring assailant of slavery, in a pamphlet published just before Wheatley's *Poems* appeared and entitled "An Address to the Inhabitants of the British Settlements in America, upon Slave-Keeping," cites Wheatley as a primary example of "as sublime and disinterested virtue" among Blacks "as ever adorned a Roman or a Christian character." He speaks of her "singular genius and accomplishments" which "not only do honor to her sex, but to human nature." Although her volume had not yet been published, several of her poems had been printed and had, according to Rush, been "read with pleasure by the public" (3). Three poets, all contemporaries of Wheatley, Jefferson, and Rush, wrote verse encomia honoring her. In the broadside, "An Address to Miss Phillis Wheatley, Ethiopian Poetess" (1778), Jupiter Hammon, the first Black to publish a poem in America, urges her to remain "a pattern still . . . to youth of Boston town" (Mulford 856). Following her death on December 5, 1784, the *Boston Magazine* for that same December printed "Elegy on the Death of a Late Celebrated Poetess," in which the author, a pseudonymous Horatio, compares Wheatley to the Greek Orpheus. In an eight-line epic simile, Horatio remarks that, "tho' her outward form did ne'er disclose / The lilly's white or blushes of the rose," Phillis nonetheless (Horatio is obviously white, for Blacks do indeed "blush"), "tun'd her sweet mellifluous lyre" and produced poetry which is "her greatest praise" (Mason 1966, xvii).

Some twelve years after Wheatley's death, there appeared in the *New York Magazine* a poem signed by "Matilda" and entitled "On Reading the Poems of Phillis Wheatley, the African Poetess." This poem begins by offering the Great Chain of Being as an explanation of the apparent inferiority of Blacks: "The unfavor'd race in shade are meant to be / The link between the brutal world and we." Then it explains that, since her arrival in the more civilized American colonies, Wheatley has become refined by her exposure to learning and Christianity and has even become a towering intellect: "A Phillis rises, and the world no more / Denies the sacred right to mental pow'r" (Huddleston 57–58). Well, Matilda was unfortunately a bit too optimistic in her assessment.

Each of these three poetic encomia calls attention to Wheatley's color and celebrates her poetry as an example of Black talent, but none of them actually presents a discussion of any of her poems or even refers to one of them. These celebrations of Wheatley, as a consequence, could have easily become at the same time applicable to the socio-anthropological argument which asserted that Blacks were equal to their white enslavers in ability and talent. Johann F. Blumenbach, a German professional anthropologist of the times from Göttingen, who is often called the father of physical anthropology, follows a similar pattern in his work, "Of the Negro in Particular" (1790), in which he states that he owns a copy of the 1773 *Poems* and that Wheatley "is justly famous for her poems which scarcely anyone who has any taste for poetry could read without pleasure." Some of these poems Blumenbach finds to be "particularly beautiful." But he mentions no poems and offers no further discussion (310).

Three amateur anthropologists, however, writing during the same period, do quote some lines of her poetry. Gilbert Imlay, one-time captain in the Continental Army before turning amateur geographer and anthropologist and subsequently the lover of Mary Wollstonecraft, boldly attacks Jefferson's position against Blacks in "Letter IX" of *A Topographical Description of the Western Territory of North America* (3rd ed., 1797), especially citing Jefferson's indictment of Wheatley. Then he writes, "I will transcribe part of her poem on Imagination [11. 13–32], and leave you to judge whether it is poetical or no." Following the quotation, Imlay comments, "I should be glad to be informed what white upon this continent has written more beautiful lines" (229–30). Imlay's *Description* enjoyed at least one German translation (1793). Thomas Clarkson, in his *An Essay on the Slavery and Commerce of the Human Species, Particularly the African* (1786; mentioned by Blumenbach), matches Imlay's enthusiasm for Wheatley, but he is more generous in his quotations. Clarkson first cites lines from "An Hymn to the Evening," " . . . to the Morning," and "On Imagination"; second he reproduces the entire testimony verifying the authenticity of Wheatley's poems which preceded the text of the 1773 volume and which was signed by the aforementioned noted Bostonians. Clarkson then rhapsodically declares, " . . . if the authoress *was designed for slavery*, . . . the greater part of the inhabitants of Britain must lose their claim to freedom" (110–12). Clarkson's *Essay* was often reprinted, even enjoying "three French adaptations by 1789" (Seeber 85n55), as the abolitionist movement gathered force in Great Britain and as Clarkson's own role in that movement became major. Even Wordsworth owned a copy.

Another work that contributed mightily to the abolitionist movement in Great Britain, and in Europe, was *Narrative of a Five*

Years' Expedition against the Revolted Negroes of Surinam (1796) by the Scot John G. Stedman. Stedman, like Imlay and Clarkson, was fond of Wheatley's "On Imagination" and quoted fourteen lines (11. 9–22). Of these lines Stedman exclaimed, "What can be more beautiful and sublime?" (363). Coleridge owned a copy of Stedman, and his *Narrative* was translated into Swedish, German (two editions), Dutch, Italian, and French (two editions). Clearly all four of these men—Blumenbach, Imlay, Clarkson, and Stedman—were concerned not with judging Wheatley's poetry but with using her work to construct their respective arguments for the equality of the races. Note, nevertheless, the participation of certain of Wheatley's texts in the flow of thought which yielded several of the European Romanticisms; indeed the lines from "On Imagination" quoted by Imlay, Clarkson, and Stedman are the salient ones wherein Wheatley does two things: she subordinates fancy to imagination—for the first time in Western literary aesthetics—and she projects her experiment with heterocosms.[3]

Over a decade later, a work appeared in Paris, *De la littérature des négres*, by Henri Grégoire (1808). Like the preceding anthropological treatises, this book was a philanthropic defense of Blacks and an attack upon their enslavement, but with a much different emphasis. As the title of the English translation indicates, *An Enquiry Concerning the Intellectual and Moral Faculties and Literature of Negroes* (1810), the faculties of Blacks are still major points of emphasis; Grégoire's method is sociological rather than anthropological. Here he finds the merits of equality of the races in the literary productions of Blacks in Latin, French, and other languages, as well as those in English. In his assessment, Phillis Wheatley's achievement in poetry is not the least successful of these literary productions.

According to his own testimony, Grégoire borrowed Blumenbach's copy of the 1773 *Poems* to make his observations about Wheatley's poetry. Grégoire's treatment of Wheatley follows somewhat the same structure as that of the previous celebrations; he gives a brief, but often inaccurate biographical sketch of Wheatley's life as a slave and her efforts toward her education, although his treatment is more extensive than that of the preceding sketches (two full pages as opposed to a few lines in the others); he quotes from her poetry and reproduces three complete poems ("On the Death of J.C. an Infant," "An Hymn to the Morning," and "To the Right Honorable William Earl of Dartmouth") rather than merely a few lines. He also takes the time to refute Jefferson's unwillingness "to acknowledge the talents of negroes, even those of Phillis Wheatley" (236).

But at this point, Grégoire departs from the pattern established by the celebrants of Black poetry and culture, his comments upon her poetry moving beyond simple panegyric toward a more judicious examination of her subject matter. Rather than merely displaying her work, he observes that her "Ode to Maecenas," which opens the 1773 volume, shows a familiarity with Horace. He comments further upon this poem that, "It is not without merit; but we hasten to subjects more worthy of her muse" (238). This French abolitionist remarks as his final evaluation of Wheatley's poetry: "Almost all her poetical productions have a religious or moral cast—all breathe a soft and sentimental melancholy" (238). Grégoire recognizes Wheatley's achievement in verse, but unlike certain celebrants before him he does not find her poems to be beautiful. He does, however, attempt to defend her poetry on the basis of its content—not merely because it is the product of a Black woman. His treatment of her more closely approaches a balanced critical assessment than those of previous readers. Grégoire was probably the first earnest apologist for Wheatley's poetry, one who based his defense upon an examination of the poems themselves.

Though the France of Grégoire was caught up in the intense turmoil of the Napoleonic era, it was, nevertheless, far removed from the cotton fields and Black bondage of the American South. He could afford to be objective in his study. But the struggle against what Melville later called "man's foulest crime" desperately needed the example of a Phillis Wheatley to advance, as convincingly as possible, the equal humanity of Blacks and whites. It was inevitable, then, that the commentary upon the life and works of Wheatley was to remain polar, that her works would continue to be used in the cause for Black freedom, and that for every celebrant of her achievement and example, a detractor would arise who would malign her work as the product of some white or who would claim that her poems were the silly effusions of an adolescent slave girl.

In this atmosphere of conflict, when Frederick Douglass was about fourteen years old, William Lloyd Garrison's *Liberation* published in 1832, from February through December, each of the 1773 *Poems*, these selections appearing at the rate of about one a week. This renewed interest in Wheatley probably motivated the 1834, 1835, and 1838 American editions of Wheatley's poetry, which include both a "Memoir" of Wheatley's life as recalled by Margaretta Matilda Oddell, a grandniece of Susannah Wheatley, and a collection of poems by the Black poet George Moses Horton. The unsigned "Introduction" to this volume, an impassioned plea for the abolition of slavery, promotes the examples of Wheatley and Horton as primary evidence for the inhumanity of bondage. One statement made in this "Introduction" is prophetic: "But even were the thrall of bondage broken, the hapless victim of slavery would find himself, in but too many cases, we fear, fettered by prejudice—despised by the proud—insulted by the scornful" (9).

Oddell's "Memoir" contributes twenty-five pages of information about the life of Wheatley, the longest account of her biography available in the eighteenth and nineteenth centuries. Her account is probably the most reliable life sketch because its author was, according to her own testimony, "a collateral descendent of Mrs. Wheatley . . ." and was "familiar with the name and fame of Phillis from her childhood" (35). But this set of observations upon Wheatley's life, useful though it is as biography, offers practically no discussion of Wheatley's poems beyond the following:

> We gather from her writings, that she was acquainted with astronomy, ancient and modern geography, and ancient history; and that she was well versed in the scriptures of the Old and New Testament. She discovered a decided taste for the stories of Heathen mythology, and Pope's Homer seems to have been a great favorite with her. (35)

Julian Mason, one of Wheatley's recent editors, echoes this last remark about Wheatley's knowledge of Pope; we will soon discover, however, that Wheatley's concentrated reading traveled far beyond Pope.

In 1849 as the storms of the Civil War were gathering force, William G. Allen, a frequent contributor to liberation journals and a professor of Greek and German at New York Central College (one of the first predominantly Black colleges), published a slender volume of selections from Wheatley, Benjamin Banneker, and George Moses Horton. The Banneker selections include his famous exchange between himself and Jefferson wherein Banneker, the author of highly original almanacs demonstrating considerable mathematical skill (and his rhetorical abilities in his letter show a writer of no small talent), deftly assails Jefferson's claim that Black Folks have no intellectual prowess, and Jefferson, in his response, comes off as a sort of wily greased pig. As for the poems of Wheatley and Horton, who wrote about forty years after Wheatley, Allen, revealing a romantic, anti-neoclassic bias, if not a measure of gender bias, declares that he regards "Horton as decidedly the superior genius" (7). While Allen's attention to Wheatley certainly kept alive interest in her, his use of her once again indicates a preoccupation with socio-anthropological concerns.

Typical of the opposite end of the spectrum of opinion is an essay entitled "Antipathy to the Negro," appearing in 1878, fifteen years after the Emancipation Proclamation. In this article, James Parton writes that Jefferson's observations upon Wheatley's poetry are essentially correct:

> The colored poet, Phillis Wheatley, had her admirers a hundred years ago in Boston, where her volume can still occasionally be found. We have carefully looked over it, and cannot deny the justice of Jefferson's remarks upon it. She was a poet very much as "Blind Tom" is a musician, her verses being the merest echo of the common jingle of her day. (Mason 1966, xlv)

Like Jefferson, Parton does not even name one of Wheatley's poems, much less discuss their content or structure. Other commentaries of Wheatley similar to those of the celebrant Oddell, and the detractor Parton, appeared throughout the nineteenth century.[4]

In 1894, Gertrude E. H. Bustill Mossell, called by Joanne Braxton, who introduced the volume, "The prototypical black feminist" (xxix), penned a sketch of Wheatley in which she holds that, although "Her verse shows the shadow of her unhappy lot," it "rises above those sorrows" which one who served as a slave could not escape (Mossell 55). In doing so, moreover, Mossell rhapsodizes that Wheatley's verse strides "on the uplifted wings of song, floats to the starry heavens and consoles the afflicted." As well, it "gives praise to the faithful ruler" [in her poem to King George III?] and breaks forth in love for the new home" (55). This last phrase must surely be an implicit recognition of Wheatley's patriotism. Trying to address the negative assessment doled out to Wheatley by Jefferson and others, Mossell asserts, "we claim for her the true poetic fire"; and in the Earl of Dartmouth piece, Mossell finds that "the perfect rhythm, the graceful courtesy of thought, [and] the burning love for freedom capture the heart" (56). Naming several others of Wheatley's poems, Mossell attests that she has read Wheatley's poetry with a keen and enthusiastic eye. In fact Mossell's portrait constitutes the most enthusiastic commentary on Wheatley I have located until very recent times.

With the approach of the twentieth century, however, we return to the earlier fundamental poles of opposition as we encounter two detractors neatly balanced by two celebrants. These four commentators upon the poetry of Phillis Wheatley are worthy of note because of their individual reputations as literary critics and because of the impact they have had upon Wheatley Studies in the twentieth century.

Moses Coit Tyler gives approximately one and a half pages to a discussion of Wheatley in *The Literary History of the American Revolution: 1763–1783* (1897). The attention he does give her has probably done more to damage her literary reputation than have the remarks of any other detractor besides Jefferson. He speaks of Wheatley as one "whose name still survives among us in the shape of a tradition vaguely testifying to the existence of a poetic talent in this particular member of the African race. Unfortunately," he continues, "a glance at what she wrote will show that there is no adequate basis for such tradition, and that the significance of her career belongs rather to the domain of anthropology, or of hagiology, than to that of poetry—whether American or African" (186). The abstruse syntax of this passage, along with the absence of any quotes from her work, suggests that Tyler has judged Wheatley on hearsay and by reputation rather than on the basis of a concrete examination of her works. Tyler acknowledges that her 1773 volume "attracted for a time considerable curiosity, both in England and America,—not at all, however, because the verses were good, but because they were written by one from whom even bad verses were too good to be expected" (187). In a note about her letters, Tyler states they are "little else than pious and almost infantile platitudes" (187n.).

William Joseph Long extends this denigration of Wheatley's literary reputation in his *American Literature* (1913), a popular history of literature of the early twentieth century. But Long is bolder than Tyler, for he does quote a few lines of her poetry (Tyler had not even named one of her poems from the 1773 volume). Long begins his two-page harangue against the quality of Wheatley's verse by describing her as one "who enjoyed a day's favor." Next he suggests that one who was "violently taken from her savage mother in Africa" (145) should display in her poems a rich variety of experience. But then, he says, a look at the "tamed" elegy "On the Death of an Infant" brings great disappointment. Finally after having found "something promising," in a few lines of "On Imagination," Long exclaims, "Here is no Zulu, but drawing-room English." Then he concludes his culturally biased, anti-neoclassic commentary by maintaining that Wheatley

> . . . sings like a canary in a cage, a bird that forgets its native melody and imitates only what it hears. We have called attention to her simply because she is typical of scores of minor poets of the Revolutionary period who, with a glorious opportunity before them, neglected the poetry and heroism of daily life in order to follow a literary fashion. (146)

The literary fashion of which Long speaks was of course that of the neoclassic idiom; Tyler's entire four-volume *Literary History* is infected with this same Romantic bias. When we couple this Romantic bias against the neoclassic idiom with the popularity these works by Long and Tyler have enjoyed—Tyler's *Literary History* has never been surpassed for its sheer detail and breadth of coverage, and he worked from original texts without benefit of Early American Imprints—we can begin to understand why the bias against American poetry composed before 1800 (not to mention the parallel bias in this country against any creative texts written before 1800, except perhaps Benjamin Franklin's *Autobiography*) continues without significant interruption even to the present day.

The indictments of Tyler and Long did not, however, remain unanswered. Charles F. Heartman produced the first collected edition of Wheatley's poems and letters in 1915. In a preface to this volume, Arthur H. Schomburg extols Wheatley: "That so young a child could be 'inspired by the Muses,' could only be in strict compliance with the maxim 'a poet is born, not made'" (10). Schomburg then accuses Long of reviving the old method of criticism in his judgment of her poetry by absolute standards. Schomburg recommends that the new method of literary criticism be applied to the study of Wheatley's works. This new method he describes as judging "a poem by relative standards, by its relation to the poet's age and the poetry of the age" (18). Although Schomburg's "new method" is certainly not new today (nor was it "new" when he wrote), one should include this approach when judging any poet. To date, few readers of Wheatley's poetry have followed Schomburg's advice, and perhaps even more regrettable is Schomburg's failure to pursue his own counsel in introducing the public to Wheatley's verse.

The second of Wheatley's celebrators of the early twentieth century, G. Herbert Renfro, surpasses Schomburg's enthusiasm for Wheatley when asserting "Nature has designed Phillis for a queen, not for a slave" (Renfro 11). Renfro makes this statement in his 1916 edition of the *Life and Works of Phillis Wheatley*, an edition that was often reprinted during the 1970s.

The general tone of his introductory "Sketch of the Life of Phillis Wheatley" is laudatory, and he makes several cogent observations concerning the light in which Wheatley's poetry should be viewed. He maintains about her condition of servitude: " . . . it was utterly impossible that her talents could be fully developed, or that she could enjoy more than a small share of the advantages common to the freer and lighter-hued daughters of the land" (13). Renfro suggests

Wheatley's manner of composition was "original, spontaneous and highly imaginative": "She would retire at night (her room furnished, by the kind indulgence of her mistress, with fire, light and writing material) and often awaken with a train of poetic fancy and ideal images which was immediately preserved" (20). In truth, Renfro has here paraphrased a portion of Oddell's "Memoir." But then he closes his sketch with this candid and fitting observation: "In the days when women were not encouraged to pursue the richer fields of science and literature, when only the wealthy and refined invaded the storehouses of ancient classics, a Negro girl became an honored precedent for an ungrateful nation" (26). Despite the sensible recommendations of Schomburg and Renfro, neither commentator actually examines one of Wheatley's poems. What each does provide, however, is a suitable and necessary response to such detractors as Tyler and Long, for their volumes make available to the twentieth century the works of Phillis Wheatley. Perhaps because of their efforts, her poetry has not become forgotten.

The tide of later twentieth-century opinion about Wheatley alters considerably from the clear poles of opposition of the first 150 years of commentary. Both detractors and celebrants relax their positions; the detractors become tolerators, and the celebrants, defenders. The members of these new camps, nevertheless, often continue to remain mere commentators, avoiding any attempt to elucidate her texts. Of the writers about Wheatley's poetry after 1920, two carry over from the old camps: one is a detractor and the other a celebrant. Both will be considered later.

Between World Wars I and II, the Harlem Renaissance greatly spurred the production of original poetry, drama, and fiction by Blacks, and scholarly research into Black authors of the past. Hallie Quinn Brown, noted educator and elocutionist, published in 1926 her *Homespun Heroines and Other Women of Distinction,* in which she claims that Wheatley, as a "poor, little orphan," "had gone through so much suffering and terror that her mind had become bewildered concerning the past" (6). As we saw in the "Introduction," Brown joins June Jordan and Donna Landry in robbing Wheatley of her African heritage. As well Brown gives the worst report of John Peters, the Black gentleman Wheatley married, that I have seen. According to Brown, Peters "failed" at business and "became very poor. Though unwilling to do hard work himself, he wanted to make a drudge of his wife" (9). Do we hear in this case a strident chord of anti-patriarchalism? We would do well to recall that, during the period Peters and our poet were married (between April 1, 1778, and December 5, 1784, the date of Wheatley's death), the American Revolution was being fought and that the American victory brought little prosperity for a number of years. In many years of studying Wheatley, I have not been able to confirm that Peters "wanted to make a drudge of his wife."

In *The Negro in Literature and Art in the United States* (1929), Benjamin Brawley gives an entire chapter to Wheatley. He outlines her biography, quotes some of her letters and poetry, and comments upon her work. His approach sets the pace for the critical commentary upon Wheatley during the period. He calls her now frequently anthologized "On Being Brought from Africa to America" a "pathetic little juvenile poem" (19) and asserts that a good many of her poems "are little more than a part of a pseudo-classic tradition" (34).

Although he never explains his term "pseudo-classic," too many commentators of this and succeeding periods have seized upon the notions he expressed—that Wheatley must somehow be considered, first, "pathetic" in her apparent failure to speak out against the oppression of her bondage, without ever attempting to reclaim the world in which she lived; and, second, since she seems to have used Pope as a model for the composition of her poems, she must be classified as a mere imitator. Brawley does not say just how her work is supposed to display this tendency toward counterfeiting. As well, his neoclassical bias is obvious. It should be noted, however, that he anthologizes a generous twenty-four pages of Wheatley's poetry in *Early Negro American Writers,* his 1935 collection.

In spite of Brawley's negative commentary upon her poems, his *Negro in Literature and Art* was very likely a disseminating force in Wheatley Studies; in the next few years she was much talked about, both favorably and unfavorably. Charlotte Ruth Wright published a new edition of Wheatley's poems in 1930. Vernon Loggins, in the following year, gave her a fifteen-page discussion in his influential *The Negro Author: His Development in America*. He describes Wheatley as "noteworthy as an accomplishment in imitation," one who had written "neoclassical sentimental verse" which offers "slight interest to the modern reader" and to which "there can at the present day be little emotional response" (16). In *The Negro Genius: A New Appraisal of the Achievement of the American Negro in Literature and the Fine Arts,* Brawley reiterated in 1937 his former opinions of Wheatley. In that same year, Sterling Brown wrote in his *Negro Poetry and Drama* that Wheatley's poetry shows her to have been "shyly imitative," one who "gave back only what she had got from others" (5–6). But J. Saunders Redding's treatment of Wheatley in *To Make a Poet Black* (1939) flatters her least. He indicts her for "wan creative energies," for "abnegation and self-pity," and for an "overemphasis of religion," "a common fault at the time" (9–11).

Although patronizingly tolerant of Wheatley's poetry, none of these critics dared omit completely mention of Black America's first writer to publish a book. So they contented themselves with merely passing her off as some sort of unfortunate accident in the history of Black American literature, who, to recall William Long's assessment, "enjoyed a day of favor" but who could only imitate what she had heard. In the final estimation of these tolerators, then, Wheatley can not be ignored because of her undeniable significant achievement in the white world of Colonial and revolutionary America, but she must be censured and her reputation discredited because her poetry reads like the juvenile production of a pathetic little imitator—in short because she, without any originality whatsoever, "writes white."

Because, without a judicious appreciation of neoclassicism or for American writing before 1800, it is so difficult to answer, this sort of condescension certainly did great harm and actually embellished the severe criticism of a Jefferson or the ridicule of a Parton. Although this condescension acknowledges her as a figure of some importance in literary history, it then soundly condemns her as not worth any further notice. This sort of relegation leads the uninitiated away from anything but a momentary glance at her work. By praising her as a founding force in Black American literature and then hastily passing over her, these early-twentieth-century tolerators teach students her name but leave them with an incomplete, erroneous, and finally negative impression of her poetry.

One can conclude with some validity that it is no small wonder Wheatley's poetry is even read today and that it is probably just short of a miracle that she began to enjoy a marked degree of popularity in the late 1960s and 1970s. Such popularity may be explained, however, by that period's expansion of interest in Black American literature and by the increasing numbers of Black Studies programs within America's institutions of higher learning. But as in the past, whenever her reputation is at its lowest, Wheatley has somehow commanded either a celebrant or a defender. James Weldon Johnson, for example, rallies to her defense in his anthology, *The Book of American Negro Poetry* (2nd ed., 1931), as we observed earlier, where he called her "an important American poet" (23).

So influential a speaker as Johnson, one with such solid critical perception, did not long remain unheard; in the next two decades, those of the 1940s and 1950s, the seeds of Wheatley's popularity during the 1970s were sown. Sterling A. Brown, Arthur P. Davis, and Ulysses Lee include three of her longer poems in *The Negro Caravan*, a classic among anthologies of Black American literature first published in 1941 and a second time in 1969. Although he reproduces none of her poems, W. Tasker Witham does give a two-page, less than enthusiastic assessment of Wheatley in his 1947 anthology *Living American Literature: Panorama of American Literature*. Langston Hughes and Arna Bontemps reproduce two of her poems in their 1949 *The Poetry of the Negro: 1746–1949* (revised and updated by Bontemps in 1970). And Shirley Graham, wife of W. E. B. DuBois, wrote a somewhat romanticized biography of Wheatley for young people entitled *The Story of Phillis Wheatley: Poetess of the American Revolution*, also in 1949, which has been reprinted at least twelve times.

Her popularity with critics during this period, however, lagged a bit behind her public popularity. Richard Wright, nonetheless, found time to make a poignant observation on the poetry of Wheatley, in spite of his well-known gender bias, in his "Introduction" to the 1945 edition of St. Clair Drake's and Horace R. Cayton's two-volume sociological treatise *Black Metropolis: A Study of Negro Life in a Northern City*. After having cited a few lines from her "On Imagination," Wright defends Wheatley's poem by stating, "Whatever its quality as poetry, the above poem records the feelings of a Negro reacting not as a Negro, but as a human being" (xxxiii).

Then, eight years later, Arthur P. Davis, one of the editors of *The Negro Caravan*, published the first article on the poetry of Phillis Wheatley to appear in a scholarly journal that was not merely a review of an edition of her poems. In this article, "Personal Elements in the Poetry of Phillis Wheatley," mentioned in the "Introduction," Davis addresses the accusations of many commentators that her poetry is coldly impersonal and that she should be seen today as "a pathetic little Negro girl who had so completely identified herself with her eighteenth-century Boston background that all she could write was coldly correct neo-classical verse on dead ministers and even deader abstractions." Davis insists that Wheatley was "not as devoid of racial and personal feeling" as commonly thought and that she speaks in her poems "of her own problems more often than is commonly recognized" (192). The first person to do so in Wheatley "criticism," Davis actually analyzes passages from her poetry and attempts to illustrate his analysis with examples from her texts. But his article is still more significant, for he is the first writer to point out Wheatley's great "concern with excellence as a poet" (195).

Davis's article struck a favorable note in Wheatley criticism as the turbulent era of civil rights and Black power was approaching. But just when her reputation promised to be given an intelligent revaluation, it received the blow of yet another detractor. Martha Bacon, in the year of the Harlem race riots, attempted to defame Wheatley's achievement in her *Puritan Promenade* (1964): " . . . posterity cannot help her poetry, Jefferson has the last word on this point. She does not bear comparison with any authentic poet" (38). Bacon is, however, the last of the hardcore Wheatley detractors, for her curse apparently fell upon deaf ears; the next fourteen years brought with them more critical and scholarly interest in Wheatley's life and works than in all the years preceding them.

Though no detractors have appeared since Bacon, the "criticism" of the late 1960s and 1970s is represented by tolerators who are answered by defenders, with one significant change. From the 1920s through the 1950s, the tolerators greatly outnumbered the defenders; these positions become reversed, however, in the 1960s and 1970s. As a result, Wheatley was granted a more important place in Black literature in particular and in American literature in general. In the "Introduction" to his edition (1966) of her works extant at the time, the spark that set off the great increase in Wheatley's defenders, Julian Mason—the first to do so—asserts that Wheatley "was more than just an imitator" (xxiii) and expresses the hope that his volume will make her works available for serious study. Indeed, it was Mason in this important edition who suggested that someone (later to be J. Shields) should investigate the possible influence of Mather Byles on Wheatley, who lived across the street from Byles.

William H. Robinson is certainly the first African American anthologist to encourage a careful reading of Wheatley's poems. In his groundbreaking *Early Black American Poets* (1969), the first such anthology to use the epithet "Black," Robinson, the most prolific Wheatley scholar to date, chooses to include ten of her poems; numbering among these are several of her most important texts: "On Being Brought from Africa to America," "On the Death of Rev. Mr. George Whitefield," "Thoughts on the Work[s] of Providence," "On Recollection," "On Imagination," and "To S.M., A Young African Painter." Calling her a formalist poet, Robinson does not condemn her for writing in the neoclassic idiom. Indeed, in his words he notes, "Her favorite vehicle is the popular pentameter couplet." But he correctly observes as well that "she uses other forms with equally charming feminine ease" (99). In defense of accusations that Wheatley was racially unaware, Robinson insists that "her racial awareness in her poetry has been documented" (98). We will encounter Robinson several more times in subsequent pages.

But it would be inaccurate and even foolish to suggest that this renaissance in Wheatley Studies was not, at least in part, directly related to the struggles and victories in the civil rights movement of Black Americans. An appreciation of Wheatley by Gerald Haslam is included in a 1969 collection of somewhat militant essays about Black authors and Black American writing, essays that are dedicated to the examination of "the problems of criticism in a field ... fraught with social, cultural and political prejudices" (Bigsby 1). Haslam first praises Wheatley as "a remarkable artist, producing poetry, which, at its best, was equal to that of any American writer of her period" (Haslam 42). Then he recalls the tone of the abolitionist anthropologists, Clarkson, Rush, Imlay, and others: "In many ways Phillis Wheatley was the most revolutionary of all Afro-American writers, for, though her overt protestations were few, the very quality of her writing made forever suspect the claim that Negroes are incapable of artistic excellence" (Haslam 43–44).

Wheatley, even at this late date, is being cited by Haslam as a "case in point," a premise in a socio-anthropological argument for racial equality. Although the citation may be of value in one way, it cannot take the place of legitimate literary criticism, that criticism which elucidates a literary text. Haslam's essay does indeed encourage readers of American literature to give more attention to Wheatley as a significant poet, but it provides these readers with little instruction as to the content, the themes, and the techniques of her poems.

Although four of Wheatley's tolerators from the 1970s quote rather extensively from her poetry, none is concerned with the explication of textual meanings; rather the references to her poems are forced to fit the particular socio-anthropological thesis of each writer. One such person is Roger Whitlow, who asserts in his critical history, *Black American Literature* (1973), that Wheatley's poems "are, in fact, more important for their themes, what she felt about the people and the religious attitudes of her age, than for the style in which they are written" (23). As Whitlow's history was often used during the 1970s as a textbook in Black American literature classes, his deemphasis on her poetry *qua* poetry is certainly disappointing and does nothing to encourage close analysis of her oeuvre. Merle A. Richmond, a second member of this group, has done the most extensive biographical study of Wheatley to date in a volume about Wheatley and George Moses Horton, *Bid the Vassal Soar* (1974). She writes about the verse of each: "What is important about the poetry is what it reveals or suggests about the slaves who wrote it, and, by extension, what it reveals about the institution of slavery" (xiii). The third, Terence Collins, insists in "Phillis Wheatley: The Dark Side of Poetry" that "Wheatley's true legacy is the testimony her poetry gives to the insidious, self-destroying nature of even the most subtle, most gentle of racially oppressive conditions" (88). Finally, Chikwenye Okonjo Ogunyemi claims in another article, "Phillis Wheatley: The Modest Beginning," that her poems are artificial and show "a complete lack of feeling and involvement on her part as a writer—all attributes of a neo-classical writer"; declaring this wholly inadequate understanding of Wheatley's poetics along with the author's gross misrepresentation of what neoclassicism was about, he then accuses Wheatley of composing her poems exclusively for a white audience, writing only "what they wanted and what they could read comfortably" (17). A *close* reading of Wheatley's poetry in her own day would hardly have produced, from white folks, a comfortable response. Like the tolerators who preceded them, the members of this group, if heeded, would direct potential readers away from Wheatley's poetry toward her biographical significance to the history of the American people, especially to that of Black America.

But this group did not become, in the 1970s, the controlling group in Wheatley criticism; indeed her defense, which picks up momentum in this decade, is spectacular. In 1971, Miram Morris Fuller published an inspiring biography of Wheatley for juveniles as part of the Americans All series. In the following year in an article for *Phylon* entitled, "Phillis Wheatley—Soul Sister?" R. Lynn Matson presented a perceptive and stimulating discussion of Wheatley's poetry and suggested that she was, contrary to accusations levied by Redding, Bacon, and many others, "very race conscious, very aware of her position as a slave, and not at all 'smug'" (223). Her thesis is forced, however, largely because of the lack of concrete evidence obtainable from Wheatley's poems and letters known at the time she wrote. Discoveries during the later years of the 1970s of previously unknown poems, and particularly of letters by Wheatley, however, support the validity of Matson's defense. Her article is important to a study of Wheatley's poetry for two further reasons. First, she observes that her "metaphors of death as a flight or a voyage over water" are identical to the metaphors that occur in Black spirituals. And second, following the lead of Arthur P. Davis, Matson calls attention to Wheatley's aspiration as a poet "to soar to Poetic heights" (229). It is in this article as well that we see the first hints that Wheatley intends to construct in her poems a subversive posture.

The year 1973, the bicentennial of the publication of Wheatley's *Poems on Various Subjects Religious and Moral*, appropriately brought forth three significant developments in Wheatley scholarship. She was celebrated in an exhibit in the National Portrait Gallery in Washington, D.C.; she was the honored subject of a four-day literary festival given by Jackson State College in Jackson, Mississippi; and she was, for the first time, the subject of a doctoral dissertation.

The National Portrait Gallery exhibit of which Wheatley was an important part included other significant Blacks who participated in or who were associated with the American Revolution, from Crispus Attucks to Equiano (Gustavus Vassa). Sidney Kaplan, the noted historian, carefully described this exhibit in the first edition of his *The Black Presence in the Era of the American Revolution: 1770–1800*, devoting by far the longest chapter in this formidable work to the exaltation of Phillis Wheatley, whom he praises most perceptively as "probably the first truly American poet in our literary history" (Kaplan, 1st ed., 150).

The summer 1974 issue of the *Jackson State Review*, published by Jackson State College, is dedicated entirely to a commemoration of the previous year's Phillis Wheatley Poetry Festival. In this issue of the journal the editors present a catalogue of the festival's participants and the historical documents displayed, and they reproduce photographically the facsimiles and transcriptions of two poems and letters by Wheatley, the original manuscripts of which were also exhibited at the festival. Of special importance to Wheatley's literary reputation is the reproduction of four selected papers about her. One of these, "In Search of Our Mother's Gardens: Honoring the Creativity of the Black Woman," by a young Alice Walker, now internationally known as an essayist, novelist, and poet, praises Wheatley for keeping alive in many ancestors of today's Blacks "*the notion of song [sic]*" (49); another by Dorothy B. Porter, "Historical and Bibliographical Data of Phillis Wheatley's Publications," calls attention to recent discoveries of editions and manuscripts of her work and records that the price of her published poems and letters, as well as of those in manuscript, has considerably increased in recent years, accompanying the rise of her fame (54–60). In a third article Margaret Burroughs argues for the connection between Wheatley and the evangelical movement of Colonial New England, a movement that was carried out under the patronage of many British Tories and was encouraged by such English Methodists as the Wesleys (albeit it should be pointed out that Charles never considered himself to be a Methodist), whose main objectives included both the saving of souls and the abolition of slavery (61–73). The last article, one by Paula Giddings entitled "Critical Evaluation of Phillis Wheatley," articulates well the critical predicament of Wheatley, particularly how she has been dealt with by her misleading, patronizing tolerators:

> Let me say here that I am not saying that there isn't an element of truth in what they have said, or that they expressed their views with malice; but that their views lacked a foresight and depth: foresight in terms of understanding the elements of criticism which serve to perpetuate our sensibility throughout literature; and depth in terms of taking into account the special forces encountered by Blacks, particularly before Emancipation Proclamation in America. (75)

Two years after the Phillis Wheatley Poetry Festival, Ann Applegate complements Gidding's paper with "Phillis Wheatley: Her Critics and Her Contribution." Applegate laments the failure of "criticism" of the past "to provide the proper literary perspective to establish her [Wheatley's] position in American literature" (123); she states emphatically, " . . . her poetry is definitely worthy of consideration in the study of early American literature" (125). All these defenders from Matson to Applegate quote some parts of Wheatley's poetry, some of them citing rather generous portions; but not one offers a concentrated interpretation of a text.

The first work of this period that examines closely the texts of Wheatley's poetry is the 1973 doctoral dissertation by Kenneth R. Holder entitled "Some Linguistic Aspects of the Heroic Couplet in the Poetry of Phillis Wheatley." Holder, who treats her use of rhyme as well as the metrical and syntactic features of her verse, intends that his work be used as a linguistic base upon which to build future studies and hopes that "Ideally, this analysis of the linguistic aspects of Wheatley's poetry will complement an analysis of her poetry as art" (14). His work challenges the contention that Wheatley is simply an imitator: "A comparison of Wheatley's poems with a selected group of poems from Alexander Pope, the English neoclassical poet whom she supposedly imitated, reveals several linguistic similarities and a few significant differences" (281). By extension, Holder's conclusions suggest that Wheatley was much more than just a good student of Pope.

William H. Robinson, author of the monograph *Phillis Wheatley in the Black American Beginnings* (1975), also defends her against the charge of imitation. Robinson acknowledges Wheatley's "profound spirituality, a characteristic that she would manifest in her life, poems and letters throughout her years" (15). Like Schomburg and Johnson before him, he urges that her work be studied within the context of her own world, "a time of almost total community upheaval: there was a war going on" (29). And finally he includes a substantial discussion of two major themes of her poetry: patriotism and piety (55ff). Even though the central thrust of Robinson's study is, according to him, to explore the "various obstacles to her finding and asserting her Black and poetic worth" (72), Robinson moves toward establishing a sober context within which serious study of Wheatley's poetry must begin—and he does deal with her poems analytically.

Gregory Rigsby's study of Wheatley's elegies, also appearing in 1975, represents the first purely aesthetic approach to her poetry. In this article, "Form and Content in Phillis Wheatley's Elegies," Rigsby catalogs her elegies according to subject matter, extends Matson's observation that Wheatley's elegies might suggest Black spirituals by asserting that her preoccupation with death may well harken back to her West African origins, and explores briefly the music of her verse. Rigsby then concludes by suggesting that Wheatley adopts several conventions of the elegy as they were known to her in eighteenth-century New England but that "the structural meaning she gave them . . . helps to give to Miss Wheatley's elegies a stamp all her own" (228).

The year 1977 saw the appearance of Bill Robinson's important *Black New England Letters: The Uses of Writings in Black New England.* The significance of this monograph for Wheatley Studies lies in its close analysis of the status of Wheatley scholarship, particularly that devoted to recovery of texts by and about her. Robinson makes herein his own contribution to this ongoing undertaking, demonstrating his extensive research occurring during his trips to England to search various archives for Wheatleyana. Robinson prints, for example, several letters by Susanna Wheatley, Phillis's mistress; John Andrews, Boston merchant and one of the signers of Wheatley's letter of attestation; and Selina Hastings, countess of Huntingdon and dedicatee of Wheatley's 1773 *Poems.* It is in these letters that we come to understand for the first time that Wheatley's 1772 "Proposals" for a volume were rejected for racist reasons and that it was the countess of Huntingdon who wanted a portrait (woodcut) of Wheatley to serve as a frontispiece to the 1773 *Poems.* Robinson concludes his thorough and helpful investigation of Wheatley with the following poignant observations:

> Since the time of this 1773 volume [Wheatley's *Poems*], successive generations of black American poets, forced to deal with successive generations of racism, have been constrained to employ

successive strategies, each in his or her own way, to create and to sustain a black American poetic tradition that would give documentation to a black past, substantiation to a black present, and hope for a black future. The anguishes and achievements, the losses and the gains involved in the construction and nurturing of such a tradition Phillis Wheatley would understand thoroughly, for, in her own way, she began that tradition. (57)

Despite the efforts of Wheatley's many defenders who have responded effectively to the attempts to discredit her work, and despite the labors of temperate critics who have demonstrated that her poetry deserves critical scrutiny, echoes of ancient condescension and undocumented charges still persisted. For example, the editors of the 1974 editions of the *Anthology of American Literature* and of *The American Tradition in Literature* followed Wheatley's tolerators by claiming that her poetry is imitative. The editors of the *Anthology* restate, on the one hand, the tedious notion that Wheatley's "work was derivative and limited, and that it relied on an often repeated store of classical allusions and ritual invocations of the Muses" (McMichael 506), as if to do so must somehow be construed to be signs of inferiority. On the other hand, the editors of *The American Tradition* think that the "range of subject matter" of her verse "is small, and mostly circumscribed by the geography and mind of New England," and that "all too often her sentiments were conventional and her expression stilted" (Bradley 138). But perhaps most damaging of all is the condescending remark found in the Bibliography volume of the *Literary History of the United States* (1974): "The Negro poetaster Phillis Wheatley (ca. 1753–1784) achieved something of a vogue with the publication of her *Poems on Various Subjects* (1773), though it received little critical notice" (Spiller 100). This observation represents the extent of comment on Wheatley in either of the volumes of this still highly influential scholarly history.

To judge Phillis Wheatley as nothing more than a mere rhymester is not to *read* her poetry and to rely upon the opinions of former hostile commentators, such as Moses Coit Tyler and J. Saunders Redding. The next twenty-five years of Wheatley commentary strive to make an end of readings based solely upon *a priori* theories, most of which were at the least undocumented and all of which have now been proved wrong; the merits or demerits of Wheatley's poetry have begun, during these last twenty-five years, to be judged according to the experience and experiment of careful analysis—the central goal of the present work.

All of the writers about Wheatley's poetry from the first two hundred years—the detractors, the celebrants, the tolerators, the defenders, and the few critics of her poetry *qua* poetry—have in two significant ways contributed immeasurably, whether wittingly or unwittingly, to the study of her work. First, the recurrent periods of controversy over the quality of her verse ensured that Wheatley's life and work have remained alive. Even at such moments when it appeared certain that her most negative commentators had laid her to rest, some enthusiastic celebrant or defender rescued her and tried to establish for her a suitable place in Early American and in Black American literature. Second, one may draw out of this controversy many of the problems encountered in an approach to analysis of her poems. These problems, particularly those of her race, her sex, and her choice of the neoclassic idiom, have mitigated somewhat during the last twenty-five years. But they, disappointingly, have hardly disappeared.

CHAPTER THREE

Wheatley Intellectually Gifted—Maybe: The Last 25 Years

THE LAST TWENTY-FIVE OR SO YEARS HAVE YIELDED A VERITABLE TREASURE TROVE OF WHEATLEY COMMENTARY, A SIGNIFICANT AMOUNT OF WHICH WE CAN RECOGNIZE AS CRITICISM IN THE good sense. Wheatley now appears in all college-level anthologies of American literature, always with several selections from her poetry and most recently with a few of her letters. The 2005 *Norton Anthology of Poetry*, which collects poetry in English from *Beowulf* through the present, has four of her poems, including "On Imagination." And she has been the subject of two articles in *Publications of the Modern Language Association* and of two articles in *American Literature*. Now we may conclude that Wheatley enjoys canonical status!

During this same period, Wheatley has become a subject for critical treatment abroad, in Europe and Africa; her extant works have appeared in no fewer than four editions; at least seven single-author American books have featured her poetry as a subject in their criticism; and she has become the primary subject of numerous scholarly articles. In 2003 she became the principal topic of a monograph by Henry Louis Gates, Jr. entitled *The Trials of Phillis Wheatley: America's First Black Poet and Her Encounters with the Founding Fathers*. So frequent has been her appearance in critical discourse of this period that we may declare Wheatley Studies have become a vogue.

Perhaps it was William H. Robinson's next three books that did more than any other publications to initiate this vogue in Wheatley Studies. *Phillis Wheatley: A Bio-Bibliography* (1981), *Critical Essays on Phillis Wheatley* (1982), and *Phillis Wheatley and Her Writings* (1984) did much to stimulate new interest. The *Bio-Bibliography* contains a wealth of information about commentary on Wheatley through 1979, while *Her Writings* reproduces, in addition to her poems (those extant in 1984) and letters, texts of collateral interest, such as Margaretta M.

Oddell's valuable *Memoir*. With Robinson's works, Wheatley scholars became equipped to pursue fairly sophisticated investigations of this fine poet's texts. But did such sophisticated investigations actually take place? What remains disconcerting about so much of this critical discourse is the persistence of a large number of errors regarding Wheatley's life and works.

These persistent errors we will take up per se shortly. Now, however, let us examine other high points of this twenty-five-year period. In 1981, S. E. Ogude, a Nigerian scholar from the University of Benin, published, in the American journal *World Literature Today*, an article entitled "Slavery and the African Imagination: A Critical Perspective"; herein he defines African literature as "the collective expression of the racial memory of black people all over the world" (24–25), thereby finding the work of Wheatley a somewhat curious manifestation of that "racial memory." Two years later Ogude came out with a book devoted to the same topic, this venture published by the University of Ife Press in Ile-Ife, Nigeria. In his *Genius in Bondage: A Study of the Origins of African Literature in English*, Ogude gives a long chapter of almost fifty pages to Wheatley. So we observe Wheatley's fame spreading to her native Africa.

A year after the appearance of Ogude's article, A. J. Nielson published the provocative "Patterns of Subversion in the Works of Phillis Wheatley and Jupiter Hammon." In his work, Nielson traces Wheatley's insistence on her Africanness, calling herself "*Afric's* muse" (97) or proclaiming "An *Ethiop* tells you" (16); such subtle hints constitute Wheatley's "recognition of the unique nature of [her] project" as "she was the first African woman to venture into print as an English language poet" (214). As well, he points out that Wheatley argues, in "To the University of Cambridge in New England," that she can feel and understand "the same conceptualizations which the white students have made use of" (215). To my knowledge, Nielsen's revelation that Wheatley was capable of, and actually deployed, subversive practices in her work is the first to appear in Wheatley Studies. Regrettably, years were to pass before we readers of Wheatley began to make good use of Nielsen's penetrating observations.

Sondra O'Neale is one of the first to follow Nielsen's lead. In "A Slave's Subtle War: Phillis Wheatley's Use of Biblical Myth and Symbol," perhaps the finest article yet to appear about Wheatley, O'Neale demonstrates admirably how Wheatley could be "ironically bitter ... about slavery," for example, in her famous letter to Samson Occom, discussed in the "Introduction." O'Neale's essay represents a particularly lucid moment in the best of Wheatley criticism.

Following closely on O'Neale's great success has been the remarkable work of the excellent scholars James A. Levernier, Mukhtar Ali Isani, and Philip Richards. In such articles as "Style as Protest in the Poetry of Phillis Wheatley," James Levernier explores connections between Wheatley and the New England clergy, while Isani has, over the years, committed himself to the recovery of several of Wheatley's poems and of texts related to her, such as the recovery of all nine of the London reviews which followed publication of her *Poems*; and Philip Richards has championed, in such articles as "Phillis Wheatley, Americanization, the Sublime, and the Romance of America," the interpretation that Wheatley represents "the corrosive force of her Americanization" (216) discernable within her oeuvre. It must not go unacknowledged that Wheatley has become a popular subject in several articles by German scholars. Helen Munzing, for example, contributed the piece, "Phillis Wheatley's Textual Hybridity" to the Volume, *Multiculturalism and the American Self*, edited by William Boelhower and Alfred Horning which was published in Heidelberg in the year 2000.

Among the several single-author books which feature Wheatley are the brilliant texts, *Written by Herself: Literary Productions by African American Women, 1746–1892* (1993) by Frances Smith Foster; *We Wear the Mask: African Americans Write American Literature, 1760–1870* (1997) by Rafia Zafar; and *Impossible Witnesses: Truth, Abolitionism, and Slave Testimony* by Dwight A. McBride (2001). Foster punctuates her contextual, biographical analysis of Wheatley with such penetrating declarations as, regarding her "Goliath of Gath," "In contrasting the physical strength and military prowess of Goliath with the relative weakness, inexperience but natural cleverness of David, her version echoes African American folktales" (21) and "she occasionally published poems that were increasingly direct and self-assertive" (43), recognizing Wheatley's bold entry into the sphere of public protest.

Zafar draws some of the most trenchant conclusions about our poet in the history of Wheatley Studies. About "To the Right Honorable William, Earl of Dartmouth," the poem in which Wheatley speaks of her having been stolen from the arms of her father, for example, Zafar states, "By casting the infamy of African kidnap in familial terms, Wheatley sets up the break between British and nascent America in terms of 'natural' rights, preceding even the publication of such ideas in Thomas Paine's *Common Sense*" (21). Her interpretation of "On Recollection" is the first in print that I am aware of to point out that Wheatley's phrase, "horrid crime," refers to slavery. So of course it follows that "On Recollection" is no innocuous little reflection on the function of memory, but rather it reveals a devastating condemnation of the oppressive institution of slavery.

A third book that does justice to Wheatley's texts is McBride's acclaimed *Impossible Witnesses*. Although he contributes to the old canard that Wheatley's poems were "most influenced by the works of John Milton and Alexander Pope" (106), McBride is one of the few who has recognized that "On Being Brought from Africa to America" is anything but harmless. Indeed, according to McBride, Wheatley addresses white racism head on in the second half of the poem (114). This critic next proceeds to demonstrate precisely how Wheatley's text elaborates his interpretation. Unlike many writing about Wheatley, whose work McBride judiciously characterizes as "a sociological graph of changing racial attitudes" (103), this critic attends to Phillis Wheatley's texts, yielding useful results.

Just half a decade after William H. Robinson's helpful *Phillis Wheatley and Her Writings*, two more editions of her extant works appeared. The year 1988 saw the publication of *The Collected Works of Phillis Wheatley*, the first volume in the now forty-volume Schomburg Library of Nineteenth-Century Black Women Writers. This edition particularly emphasizes Wheatley's struggle for freedom throughout her poetry and prose, her harvesting of classical sources, and her vast reading among such poets as Mark Akenside, Edward Young, and the Colonial American Mather Byles, as well as John Milton and Alexander Pope. In 1989, Julian Mason came out with a second edition of *The Poems of Phillis Wheatley*, which contains much useful information regarding his subject's texts. Vincent Carretta edited in 2001 a fourth edition of Wheatley's extant works entitled, *Phillis Wheatley: Complete Writings*, which includes her recently found "Ocean." While any new edition of Wheatley's works assuredly marks a welcome event, Carretta's claim in his title that he has collected his subject's complete writings is at best misleading; many of this prolific poet's poems and letters are yet to be located and will doubtlessly continue to surface.

Wheatley's treatment in literary encyclopedias has improved remarkably since J. Saunders Redding's jaundiced assessment in the 1982 *Dictionary of American Negro Biography*. Now we know, for example, that Wheatley was no Loyalist, as Redding had claimed. The second, 2001 edition of *African American Writers* contains a twenty-page (two-column) article on Wheatley, one of the longest essays in the volume; this article devotes ample space to Wheatley's African origins and to her elegies. *The Oxford Companion to African American Literature* (1997) gives Wheatley major author treatment.

Despite all the positive attention she has received, the Wheatley vogue is severely marked by what can only be described as a failure to take Wheatley seriously. Where many readers writing about Wheatley during these last years run into difficulty is with the basic facts of her life and work, with a reliability on erroneous conventional wisdom, with a failure adequately to contextualize her life and work, and with the intractable echoes of socio-anthropological issues. While editors David Lehman and John Brehn see fit to include two Wheatley poems ("On Being Brought from Africa to America" and "To the Right Honorable William Earl of Dartmouth") in their 2006 *The Oxford Book of American Poetry*, for example, in their brief introduction to her selections they number the poems by her in the 1773 *Poems* to be thirty-nine when she only wrote thirty-eight, and they give the date of her manumission as 1778, when we have established that date as shortly before October 18, 1773, after her return from London. In *The Poetry of Slavery: An Anglo-American Anthology, 1764–1865*, a brilliant collection, Marcus Wood opens his four selections from Wheatley's *Poems* with these trenchant remarks:

> Wheatley is now one of the most celebrated of the early African-American authors, and holds an iconic place within the Anglo-American literatures of the slave Diaspora. There is, however, intense and continuing debate over both the literary status of her work, and the extent to which it is engaged with a critique of slavery in ways which would now be considered politically cogent. (404)

The phrasing following the last conjunction "and" signals the problems manifested throughout the reminder of Wood's prefatory material. Why must we today exact that Wheatley, who lived and wrote over 220 years ago, be "considered politically cogent" for our time? Indeed were she as candid in her manner of expression—that is, in her protest against slavery—as even George Moses Horton in the early nineteenth century, she would almost certainly not have been permitted to publish anything. We can come to this understanding only by contextualizing her work within the time of her writings.

In the next paragraph of his preface, Wood claims that Wheatley knew both Latin and Greek (404). That she knew Latin cannot be doubted, but I have not been able to confirm that she had Greek as well. This notion regarding Greek is at best an unsubstantiated, early claim from nineteenth-century commentary that has been repeated so often as to have become conventional wisdom. Later Wood declares Wheatley gained her freedom "Three years after returning to America" (406), when by her own testimony, she states that, by October 18, 1773, less than two months after her return from London, "my Master has, at the desire of my friends in England given me my freedom" (170). Associated with this blunder is Wood's assertion in his "Chronology," which precedes the texts of his anthology, that Wheatley's 1773 *Poems* was published "by a black ex-slave" (iii). Overlooking the obvious three-year differential between publication and Wood's claim for "ex-slave" status, Wheatley was certainly not an "ex-slave" when her volume first appeared. Such basic facts, both of major importance to Wheatley, could have been easily ascertainable to anyone willing to find them.

Perhaps the most glaring error of fact regarding his subject is Wood's truly irritating spelling of Phillis as "Phyllis"—an error he makes with stubborn consistency, even ignoring the spelling of "Phillis" by Jupiter Hammon, also a subject of Wood's collection, in his "Address to Miss Phillis Wheatly [sic] Ethiopian Poetess in Boston." We are left to think, I suppose, that Wood believed Hammon's rendering to have been a misspelling (410). Wood does, however, mitigate somewhat his disappointing treatment of Wheatley by commenting in his closing that "as more close literary studies of the poetry emerge, it is becoming increasingly evident that the formal and technical range of Wheatley's poetry is quite exceptional" (406).

Two recently published general anthologies of poetry demonstrate disappointing treatments of Wheatley. The temper of these disappointing treatments regrettably registers an all-too-frequent handling of her life and work. To be sure, any serious reader of Wheatley must indeed be pleased to find that she has been included in such prestigious locales as *Poems, Poets, Poetry: An Introduction and Anthology* (second edition, 2002), edited by Helen Vendler and *The Norton Anthology of Poetry* (fifth edition, 2005), edited by Margaret Ferguson, Mary Jo Salter and Jon Stallworthy. Wheatley's serious readers, nevertheless, hope to find that, when she is anthologized, the critical apparatus that accompanies her work will, at the very least, be judicious.

Vendler selects for her collection Wheatley's most frequently anthologized poem, "On Being Brought from Africa to America"; unfortunately this poem is perhaps her least understood, and Vendler's use of it sounds a typical chord. Consisting of two four-line stanzas of what appears to be vastly different thought, this cleverly crafted poem invites its readers not to recognize the contrast, at least not immediately. Here, as at several other moments in the 1773 *Poems*, Wheatley's text brilliantly diverts the attention of her principal, white readers by projecting a façade of innocuousness. Basically speaking, the first stanza, probably all there was of the poem when first named in the 1772 *Proposals* as having been composed in 1768 and entitled "Thoughts on Being Brought from Africa to America," looks as if it tells the tale of a recent convert to Christianity. By 1773, some five years later, Wheatley had left behind her period of juvenilia, during which her major project was trying to convince white folks she was just as "good" for God's grace as were they.

By the period of her interiorized maturity, from late 1771 through to her manumission shortly before October 18, 1773, her patience with the so-called religious community of white folks was virtually terminated. In other words, Wheatley, during her first period of maturity, became heavily engaged in a search for her own idea of God. Such significant poems as "On Imagination" and "On the Death of Dr. Samuel Marshall" display barely a hint of Christianity. So we should not be surprised to discover a bit of a conflict regarding Wheatley's commitment to Christianity in this text. Indeed, when we look up "pagan" from the first line, "'Twas mercy brought me from my pagan land," we find some unexpected information. "Pagan," in the phrase "my pagan land," derives from the Latin "paganus," which identifies a rustic or rural villager—certainly not a Christian heathen, a later, early Christian application. Given Wheatley's unquestioned knowledge of classical Latin, it would be less than sound to presume that Wheatley did not have access to this knowledge. So if Wheatley is simply identifying her land as a rurality rather than as a residence for heathens, such a possibility cracks wide open the subversive meaning of this poem. This initial stanza further details that, having arrived in the wonderful land of Christ, she was taught about the Godliness of the "*Saviour*" and his wonderful promise of redemption. But what, pray, have all the wonderful promissory claims actually "brought" her (pun intended)? The second stanza, as we will soon learn, states blatantly that many of these "wonderful" Christian types have labeled her and other Black Folks the bearers of an *evil* color.

The poet has in the first stanza, nevertheless, relied on the white folks' preoccupation with a dominating pagan vs. Christian mentality to lead them away from ferreting out her intense rejection of their oppressive behavior. Now, when we combine her knowledge of classical Latin with her development of a syncretized religious consciousness (her integration of Christianity, Islam, hierophantic solar worship, animism, and classical myth), the next stanza, probably added for the 1773 *Poems*' version, carries much more power than conventional wisdom has assumed.

The tone of the second stanza shifts abruptly from apparent harmlessness toward aggression, an aggression masked by the ostensibly passive tenor of the first stanza. "Some view our sable race with scornful eye"; so begins this somewhat militant stanza. Having figuratively "gotten permission" to declare herself, as she had in "To Maecenas," where she asserted to her white readers that she will make herself a mature poet "While you, indulgent smile upon" her success, Wheatley calls her Black brothers and sisters members of the "sable race." This elevated dignification of the color "black" she next starkly contrasts with an overheard denigration of that color: "'Their colour is a diabolic die.'"

Outraged by white folks' racist characterization, Wheatley next admonishes, "Remember, *Christians, Negros* [sic], black as *Cain* / May be refined and join th' angelic train" (18). Note that Wheatley's "Remember" is cast in the imperative mood. Perhaps even more significant is the separation this command achieves. That is, Wheatley's demand that "Christians" recognize the alleged availability of salvation for all believers distances her from the Christian community which has already separated itself from her and her Black brothers and sisters, if only by the perceived "evil" nature of their color. When we place this poem within the context of Wheatley's evolving religious consciousness and take into account the subversive nature of her poetry composed during her first period of maturity, "On Being Brought from Africa . . ." wields a powerful message.

For not only does Wheatley directly chide the so-called Christian white folks of Boston *and* London, but she sets herself over and against such "Christian" persons who fail to recognize her human equality, as well as that of all Blacks. So it becomes doubtful as to whether Wheatley continues, in 1773, to number herself among the Christian community, or for that matter to be satisfied with the Christian religion as it may be identified by its white advocates.

Just so, we discover that this poem is much more complex than Vendler's flawed judgment that we should read the poem as "Phillis Wheatley's advocacy of Christianity over paganism" (293). This misleading comment represents the extent of Vendler's remarks regarding Wheatley. In this instance, Vendler clearly fails as a serious reader of Wheatley when she continues to press for the conventional interpretation of this piece and when she gives no thought to how contextualization could help to shape our understanding of "On Being Brought. . . ."[1]

A better grasp of Wheatley's shift away from being a kind of accommodationist toward her subversive posture can now be offered for why she dropped the earlier 1767 poems, "An Address to the Atheist" and "An Address to the Deist"; these naïve statements from her juvenile period no longer serve her determination to seek liberation though her written words. Indeed, "On Being Brought from Africa to America," *revised,* can now be viewed as another sign of her rejection of white folks' Christianity *but not necessarily of Christianity itself.* As we will find out in a later chapter, Wheatley embraces Christianity as a part of her syncretized idea of God.

"On Being Brought from Africa to America" is also included in the fifth edition of *The Norton Anthology of Poetry,* along with three other poems, one of which is her most important work, "On Imagination." Finding four of her poems in this august collection is for all serious readers of Wheatley assuredly gratifying. So when the editors take the trouble to trace some of the final lines of "On Imagination" to a brief passage in Milton's book 9 from *Paradise Lost,* I, for one, was quite pleased, as most editors of large collections do not give her work such attention. Another factor that falls neatly into place in this particular exercise in source hunting is the fact that the *Anthology* includes all of *Paradise Lost*'s book 9, enabling the editors to draw connections between these two poets' works within the same text.

A closer reading, however, begins to reveal a few problems in this seemingly fortuitous connection. The problems that arise are signaled by the editors' biographical sketch of Wheatley. They call John Wheatley, her owner, a tailor, for example, when the Wheatleys owned two merchant ships which created valuable contacts for them in London, even enjoying the friendship of Brook Watson, famous for his merchant marine exploits in America and the Caribbean and a sometime major of London. This same Watson bequeathed Wheatley a copy of Milton's *Paradise Lost* during her visit to London. Claiming that Wheatley was "Influenced by John Milton and Alexander Pope," the editors "accuse" Wheatley of using "highly artificial diction," without saying exactly of what this practice consists. Such expressions that Whatley does use, and which Wordsworth would have called "poetic diction," include "finny race" and "feathery race." These expressions were standard poetic idioms of the day deriving from British neoclassical praxis, as the editors of *The Norton Anthology of Poetry* know very well.

Subsequently the editors opine that, despite her "artificial diction," Wheatley employed an emotionally restrained, highly accessible plain style," failing to explain the obvious contradiction. These problems, coming from a lack of knowing the facts and from a reliance upon conventional wisdom, predict that these editors may encounter difficulty when trying to identify Wheatley's sources.

The editors offer what looks like, on the surface, a plausible source for Wheatley's lines: "Winter austere forbids me to aspire / And northern tempests damp the rising fire; / They chill the tides of Fancy's flowing sea" (11. 50–52), the sea of her inspiration. According to the editors, Wheatley "here alludes to and revises Milton's famous lines to his Muse (his source of inspiration) expressing his fear that he is too old, or born in a time and place too inhospitable to epic productions, to accomplish his poetic aims." The lines from book 9 of *Paradise Lost* read: My muse appears not to be functioning at its best because "an age too late, or cold / Climate, or years, damp my intended wing / Depressed" (*Norton* 426). While "cold/climate," "damp," and the subject of inspiration do indeed interplay here, what should we understand about Milton's advanced age (in his sixties) and Wheatley's youth (nineteen or twenty); or Milton's assertion that the age of the world may be too late for epic ventures and Wheatley's determination, in "To Maecenas," "Goliath of Gath," and "Niobe in Distress . . . ," to work undauntedly with epic materials? The cold Wheatley speaks of in "Winter austere" she had already introduced much earlier in the poem: "Though winter frowns to Fancy's raptured eyes" (1. 23). Therefore, what this poet is doing in her conclusion is drawing an obvious connection between her earlier disempowerment that cold, white folks would impose on the operation of her fancy, which her imagination and fancy manage to overcome for some thirty-seven lines but which she cannot indefinitely sustain—both because the two heterocosms she elaborates are mythological constructs, like the later heterocosm Keats creates in "Ode to a Nightingale," and because white oppression is less than supportive of her enterprise. There is, then, evidence within Wheatley's text and in her life conditions which erodes the notion that Wheatley is rewriting Milton. I am *not* trying to suggest that the *Norton* editors are completely mistaken in their judgment; perhaps a palpable influence of Milton's text, one she knew well, does manifest itself here. What I am suggesting, however, is that, once again, Wheatley's texts are more complicated than careless readers are aware.

Their less than precise reading leads the *Norton* editors to draw another questionable interpretation. Wheatley's final line of "On Imagination," which completes the above three-line passage, reads, "Cease then, my song, cease the unequal lay" (1. 53). In her use of the adjective "unequal," so say these editors, Wheatley echoes "Milton's acknowledgment of his inability to write without the help of a power greater than (unequal) to his own" (*Norton* 723). A cursory glance at Wheatley's entire extant oeuvre quickly teaches us that this poet has, on numerous occasions and in great detail, enumerated the office of poetic afflatus; as a matter of fact, it is safe to say that Wheatley is preoccupied with this subject. The point here is that she certainly did not require a Milton, or even a Pope, to instruct her upon the gravity of this subject. Wheatley's phrase "unequal lay" may be constructively read as a comment by the poet that no one can indefinitely sustain the mythological, artificial world of a heterocosm. Only a lack of familiarity with this poet's work would explain why these editors have given these troubled readings.

Wheatley receives less than stellar handling in two collections of essays about African American authors in general. In the important collection *American Literature, American Culture,* edited by Gordon Hutner, who also serves as founding editor of *American Literary History,* Hutner excerpts a portion of J. Saunders Redding's 1939 *To Make a Poet Black,* which deals with Jupiter Hammon, Wheatley, and George Moses Horton. Of these three early African American poets, Redding saves all his vitriol for Wheatley. He finds, for example, that "Not once ... did she express in either words or action a thought on the enslavement of her race; not once did she utter a straightforward word for the freedom of the Negro" (Hutner 278). Speaking of "her wan creative energies" (Hutner 279), Redding invites his readers to believe that she "wrote white." To be sure Redding's vituperation may be explained, in part, by the fact that certain of Wheatley's texts—the "freedom" letter to Occom and the elegy on David Wooster, for example—were not known in 1939. We have already seen, however, that the serious reader of Wheatley should have recognized a modicum of subversion in the 1773 *Poems.*

Later in his chronological collection of essays, Hutner includes "Writing, 'Race,' and the Difference It Makes" by the renowned scholar and critic Henry Louis Gates, Jr. While this well-known essay does indeed give Wheatley better, more sympathetic press, it, by itself, does not rescue her from Redding's jaundiced and inaccurate assessment. Indeed, the purpose of Gates's fine essay is not to absolve Wheatley; rather he wants to demonstrate, and he does so admirably, that central to so-called Enlightenment thought was the project carried out by such intellectual giants as Hume, Kant, Jefferson, and Hegel, of proving the Black race's inferiority. The reader of Hutner's popular and prestigious six-hundred-page anthology is presented with no additional perspectives on Wheatley; therefore, readers are encouraged to take away only Redding's misleading evaluation.

Within his collection *African-American Poets: Phillis Wheatley through Melvin B. Tolson,* Harold Bloom gathers two essays about Wheatley: Sondra O'Neale's brilliant "A Slave's Subtle War: Phillis Wheatley's Use of Biblical Myth and Symbol" and Julian Mason's not-so-brilliant "'Introduction' to *The Poems of Phillis Wheatley.*" As Bloom's biographical note on Wheatley numbers among the most friendly and accurate brief notices I have found, his choice of the Mason piece leaves me puzzled and certainly disappointed. For the most part, Mason's statements of fact are reliable; when he attempts to detail facts about her educational background, however, he claims that Mary Wheatley, one of two children by John and Susanna Wheatley (Nathaniel, her brother was her twin), tutored Phillis in "studying the Bible, English (language and literature), Latin (language and literature) . . ." (Bloom 49).

Having checked the records of the Boston Latin Grammar School, during the 1760s and 1770s, I have not been able to establish that Nathaniel Wheatley, much less Mary (women were not permitted to attend the Latin grammar schools), ever matriculated with Boston Latin. Unless the Wheatley twins were privately tutored in the ancient languages (possible for Nathaniel, but unlikely for Mary) and given the fact that neither John nor Susanna appear ever to have studied anything beyond the Dame or Petty school curriculum (in which children from ages three to six or seven were taught to read the King James Bible and sometimes a little writing), Mary Wheatley was probably not equipped to tutor Phillis in Latin.

A more probable scenario is that the young and talented girl received instruction in Latin and in poetics from Mather Byles, a nephew of Cotton Mather, a congregational minister and a graduate of Harvard College; as Byles lived across the street from the Wheatleys and had been a prolific poet and champion of poets in his younger days, it is plausible that Byles took an interest in helping to shape Wheatley's budding talent. It is certain that Wheatley constructed her 1773 *Poems* (arranged her volume) after the example of Byles's 1744 *Poems on Several Occasions* (Shields, "Phillis Wheatley and Mather Byles" 1980).

Mason's declaration that Wheatley "wrote too many run-of-the-mill elegies" (Bloom 59) indicates a lack of understanding that Wheatley's motive for writing elegies probably derived from her experience in her native Gambia. That experience almost certainly taught her that, then as now, women in Africa held or hold the responsibility for delivering elegies. In other words, Wheatley felt an obligation to compose elegies, and all indications are that she knew each of her subjects.

Just such a misunderstanding, stemming from Mason's failure to contextualize Wheatley's motives for writing, probably led Mason to conclude that Wheatley "must be labeled as primarily an occasional poet" (Bloom 59), when, as we have already repeatedly observed, Wheatley actually chose her subjects with deliberate care. Her elegies were anything but occasional. This word "occasional," of course, connotes a lack of purposefulness or personal involvement with the subject treated along with a surrender of agency to some external force. Particularly during the period of Wheatley's interiorization, her first season of maturity, her topics were chosen with the subversive intention to explore the range of freedom she could realize within texts she created. Once again her poems were, more often than not, anything but occasional.

The word "occasional" also connotes a measure of public performance; that is, occasional poetry usually targets a public audience. Wheatley, knowing full well that white folks would not take her work seriously, used this knowledge to develop a "public-looking" style that would enable her to pursue topics of profound concern, such as the problem of freedom. As we have only recently recovered her subversive strategy, Wheatley's readers have failed to grasp two major realities about her work: first, that it was not as occasional as taught by conventional wisdom; and second, since it was not as public as thought, she owed less to Pope and Milton, two very public poets (for the most part), than has been alleged ad nauseum.[2]

From late 1771 until the appearance of the 1773 *Poems*, Wheatley usually wrote poems about her own struggle for freedom, which we may say metonymically represents the freedom struggle borne by all Black slaves. So how imitative of either Pope or Milton can Wheatley have been? It is one thing to maintain Wheatley went to school to Pope's expert sound techtonics, as many poets have (recall Pope was Byron's favorite poet), but it is quite another to hold that she slavishly imitated him. Yet Mason insists, "Pope's translation of Homer was the single most important influence on her works" (Bloom 60). He subsequently expands on this notion, a function of conventional wisdom, to levy this statement: "Certainly Pope's relatively fixed formulas for neoclassical poetic music found a ready response in this young African girl's natural imitative ability" (Bloom 60). These unfortunate remarks most regrettably resonate with Thomas Jefferson's insistence that Black Folks, while proficient in memory, have no innate capacity to create (see *Notes* 187–90).

Hardly less unfortunate is Michelle McKay and William J. Scheick's article, "The Other Song in Phillis Wheatley's 'On Imagination,'" published in *Studies in the Literary Imagination*. I make much of this highly questionable tract for three reasons. First, it amply displays each of the four factors that identify a lack of serious investigation: inaccurate facts, a reliance on erroneous conventional wisdom, an obfuscatory preoccupation with sociopolitical concerns, and a failure to contextualize her life and work.

Second, on a first or cursory reading, this piece exhibits the slick, even at times seductive, "look" of a potentially authoritative and influential performance. My perspective here is based on concrete experience. Whenever I have used this article, reproduced in its entirety, in my graduate seminars (I have done so now some four times), *all* my student colleagues, even the very brightest, are fooled by its authoritative veneer; indeed, not until we "read" it deliberately in class does this article's seductive mask become lifted.

Third, as "On Imagination" is Wheatley's single most important and perhaps her finest poem, it becomes vital that we approach it not with the carelessness manifested by this "interpretation," but with the deliberation and probity it deserves. For these reasons, exposure of this piece's many ills becomes both compelling and necessary.

The authors open with a quotation from W. E. B. DuBois's *Souls of Black Folk* (1903), wherein he describes his sense of "double-consciousness." The problems begin here. DuBois is speaking from the perspective of a Black man who has been promised full citizenship, but Jim Crow restrictions and racist attitudes have, throughout his life, limited the real benefits of full citizenship enjoyed by white men. In *The Black Atlantic: Modernity and Double-Consciousness,* Paul Gilroy asserts that DuBois "produced this concept . . . to illuminate the experience of post-slave populations in general" (126). DuBois's frustration and bitterness was, and even continues to be, felt by all Black men. While Wheatley certainly did feel much bitterness (as in "On Recollection"), she was both a slave and a woman. As such, she was not promised freedom, at least not when she composed "On Imagination," and then denied its fullness, and as a woman her expectations for the exercise of freedom were probably curbed even further. In other words, DuBois's double-consciousness concept indicates a considerable expression of outrage which Wheatley's circumstances of over 120 years earlier could not have exacted. This comparison between DuBois's duality and the two voices, one white and the other Black, that these authors claim to "hear" in "On Imagination," therefore, comes across as weak at best.

In the third paragraph, the authors adopt a habit of stylistic construction which, from its first appearance, erodes their entire enterprise. According to them, "By her own account, she seems to have been robbed of her memories of Africa, with one exception: a recollection of her mother offering libations to the rising sun." Then immediately following this assertion, they pronounce "Bereft of her African heritage..." (McKay and Scheick 71). Somehow, I know not how, the speculative "seems" has miraculously transformed to the factual "Bereft."

Further contemplation of this passage causes me to ask, when in her "own account" has this "robbery" occurred? How? What I see clearly in her poetry is the memory that the elegiac mode she so persistently evokes presses itself on her as a cultural memory, almost a reverence, for her African homeland; that her penchant to place "words" in the mouths of her deceased subjects suggests a residual African animism (ancestor worship); and that her unmistakable emphasis on solar imagery derives from her African culture's practice of hierophantic solar worship. Here we have viewed several indications of just how strong was the memory of her native Gambia. Actually, the "exceptional" memory *partially* described by these authors should have led them to recognize that pouring out libations to a rising sun does indeed manifest worship of the sun.

But what they fail to include in this memory of her mother is that, after the libations, she prostrates herself in the direction of "his"/its rising; that direction would, of course, have been toward the east, hence toward Mecca. This ritual strongly suggests the first of Islam's five daily prayers, and Islam had indeed penetrated the Gambia region some two and a half centuries before Wheatley's birth (McEvedy 64, 76). The indecipherable characters the eight-year-old Wheatley was observed to be writing with charcoal on a wall were very likely to have been Arabic. As the next chapter takes up her African origins per se, it is significant to say at this point that Wheatley carried with her a considerable memory of her African homeland.

The authors' claim that Wheatley was "robbed" of her African heritage reveals their general determination to argue that white folks had such decisive control over Wheatley that the "power" of imagination represents white authority, thereby relegating the inferior fancy to Wheatley herself. To be sure, this notion does *rob* Wheatley—of her own agency! It is, nonetheless, to these authors' credit that they try to establish that Wheatley's "so-called" second voice, fancy as opposed to imagination, "expresses a personal and courageous message" (McKay and Scheick 73). But they misstep when they hold that "slavery-like bondage" characterizes fancy when the poet observes that, as the fancy wanders about in search of some diverting, "lov'd object," its (the fancy's) "silken fetters," the property of fancy, "all the senses bind" (65).

The mental operation of fancy here closely resembles that expressed by Mark Akenside in the line, "The silken fetters of delicious ease" in his extremely popular (for its time) 1744 *Pleasures of Imagination* (book 2, 1. 562). As we begin to read Wheatley with an eye to her subversive strategy, I suppose it does become tempting to see subversion behind every syllable. To do so in this context, however, displays a failure to read the text closely enough. Clearly Wheatley is presenting an analytical discussion of how she understands fancy's role in the service of the poet. And note that I have shown these "silken" chains, which are *not* chains but a suggestion of the next line's "soft captivity," are certainly the property of fancy! The "silken fetters" and "soft captivity" of which Wheatley speaks are, then, functions of a "delicious ease," occurring as a result of heightened poetic afflatus—not signs of a "self-enslaving inclination" (McKay and Scheick 74). Indeed any enslavement that may figuratively take place here remains merely figurative, resulting from the poet's analysis of *her* intellectual property.

These authors get into deep trouble on the fourth page of their article when they claim that the imagination exercises the "cold majesty of the imperial queen who is situated in the remote freedom of 'refulgent heights'" (74). This phrase, "refulgent heights," appears in the poem's second stanza:

> From *Helicon's* refulgent heights attend,
> Ye sacred choir, and my attempts befriend:
> To tell her glories with a faithful tongue,
> Ye blooming graces, triumph in my song.
>
> (65)

Just a glance at a classical dictionary, say Margaret C. Howatson's *Oxford Companion to Classical Literature,* would have identified "Helicon" as the mountain home of the muses, *not* the residence of imagination per se; and of course every schoolgirl and -boy know that "sacred choir" is synonymous with the nine muses. Curiously, the only classical resource listed in the authors' bibliography is Edith Hamilton's *Mythology* (1940). The listing of this children's handbook demeans Wheatley's prodigious knowledge of ancient classicism, essentially adding injury to insult.

The second stanza of "On Imagination," therefore, serves as Wheatley's elaborate invocation to the muses. The authors compound their blunder when they declare, "Since Imagination and Fancy are both gendered as female, the phrase 'To tell her glories' presents a pronoun that remains referentially uncertain" (McKay and Scheick 74). At this point I find myself bewildered. If we should give this stanza as a sort of "trick" exercise, "find the antecedent," to an eighth-grade class in basic grammar, our brightest students would surely recognize that these four lines, in and of themselves, have no antecedent, as the noun to which the pronoun "her" refers must be somewhere above and beyond these four lines. We would, to be sure, award these brightest scholars an "A." But as for these authors . . . ? As there is no gendered noun, in these four lines, we must, of course, seek the antecedent for "her" in the preceding stanza where we find a gendered noun in "queen" whose referent is unquestionably the title's "Imagination." Frankly, as the authors base the remainder of their argument on this unfortunate misreading, their presentation crumbles precisely at this point.

The many other errors which we encounter in this piece are so numerous that to belabor their exposure for long could be thought to approach cruelty. With an eye toward preventing this sort of poorly argued interpretation, I am, nevertheless, obligated to direct attention to what are perhaps the most glaring problems remaining. We soon come to find Wheatley is a "fettered soul," without ever being told *how* we reached this chained destination. Somehow from the line, "Though *Winter* frowns to Fancy's raptur'd eyes" (66,1. 23), fancy has become "frozen," when what happens next in the poem is that, in spite of a forbidding Winter, the poet constructs a warm and delightful heterocosm, a demonstration of the poet's power to "amaze th' unbounded soul" "with new worlds" (66,1. 22). Note the word "unbounded" here; Wheatley frees her very soul, even if only temporarily, for the duration of her heterocosmic moment.

In addition to the irritating repetition of the subjunctive constructions, "may be," "can be," and "must be," we find the repetition of an unabashed hostility toward neoclassicism in general. The eighteenth-century's literary efforts are condemned again and again in such phrases as "the tawdry ornamentalism of neoclassical tradition" (McKay and Scheick 79), the "arid neoclassical tradition" (76), and "passionless neoclassical verse" (McKay and Scheick 82). And I am still trying to fathom what these authors mean by the oft-repeated "Anglo-American literary tradition," which they never attempt to explain.

On a final note, McKay and Scheick rehearse Mason's notion that Mary Wheatley taught Phillis Latin: "She had studied Latin with Mary Wheatley" (83). I should like to add, nevertheless, that these authors do insist that Wheatley in fact knew Latin, unlike Carla Mulford, who in her introductory material to Wheatley from her *Early American*

Writings assures all students of Wheatley that she only "read classical writers in translation" (888). So we observe in "The Other Song in Phillis Wheatley's 'On Imagination'" errors of fact, a dependence on conventional wisdom, a desire to draw on sociopolitical concerns (especially in the DuBois comparison), and *a failure to contextualize her texts.*

In his "authoritative" *Authority and Female Authorship in Colonial America,* Scheick draws on his erroneous conclusions in "The Other Song . . . ," thereby only compounding his failure to grasp Wheatley's important "On Imagination." While I must say I like Scheick's observation that in "On Being Brought . . ." "Wheatley's persona . . . challenges the critical complaints that her poetry is imitative, inadequate and unmilitant" (124) and that we may perhaps "expect too much if we insist that Wheatley conform to the current agendas for and readings of the social text of our time" (127), such positive perspectives do not ameliorate the several troublesome readings Scheick makes in his chapter on Wheatley.

In his discussion of "Goliath of Gath," for example, three times Scheick refers to the poem as "Goliath and Garth," paralleling the sort of careless usage we have seen all too often characterizing other critics' misspelling of "Phillis." About this same poem, Scheick insists upon calling this 222-line poem a biblical paraphrase, rather than the epyllion that it is. To be sure, Wheatley's source for "Goliath of Gath" is 1 Samuel 17; yet the poem in Wheatley's 1773 *Poems* has become so fleshed out by many interpolations obviously adapted from classical epic that to ignore the proper identification of "Goliath" as an epyllion or short epic is simply to miss the several opportunities for Scheick to have enlarged and reinforced his standing, though otherwise more convincing interpretation.

Scheick's reading of "On Being Brought to America" is in turn marred by claiming that Wheatley's use of "refined" (as "refin'd") in the last line derives from a passage in Isaiah and that "train" in the same line springs from another passage in Isaiah. A glance at a concordance of the Bible (including the Apocrypha) quickly reveals that "train" appears in 1 Kings 10:2; Judith 7:18; and Additions to Esther 15:4, while "refined" may be found in Isaiah 25:6; 1 Chronicles 28:18; 29:4; and Zachariah 13:9. I submit, moreover, that Wheatley would have easily encountered both these words in Pope, Hobbes ("train" as "trayne"), and in Henry Home, Lord Kames, among many others. Why *must* Wheatley's use come from Isaiah?

As for "On Imagination" Scheick repeats his notion that "Fancy" is "Devalued and subservient," thence serving "as a trope for suppressed

African American sentiment," and that "Anglo-American neoclassical culture" suppresses "human feeling" (125). Seldom have I encountered such blatant hostility toward neoclassicism. Once again, as well, we find ourselves exposed to such ineffective conditional constructions as "must have had in mind" (twice) and "may contain aesthetic allusions" (122–23). I should be pleased to discover whatever on God's green earth Scheick means by "aesthetic allusions." While Scheick's intentions to find insightful political commentary within Wheatley's oeuvre may, in the effort, be admirable, the execution is finally neither admirable nor convincing. Other critics of this most recent period in Wheatley Studies have proved more successful.

In *The Collected Works*, I observed that, for too long a time, Wheatley's political poetry had been ignored. Since that time, many have taken up the cause of recognizing Wheatley's major preoccupation with American political patriotism. Indeed, contrary to J. Saunders Redding's claim that Phillis, like the rest of the Wheatleys, was a Loyalist, not a line of her extant work affirms Redding's unjustifiable opinion. Redding's inaccurate judgment also does not take into account the fact that Mary Wheatley, whose twin was Nathaniel, married one of the most fiery American Patriot ministers, John Lathrop. As critic after critic has recently demonstrated, Wheatley was, as a well-known, publishing poet, a positive influence on the evolving Revolutionary War. Tom Paine, for example, published her panegyric (praise poem) to General George Washington in *The Pennsylvania Magazine/American Monthly Museum* for April 1776.

Such articles as Betsy Erkkila's "Phillis Wheatley and the Black American Revolution," Daniel J. Ennis's "Poetry and American Revolutionary Identity: The Case of Phillis Wheatley and John Paul Jones," and Peter Coviello's "Agonizing Affection: Affect and Nation in Early America," place Wheatley in the foreground of American Revolutionary politics. Erkkila examines some of Wheatley's political poems against the Revolutionary War's "two primary social tropes: the family and slavery" (225). Regarding Wheatley's role Erkkila builds her case toward making the pivotal observation that Wheatley's fervor for freedom leads her to construct "a poetics of ascent" (232). Following this juncture, Erkkila brings her readers to the concluding moment of her essay when she declares that Wheatley has, with the assistance of the rhetoric of American Revolutionary politics, actually "shaped a poetics of ascent and liberation" (236).

I certainly do agree that these momentous phrases indeed capture the thrust of Wheatley's entire poetic undertaking. What I find disturbing here, nevertheless, is the fact that my 1978 dissertation was given the title *Phillis Wheatley's Poetics of Ascent*, that many writers about Wheatley have subsequently referred to it, that I announced in my 1988 *Collected Works* the title of my then-forthcoming *Phillis Wheatley's Poetics of Liberation* (327n15 and 329n26), and that Erkkila's article did not appear until 1993. As well, I can find not a single hint of any reference to John C. Shields or any of my work in Erkkila's essay.

While I celebrate any and all efforts to foreground the contribution of Phillis Wheatley to the American adventure in freedom, especially those efforts in the three articles named, I do have a few misgivings with the last two articles. These misgivings I shall address now. My own effort here is not to find fault but to clarify, as much as is possible, Wheatley's role as a politically astute Black woman whose primary objective was ever to promote liberation for all Americans, regardless of color. Daniel J. Ennis's article explores the literary relationship between Wheatley and John Paul Jones, who had in late October 1777 written a letter to Phillis in which he enclosed a few adulatory verses of his own composition. The cover letter of this missive calls Wheatley "the Celebrated Phillis, the African Favorite of the Nine [muses] and of Appollo [sic]" (Ennis 85).

We should recollect that Wheatley knew several more of the principal players in the American Revolution, including such dignitaries as George Washington, named above, who received Wheatley at his Cambridge, Massachusetts, headquarters sometime during the middle of March 1778; Benjamin Franklin, who called on Wheatley while in London in early July 1773 and to whom she would later dedicate her second volume of poems, proposed on October 30, 1779, but regrettably never published; David Wooster, merchant and major general of six regiments in Connecticut whose death occasioned one of her most passionate statements about freedom; and John Hancock, who signed her "To the Publick." When we add the name of John Paul Jones, we find that Wheatley did indeed number among her acquaintances an impressive group of famous Americans. So Jones's identification of Wheatley as "Celebrated" was no exaggeration.

We should also note that all these famous gentlemen were thoroughly political beings. That she caught the appreciative attention of John Paul Jones certainly does attest the extent of her fame and suggests a touchstone of her influence. In "Poetry and American Revolutionary Identity," Ennis rightly makes the point that at the present time, "Most critical commentary on Wheatley agrees that there is something constructed and/or artificial about who she is" (91). Self-fashioning and the nature of how Wheatley negotiates the white world, which would, if it could, control her, characterizes a major part of this volume. I am moved to query about all this self-fashioning phenomenon whether there has ever been any public figure in the history of mankind who has not engaged the phenomenon of self-fashioning?

The point to be made here is not simply that Wheatley is concerned with self-fashioning, but that Wheatley's position as a Black woman slave (until her manumission) who is the most capable poet of her time presses upon her a set of unique problems, the most difficult of which is how she can be true to her self, how she can carve out a space for her personal self which will, at the same time that she achieves expression of this loyalty to self, enable her, during the first period of her maturity, to continue to publish. Of course, she refuses to *lie* about her politics or any of her artistic interests. So she goes underground; that is, she chooses subversion. This subversion she applies, as we have seen and will see again and again, to the most personal of her poems. As well, this subversion derives largely from her understanding of Vergilian pastoral (eclogues), hence the artificiality which has, in the past twenty-five years, become increasingly apparent as we attend more concentratedly to her texts.

Ennis suggests that Wheatley's final couplet ending her poem, "To His Excellency General Washington," carries "a sense of paternal monarchalism." (93). While "A crown, a mansion, and a throne that shine, / With gold unfading, Washington, be thine" does indeed advance a monarchical perspective, before we label Wheatley a monarchist, we must recall that Washington himself passed a copy of Wheatley's tribute through such channels that its publication became virtually assured (see *Collected Works* 304–5 for details); that Washington eventually was offered a crown; that Washington's refusal did again, eventually, redirect the Founding Fathers' focus on republican rule for the United States; and particularly that the kind of government that would replace colonialism in America was, before that fateful summer of 1787 during which our Constitution was shaped, a matter of profound fluidity. If Wheatley looks like a monarchist, even if only briefly, we would do well to assume that she, like so many others, was merely responding to the shifting political currents of her time.

I also have a significant problem with Ennis's promotion of Vincent Carretta's "useful term 'Afro-British' to describe writers like Wheatley" (97). While I would endorse the use of "Afro-British" to encompass a writer like Olaudah Equiano, I am uncomfortable with such a descriptor for Wheatley, principally because she always saw herself in terms of the description Samuel Cooper and others articulated as early as the 1761 *Pietas et Gratulatio*. Therein, as we observed in a previous chapter, the phrase, New England, was dropped for the then becoming preferred "Columbia," which took into account all the Atlantic colonies. Wheatley's intimacy with Cooper and the Lathrops (Mary and John), along with the tenor of the entirety of her poetry concerned with American patriotism, argue against the notion that Wheatley herself could ever possibly have been content with being called "Afro-British."

I should like to remind all serious readers of Wheatley that, in the second period of her maturity when she, for the most part, dropped her subversive voice, this staunch American patriot penned the lines: "For *Galia's* [France's] Power espous'd *Columbia's* Cause, / And newborn *Rome* shall give *Britannia* Law" (154). Even as early as "America," Wheatley's position toward Britain was one of American Patriot resistance to British "tyranny"; here in 1768 she already approvingly gives the British "child," "americus," the title "rebel" (134). Perhaps this desire to ascribe to all writing by Americans recorded before July 4, 1776, the label "British" derives from the evident, recent fashion among many, but not all, Early Americanists; this "fashion" helps to promote, in my estimation, an illogical historical position that America was only British and therefore derivative of Great Britain up until the Declaration of Independence was approved.

At that fateful moment, however, when all signatures had been affixed, nothing less than a Divine Transubstantiation took place, wherein all that had been British on July 3, 1776, and before, miraculously transformed into what now became identifiably American. The absurdity of such a position is surely self-evident. When we combine this understanding with the fact that Wheatley wrote several more poems in support of American independence *after* July 4, 1776, and that her second volume of poems was to have been dedicated to Benjamin Franklin, the absurdity of calling Wheatley Afro-British redoubles.

The last of the three articles named above, Peter Coviello's "Agonizing Affection: Affect and Nation in Early America," is more complex than the first two. Attempting to analyze the role of what Coviello calls the "collective affect" (440) during the era of the early republic, he cites John Winthrop's 1630 homily, "Modell of Christian Charity," then comes back to Phillis Wheatley and Thomas Jefferson's devastating judgment of her and the Black race in general. In his journey backward to Winthrop, he notes the Revolutionary era's preoccupation with "The dangers of an excess of feeling," which Coviello claims "often came to be *racialized*" (441); such was certainly the case of Jefferson in his infamous chapter 14 of *Notes on the State of Virginia*.

While recalling Jonathan Edwards's *Treatise on the Religious Affections*, Coviello curiously remarks nothing about Edwards's condemnation of an unsanctified imagination nor anything about Phillis Wheatley's "On Imagination"; the truth is, as we have already found in a previous chapter, the eighteenth-century attitude toward imagination, at least until after Wheatley's *Poems*, was often one of trepidation and distrust of a faculty that allegedly gave rise to disorder and chaos. In a study of emotion during this time, the lack of any mention of the operation of imagination is conspicuous by its absence.

Coviello's emphasis on civic or political virtue, without ever really trying to define this concept, begs for a knowledge of the undeniable and major impact during eighteenth-century America of the myth of Aeneas. As I have determined in *The American Aeneas* (especially in chap. 4), civic virtue was, in America particularly, understood as a slightly modified *pietas*, manifested by the devotion of Vergil's hero in the *Aeneid* to the gods (to God in American terms), to family and friends, and to country. The pervasive influence of ancient classicism from about 1720 to 1800 in America has been forgotten in recent times, probably because of the overwhelming hegemony of the Adamic myth, signaled by the magisterial work of Perry Miller and his disciples.

Knowledge of the powerful role of classicism in America, had he possessed it, may have led Coviello at least to question whether Winthrop's statement in "Model of Christian Charity"—that the colonists aboard the *Arbella* were, in 1630, embarking upon the construction of "a Citty Vpon a Hill" (456) exclusively in terms of Matthew 5:14, part of the Logia of Jesus of Nazareth ("A citie that is set on a hill, can not be hid" [Geneva Bible])—was strictly biblical and therefore Adamic, or whether the notion of a city on a hill may well have had, and probably did have, connotations to the classical world's preference for strategic, urban constructions. Recall Rome was built on seven hills.

Absence of any awareness of the importance classicism exercised in the Revolutionary period has caused Coviello, and others of his generation, not to question the principle that "the nascent nation-language," as every schoolboy and -girl have been brainwashed to know, has "its provenance in specifically religious discourse." If *The American Aeneas* has accomplished anything, it has exploded, for all time, the notion that our country was founded on exclusively

Adamic principles. And if this book accomplishes anything, it will be to prevent such narrow-minded judgments regarding "Wheatley's evangelical religion" (459). In the previous chapter, we learned that Wheatley's complex religious consciousness was instructed by much more than evangelical Christianity.

Knowing that Wheatley is considerably more complex than conventional wisdom has, for too long, dictated could have led Coviello to have found Jefferson's jaundiced view of what Jefferson and Coviello both believe to have been Wheatley's orthodox evangelism to reveal more about Jefferson than about Wheatley. In other words, tracing in Wheatley's texts a multiple, syncretized idea of God could have exposed just what kind of reader Jefferson was—one whose wonderful genius (ha, ha) for levying critical literary judgment brought him to pronounce a defenseless African American woman a fraud and a cheat. What a brave man! What actually appears to be the truth behind Jefferson's attack on Wheatley is the fact that, as a slaveholder, the existence of a literate slave who can compose publishable poetry poses a threat to his chosen way of life.

While Coviello's provocative remarks about issues of grief and loss in Wheatley are indeed admirable, the strong political strain in Wheatley's texts, nevertheless, remains stubbornly pro-American and patriotic, and corresponds to the three periods of Wheatley's career, those of her juvenilia, of the first interior period of her maturity, and of the second, public period of her maturity. Always, whenever she speaks in terms of "wishes for the common good" (74), her approach, even in her juvenilia, is direct and collective. As she enters her first mature years, after she begins to realize she has not been accepted by the Boston bunch, she analyzes her victimization at the hands of the institution of slavery, causing her to search with great intensity for an interior space whence *she* may be free. Following her manumission, she quickly becomes emboldened to speak out with considerable force for liberation for all persons of color.

In his provocative and admirably analytical book, *Impossible Witnesses: Truth, Abolitionism, and Slave Testimony*, Dwight A. McBride has a chapter on Wheatley which he calls "Appropriating the Word: Phillis Wheatley, Religious Rhetoric, and the Poetics of Liberation." Significantly, unlike Erkkila, McBride cites my *Collected Works* numerous times. But more to the point, McBride points out that, even in her elegy on Whitefield from her late juvenile period, and as Whitefield was perceived to be "a friend to the African," Wheatley's very act of choosing to write a poem on the voice of the Great Awakening registered "a political statement." Certainly the London version of this elegy, which carried the antislavery lines

> Take him, ye *Africans,* he longs for you,
> Impartial Saviour is his Title due.
> If you will walk in Grace's heavenly Road,
> He'll make you free, and Kings, and Priests to God.
>
> (210)

differs strikingly from the version in the 1773 *Poems,* which replaces, "He'll make you free, and Kings, and Priests to God," with the less activist line, "'you shall be sons, and Kings, and priests to God'" (23).

While Wheatley could have well approved the "make you free" phrasing, the broadside version which was published in 1770, also in October, has the same line, "You shall be sons, and kings, and priests to GOD" (208) as in the 1773 *Poems.* My guess is that some well-meaning abolitionist in England penned the unambiguously antislavery line. As a slave herself, Wheatley would most probably not have wished to attract direct attention to her personal predicament. To have done so during her years of immaturity, such an obvious bid for manumission could have resulted in severe limitations upon her capacity to appear in print. Her choice of the subversive mode which characterizes her first period of maturity also argues the further the unlikelihood of her delivering an unmasked plea for freedom during her early years of publication.

What Wheatley did appear to be most concerned to accomplish in her early poems, besides her quest for approval from the Boston, white folks Christians, was a traceable declaration of American patriotism. A reliable touchstone for her public American, patriotic views is the projected arrangement for what would have been her first volume, proposed on February 29, 1772. This volume, had it received enough endorsement, would have been radically different from the 1773 *Poems.* For it would have included "On America," which enumerates the American angst against harsh British taxes; "To the King's Most Excellent Majesty," which celebrates the 1768 repeal of the Stamp Act; "On the Death of Mr. Snider Murder'd by Richardson," which extols Snider as "the first martyr for the common good"; "On the Arrival of the Ships of War and the Landing of the Troops," which if located would almost certainly have conveyed the indignity of Boston patriots; "On the Affray in King-Street, on the Evening of the 5th of March," which definitely (if authenticated) would have lionized Crispus Attucks and others, victims of the Boston Massacre; and finally "To Samuel Quincy, Esq; a Panegyrick," which is not extant but would have been a praise poem about the attorney (Quincy was also the attorney for the Wheatleys) who defended those survivors who joined Attucks and others in the "Affray."

If indeed these six obviously strongly patriotic poems had all appeared in Boston in this first proposed volume, Wheatley would have almost certainly received the title, harbinger of the American Revolutionary War—not harbinger of the American Colonial Rebellion. Among those political poems named above in the 1772 "Proposals," the 1773 *Poems* numbered among its selections only the laudatory and certainly apposite (because for a British audience) "To the King's Most Excellent Majesty." Wheatley continues, nevertheless, in the remainder of her oeuvre to register enthusiastic endorsement for the American patriot cause exclusively in such poems as "To His Excellency George Washington," "On the Capture of General Lee," "On the Death of General Wooster," and "Liberty and Peace." Critics are certainly correct to focus attention on Wheatley's "poetry of politics," but much more work is yet to be accomplished.

Following the examination of 190 years of commentary by detractors, celebrators, and tolerators, we have finally encountered legitimate criticism (that which actually investigates Wheatley's texts) beginning with Arthur P. Davis's 1953 analysis of the personal element in her poetry. Happily, after Davis's groundbreaking study, we have observed, in articles and single-authored books, the publication of many other well-constructed analyses of Wheatley's texts. Despite the publication of many positive examples of good criticism, an article like that by McKay and Scheick about Wheatley's "On Imagination" presents a clear example of poor scholarship and worse analysis. It is certainly one of the desiderata of this volume that it contribute to the elimination of such undeserved misreadings. As well, all subsequent readings of Wheatley's fine works should become complicated by a more detailed awareness of her African heritage and by an acknowledgment of the three periods of her spiritual and intellectual evolution.

CHAPTER FOUR

African Origins

O N JULY 11, 1761, PHILLIS WHEATLEY ARRIVED IN BOSTON HARBOR ABOARD THE SLAVE SCHOONER *PHILLIS;* WITH NOTHING MORE THAN A SCRAP OF DIRTY CARPET TO CONCEAL HER nakedness and within three weeks of her arrival, she was sold on the block "for a trifle" to the wealthy Boston merchants John and Susannah Wheatley. Named for the slaver which transported her, she was brought to the Wheatley mansion on the corner of King Street and Mackerel Lane (now State and Kilby streets) where she met the twins, Mary and Nathaniel, the only children of the Wheatleys. It is supposed that Phillis was at the time about seven or eight years old, "from the circumstance of shedding her front teeth." All she is thought to have recalled to her white captors about her native land is the memory that "her mother *poured out water before the sun at his rising*" and then "prostrating herself" just outside her hut toward the sun at his rising (italics are Oddell's);[1] moreover, in a poem, "Phillis's Reply," she, when about twenty-one, names Gambia as the land of her birth and writes a poetic description of it which plausibly resembles today's Gambia. Candid references in her own writings to the land of her birth are, nevertheless, tantalizingly few and may indicate a reluctance on her part to share with her predominantly white audience, the same people who would keep her in bondage, what other warm memories she may have had of her African homeland.

Whatever her motives for not recording additional details, she doubtless could have recalled many; for, even if one allows a period of time for her restraint in one of the infamous African barracoons or barracks of temporary confinement before sale and transport to an oceanbound slaver, Wheatley must have, by the age of seven, acquired some knowledge, at least in a general way, of the customs and mores of her people. In "To the . . . Earl of Dartmouth," she affectively describes the slaver's heart, "more than Stone, ne'er [by] soft

Compassion mov'd / Who from its Father seiz'd his much belov'd" (218; earlier version). Not only did she have a mother who honored the dawn and a father who fought against the capture of his daughter, but she belonged to a people who spoke a language, worshiped the deity, observed common rituals and customs, and worked together toward the achievement of common goals. In short, for the first seven years of Wheatley's life, we can almost certainly posit that she was a nurtured member of a specific African culture.

Undeniably the influence of the British, American, and classical worlds on Wheatley's writing was decisive. But to ignore the fact of her African origins is first simply dishonest and second to do her work grave injury. *Because she has left regrettably few details of the land of her origin, concentration beyond the acknowledged fact of her birth in Africa necessarily leads into speculation.* I shall employ caution, therefore, as I move from the few but provocative details concerning Africa she does provide toward an investigation of the geographic location of the land of her birth, the people of that land, their religious practices, their intellectual and artistic pursuits, and particularly the habits of their oral literature. While there may be consolation in knowing this journey must be brief, its progress yields several, perhaps unexpected, rewards.

Investigating the inertia of Wheatley's African heritage[2] must properly begin with her own testimony that Gambia was her homeland. While Julian Mason, a recent editor of Wheatley's poems, warns against accepting "her reference to Gambia as specific evidence for her homeland" and suggests that this reference "may be a poetic pose" (Mason 1966, 87n), William H. Robinson, another recent editor, maintains that the poet may here be making "reference to her remembered African homeland." A careful scanning of the poems shows that each of the other seven times she specifically cites her racial origins, she does so by employing the adjective "Afric" five times, the noun "Ethiop" once, and the noun "Ethiopians" also once. Her use of "Ethiop" and "Ethiopians" certainly constitutes a poetic pose, adopted perhaps from her reading of the King James Bible. Not at any other time, however, is Wheatley so specific about her origins as when she names Gambia as her native land. Robinson in his discussion of the allusion to Gambia points out that, even if this memory of Gambia were not a personal one (which seems doubtful to me), she could have inquired of the Fitch family, whose head Timothy was the owner of the *Phillis* (the slaver that brought Wheatley from Africa to America) what was the land of her birth. Indeed, on the very voyage that resulted in Wheatley's transport, Timothy Fitch had expressly instructed his captain Peter Gwin to secure his cargo of "slaves from the coasts of Senegal and Gambia." But then Robinson judiciously observes the location of Wheatley's purchase "need not have meant that she was a native of that locale. Slaves were often brought from miles distant from coastal locales where they were bought by European slavers."[3]

It is Wheatley's close description of her homeland which, nevertheless, most substantially challenges the suggestion that in naming Gambia as the land of her birth, she may simply have been striking a poetic pose. She distinguishes "pleasing Gambia" as the land of "spring's luxuriant reign" where gay meads smile and streams flow tunefully the year round—quite a contrast to rainy, snowy Boston. Next she emphasizes the spontaneous regenerative power of Gambia's "soil" which "yields exhaustless stores" (Wheatley 144), and she is also careful to point out the interdependency of the soil's productivity and the sun's life-giving energy. Then she concludes this recollection of her Gambian homeland by specifying that the particular place of her origin was "devoted to the God of day" (144). Her last observation is in perfect accord with her principal biographer's remark that "her mother *poured out water before the sun at his rising.*" The picture the poet draws of smiling meads, tuneful streams, and warm life-sustaining sun, as well as perennial, self-recreating springtime, sounding much like classical pastoral, may have become a bit romanticized between 1760 and 1775; but it is, nevertheless, thoroughly compatible with the present-day description of Gambia.[4]

When the evidence adduced by Robinson that Wheatley's purchase may have occurred either in Senegal or in Gambia is combined with the description the poet gives of her homeland in "Phillis's Reply," the scales lean toward Gambia as the land of her birth. Two additional pieces of evidence support this conclusion. First, the Gambia River's easy navigability suggests it made Blacks living along its banks the relatively defenseless prey of unscrupulous white (and Black) slavers. Second, when Oddell cites Phillis's "humble and modest demeanor" as a primary selling point which prompted the Wheatleys to buy her (Oddell 11-12), one recalls Carter G. Woodson's remark that New England colonists interested in acquiring slaves just prior to the Revolution "imported . . . Gambia Negroes, prized for their meekness" (Woodson 70). Although Oddell's observation may as easily reflect Phillis's outright fear as "meekness," the point to be made here is that the weight of evidence tips the scales toward Gambia as the land in which Wheatley spent the first seven years of her life. It is also worth noting that, based on her recall of fecund meadow lands, it is highly probable that she lived in an agricultural community, redolent of docile, grazing cattle and fields rich with undulating grains. Such a probability helps to explain the solar worship to which the poet indicates her countrymen and especially her mother devoted themselves.

Having established the land of her origins with some degree of probability, consideration of the African people to which she belonged can now be pursued. Owing to her particularly fine features, thin lips, narrow nose, and high forehead, as revealed in the portrait that introduces the 1773 volume, she may well have been of the Fulani people,[5] who lived on the meadow lands along the Gambia River, as well as in parts of modern-day Guinea-Conakry, Burkina Faso, Mali, Nigeria, Niger, Cameroon and Chad (Young, *The Fulani Peoples* 1), and who were especially well known as the most productive cattlemen and cultivators in Gambia (Quinn 21). The Fulani of the eighteenth century lived in a clearly stratified society of freemen, serfs and slaves; the freemen were further divided into a ruling class and ordinary farmers (Trimingham 132). The religion of the Fulani during the first three quarters of the eighteenth century was a syncretistic amalgam of animism, fetishism, and Islam, which was gradually turning toward an emphasis on Islam (Quinn 21; Trimingham 21–46; and McEvedy 76, 84).[6] As well, it was the Fulani who were "responsible for introducing and spreading Islam throughout much of western Africa" (Young, *The Fulani Peoples* 2). I should be delighted to have some better prepared student of Wheatley prove me wrong, but for now and as regards the remainder of our consideration of Wheatley's African origins, I am going to assume that Wheatley was of the Fulani peoples.

Although Wheatley's eighteen extant elegies, constituting a third of her total verse, fall generally into the tradition of the Puritan funeral elegy, the emphasis she gives in these poems to the celebration of the dead is assuredly compatible with the African practice of animism. For that matter, this preoccupation with death accords well with Paul Gilroy's observation in *The Black Atlantic* that "The turn toward death . . . points to the ways in which black cultural forms have hosted and even cultivated a dynamic rapport with the presence of death and suffering." Indeed the subject of death "emerges continually in the literature and expressive cultures of the black Atlantic" (198).

To be sure, Wheatley would have likely composed her elegies in the manner she chose, whether or not she carried along any vestiges of African animism. But the fact that her mother cultivated solar worship is compelling, especially since solar imagery constitutes the most prevalent image pattern in her poetry. The sun as life-giving warmth, as Apollo, Phoebus, or Sol, and occasionally as a pun on Son of God functions in her poems as energy of inspiration, attitude of reverence, and force of sublimity; in sum, solar imagery points the direction of her liberation poetics. Sun worship combines the two primitive religious practices of animism and fetishism, wherein the sun is celebrated as the life-giving (and sometimes life-denying, but never in Wheatley's poetry) principle imbued with spiritual and mystical powers.[7] When it occurs, it manifests a more sophisticated mode of worship than either animism or fetishism alone and becomes what Mircea Eliade terms a hierophany or supraprimitive modality of the sacred. In *Patterns in Comparative Religion,* Eliade observes that "sun worship is in fact to be found in very few parts of the world" (124) and that "Unlike other nature hierophanies, sun hierophanies tend to become the privilege of the closed circle of a minority of the elect" (150). It is probable then that Wheatley's family comprised members of the ruling class.

Curiously, Oddell depicts Wheatley's mother not only as pouring out water to the sun at dawn but then as "prostrating herself" (Oddell 13) toward that object, a circumstance that suggests a combination of rituals rather than the practice of a single one. Merle A. Richmond has determined that such prostration "suggests the Moslem ritual welcome to the new day" and that Wheatley's parents must therefore have been Muslims (12). The ritual here described, however, is more complex than Richmond has indicated. Even though the prostration at dawn appears to depict the first step in the Islamic daily ritual obligation of prayer (Farah 134–50), pouring out water to the sun points toward the fetishistic animism of an elite cult. At dawn Wheatley's mother would have turned her body toward the east, also the direction of Mecca. Quite likely the process of worship Wheatley recalled represented the syncretism of elements of solar worship and Islam. Knowledge that the Fulani peoples of the eighteenth century and before were experiencing a gradual turn away from animism toward Islam reinforces such a view. In any event, the probability that Wheatley's parents practiced a syncretistic form of worship that focused attention on the sun, especially the dawn, may account first for the poet's apparently easy accommodation of Christianity to whatever faith the inertia of her African heritage would have caused her to recall, and second may particularly explain the ultimate source of the dominant image pattern of her verse.

In addition to her affinity for elements of religious practice among the Fulani, Wheatley demonstrates certain intellectual and artistic interests that parallel similar pursuits among the peoples within the Gambia region. In "Thoughts on the Works of Providence," for example, she displays a more than common knowledge, certainly for a woman of the times, of astronomy and of the aesthetics of the infinite. Based on her African background, it comes as no surprise that she discovers God's providence "Shines most conspicuous in the solar rays" (44). Perhaps unexpectedly, however, is her celebration of God's works in nature in terms of "unbounded space"; for behind and above "the solar rays" is the Deity "Which round the sun revolves this vast machine, / Though to his eyes its mass a point appears." The "vast machine" or planet Earth moves "through her orb . . . with easy grace / Around her *Phoebus* in unbounded space" (43–44). Immediately, the rhetoric of Newtonian physics comes to mind, though I submit there may well be another, complementary source for Wheatley's interest in astronomy.

In an early African travel narrative, *A Voyage to Senegal . . . and the River Gambia*, published in London in 1759 but based on a journal kept during the fall of 1751, about two years before Wheatley's birth, the author, M. Adanson, then a correspondent for the Royal Academy of Sciences, observes that the Blacks he encountered showed a sophisticated understanding of astronomy, pointing out to him "the stars that form the chief constellations, as Leo, Scorpio, Aquila, Pegasus, Orion, Sirius, Procvon, Spica, Canopus, besides most of the planets, wherewith they were well acquainted" (253–54). Then he adds, "It is amazing that such a rude and illiterate people, should reason so pertinently, in regard to those heavenly bodies: for there is no manner of doubt, but that, with proper instruments and a good-will, they would become excellent astronomers" (254). If Adanson knew of the penetration of Islam into the region, he does not offer that knowledge as a possible explanation for such specific familiarity with the principles of astronomy; for with their Muslim faith the Arabic peoples had brought into West Africa both their excellent understanding of the heavens and literacy, at least to some of the West African aristocracy and particularly to the Fula peoples.

If Wheatley had been taken from the bosom of an aristocratic Fulani father, her later familiarity with Newtonian physics, information available to her as an inevitable concomitant of eighteenth-century Enlightenment, can be construed as simply the continuation of an interest prompted by her African origins. And it is also provocative to speculate that she may have come to America carrying with her a rudimentary knowledge of Arabic script adapted to the Fulani language,[8] hence in some measure explaining her immediate aptitude shown the Wheatleys both for writing and for reading the English language. Margaretta Oddell, "a collateral descendant of Mrs. Wheatley" (Phillis's mistress Susannah), who was by her own testimony "familiar with the name and fame of Phillis from [Oddell's] childhood" (Oddell in Robinson 450), has recorded that, soon after Phillis's purchase, she "was frequently seen endeavoring to make letters upon the wall with a piece of chalk or charcoal" (Oddell in Robinson 431). The implication here is that Phillis was attempting to trace English characters; given the spread of Arabic literacy into the Gambia region just before Wheatley's infancy along with her probable biological membership among the Fulani elite, one may with good reason posit that Wheatley was attempting to draw out not English but Arabic script. In addition, Oddell presents in her sketch a picture of the very young Wheatley being "beguiled from the hut of her mother" and subsequently finding herself sold into slavery. As the hut was, according to Riesman, the location at which women performed prayer or "in front of the doors" of their hut (168), and as the hut itself was constructed by women who therefore came to symbolize "that feminine work tends toward the creation of culture, that is to say it transforms nature, or bush, into culture, or village" (64), Oddell's observation reveals an uncanny awareness of the significance the hut played for Wheatley's African culture and particularly for the young, budding African poet. The importance of Wheatley's mother's hut strikingly parallels the cultural responsibilities embracing Native American women of the North American plains before and after Wheatley's era, until the interference of white folks during the late nineteenth and early twentieth centuries.

At any rate, Adanson also speaks of "the amusement I received from the fables, dialogues, and witty stories, with which the Negroes entertained each other alternately, according to their custom" (252). In a later travel narrative, *Travels in Africa to the Sources of the Senegal and Gambia*, in 1818, G. Mollien describes being awakened one morning by the singing of a Black king's *griot*, or poet-musician, who "was accompanied by a number of female singers." Then Mollien relates, "I dare not repeat the panegyrics which they bestowed on me" (29).

In themselves neither of these African travel narrative passages is remarkable. As introduction to the kind of music and poetry with which Wheatley as a seven-year-old would undoubtedly have been thoroughly familiar, however, these illustrations are of particular significance. They attest the pre-nineteenth-century (and even continuing) practice of sharing, in some traditions among African peoples, of the roles of oral poets. It is possible Adanson witnessed the chanting of fables or proverbs and historical dialogues consisting of exchanges in which listeners corrected one another's memories regarding the history of that particular group or the details of some humorous anecdote. Mollien's description is more to the point, however, first because he identifies the panegyric (praise poem) which, according to Ruth Finnegan in *Oral Literature in Africa*, "is one of the most developed and elaborate poetic genres in Africa" (111) and second because, in the phrase "was accompanied by a number of female singers," he signals the participation of women in the making of music and poetry in the very region from which Wheatley probably descended.

Although it is plausible to posit that, as a student between the ages of one and seven, Wheatley absorbed from her African years images of the land of her birth, especially of its worshiped sun, and retained memories of the intellectual and artistic pursuits which characterized the people of that land—whether or not it was in the vicinity of the Gambia River—her internalization of the habits and traditions that distinguish the practice of West African oral literature is of paramount importance to her extant verse performances. Examination of eighteenth-century West African oral literary forms and of their possible relationship to this Colonial American Black woman's poetry, therefore, demands detailed attention. This treatment of the possible relationship between her African literary origin, on one hand, and on the other, her poetical praxis—that is, her perception of her role as poet, the intensively musical strain pervading her verse, and the structures of her panegyric poems, of her epyllia and especially of her elegies—reveals several substantial parallels.

In *The Black Mind: A History of African Literature*, O. R. Dathorne writes that the traditional African oral poet "was expected to reorder the group experience . . . because he was ultimately responsible to that absolute ideal of art present in the collective memory of the tribe" (7–8). The oral tradition consequently produced by the African poet of tradition is perhaps inevitably "extremely earthbound and is linked to social functions" (17). When this "collective memory" became displaced, that is, when Black men, women, and children were enslaved, it is hardly accidental, then, Dathorne continues, "that the first Black writers in Latin, English, and French were group spokesmen and directed their praise toward objects and people within the new cultures in which they found themselves" (57). Hence we observe Wheatley in 1770, in "On the Death of Mr. Snider Murder'd by Richardson," celebrating "the first martyr for the cause" (136–37) of the American Revolution (perhaps in the first poem of the Revolution), later praising Washington in "To His Excellency General Washington" as the newly appointed "Generalissimo of the armies of North America" (145–46), and in the last years of her life extolling in "Liberty and Peace" the achievement of American independence.

Throughout each of these poems surges a strong disposition, perhaps predisposition, toward explication of the moral ramifications of the events each describes. For example, "On the Death of Mr. Snider . . ." opens with this arresting pair of couplets: "In heavens eternal court it was decreed / How the first martyr for the cause should bleed / To clear the country of the hated brood / He whet his courage for the common good" (136). From this religious sanction of the "cause . . . for the common good," the poet moves in "To . . . General Washington" to a portrait of the commander-in-chief who proceeds against Britannia's "thirst for boundless power . . . with virtue on thy side" (146). The 1784 "Liberty and Peace," one of her last poems, addresses the economic strains of the new country by predicting that, having just defeated indomitable Britannia, America can now receive "from each [foreign state] the full commercial Tide" (154) and so bring about a "Train [of] Commerce and Plenty" (155).

Then the poet enumerates how the American victory came about as an inevitable result of moral virtue overcoming "the fierce wrong," the "Thirst for boundless power," and the menace of the "Tyrant's Law." Evidence for this essentially moral victory over Britannia may be most clearly adduced, according to the poem, from the fact that France, among other countries, rose to defend the American cause. To be sure, France had several other reasons than simple support of a moral cause against tyranny for its participation in the Revolution; and it is plausible that Wheatley was fully cognizant of these extrinsic motives. Obviously, however, her purpose in this poem is not to pursue an analytical explication of the politics which did in fact play a decisive role in the eventual American success. What she hopes to accomplish in "Liberty and Peace" is to present impassioned reinforcement of America's efforts to pick itself up from the rubble of war and subsequently to move toward the establishment of "newborn Rome," a new country out of the ashes which will serve as the world's temple of freedom. So exalted by divine sanction is this new experiment in freedom that Britain must now "submit to Heaven's decree, / That bids this Realm of Freedom rival thee" (155). Wheatley has here, as was the case in "On the Death of Snider" and in "To General Washington," attempted to provide strong moral justification for acts in behalf of the American Revolution; and, as Dathorne has described the African poet's function, she has tried "to reorder the group experiences" of a shaken but resolute people.

From this delineation of Wheatley's role, again in Dathorne's words, as that of an "extremely earthbound" poet whose thoughts are palpably "linked to social functions," we turn to consideration of similarities between the musical quality of the African American's line and that of African oral poetry. All of Wheatley's poetry resounds with the unmistakable strains of a keen musical sense. I am hardly the first to offer this observation. While delivering a paper for the Phillis Wheatley Poetry Festival, celebrating the two hundredth anniversary of the publication of her 1773 *Poems on Various Subjects, Religious and Moral,* Alice Walker, the renowned Black writer of poems, essays, and prose, addressed Wheatley over the centuries with this fitting encomium: "It is not so much what you sang, as that you kept alive in so many of our ancestors the notion of song."[9] Ruth Finnegan emphasizes the essential function of music to the sort of African oral poetry Wheatley doubtless heard repeatedly throughout her first seven or eight years. "Indeed," Finnegan notes, "much of what is normally classed as poetry in African literature is designed to be performed in a musical setting, and the musical and verbal elements are thus interdependent."[10] In *Black African Literature: An Introduction,* J-P Makouta-Mboukou emphasizes the moral function of songs sung by African folk poets when he writes, "Traditional songs . . . convey a moral—a warning, ridicule, criticism, entreaty, flattery, thanks, abuse, defiance, a demand, repulsion" (21).

Wheatley's early "On Being Brought from Africa to America" illustrates all these elements. As this poem's first version was written in 1768 when she was only fourteen or fifteen, this piece is indeed a bold expression for a young slave girl. This decidedly personal lyric (bearing some relation to a confession) opens with these apparently innocuous couplets: "'Twas mercy brought me from my Pagan land, / Taught my benighted soul to understand / that there's a God, that there's a Saviour too: / Once I redemption neither sought nor knew" (18). Taken by themselves, these lines seem to attest the enthusiasm of a sincere convert to Christianity. But this young poet, even at age fifteen, is hardly naïve, as the remaining lines reveal. Having ostensibly given herself as a suitable example of the success of Christian evangelism or, to place this first half of the poem within the context of Makouta-Mboukou's description, having offered thanks for her conversion, she subsequently moves into a direct indictment of "some" white Christians.

In the first line of the second half of this eight-line lyric, the poet declares: "Some view our sable race with scornful eye." It is, then, those numbering among "some" whom the poet appears to want to address in this poem. Note the inclusive pronoun "our"; so this poet is under no delusion that she, a Black woman, has herself somehow merited exclusion from the gaze of this collective "scornful eye." Then she completes the couplet by quoting, as if to record an aspersion overhead, "'Their colour is a diabolic die.'" While pointing out the connotations of "nobility and natural dignity" provoked by the attributive "sable," on the one hand, and the association of evil and filth inherent within "diabolic," on the other, James A. Levernier has cogently argued that Wheatley's use of the noun "die" here indicates an attempt on the part of the poet to advance a sophisticated irony. "Like the black slaves brought to America," writes Levernier, "indigo *dye* and sugar *cane* [sic] were products of the triangular trade." This critic then correctly informs us that true Christians among pre-Revolutionary American colonists—that is, those other than Wheatley's "some"—boycotted goods produced in the Indies on dye and cane plantations, where the labor was carried out by Black slaves (Levernier, "Wheatley's ON BEING BROUGHT" 26).

Wheatley closes this brief but pithy lyric[11] with this undisguised imperative: "Remember *Christians, Negros,* black as Cain / May be refin'd and join th' angelic train." What has opened with the spirit of apparent confessional closes with an admonition to all whites who, without legitimate grounds, would raise themselves above Black people. For according to the Christian message as this young girl has received it, God makes no distinction between white and Black; and just as white believers are promised "redemption," conversion has taught this Black poet that, contrary to those whites whose racial bigotry would consign all of her color to hell, implied by the word "diabolic," believers, all true believers, alas even "*Negros,*" "May be refin'd" or raised to a higher spiritual state equal to that of any white believer.

It is worth repeating that, in our earlier discussion of "On Being Brought . . . ," we noted that Wheatley's use of the phrase "pagan land" looks innocuous enough, at least on the surface. When we discover the derivation of "pagan," however, a different reading arises. And it is worth pointing out that many such occasions recur throughout Wheatley's oeuvre—that is, *occasions wherein knowledge of a particular word, particularly as understood in Wheatley's world, often alters our reading of her texts.* In classical Latin, "paganus" usually identifies land beyond the urban area occupied by a country community. The Christian use of the word gradually came to refer (around A.D. 400) to non-Christians.

So if Wheatley merely characterizes her homeland as rural as opposed to a Bostonian urbanity, then she could well be subversively suggesting to her white audience that her difference from white folks and their exclusionary Christianity is merely as inconsequential as the parameters of geography. As the remainder of the poem seems to extol the Christian message but then sharply criticizes an evidentiary hypocrisy, one promising equality for all but then denying that equality to persons of color, Wheatley's geographic origins are just as "other than" as her color. Given this reading, the poet's African origins are, or *should be,* just as meaningless as if she had strolled into urban Boston from the outlying countryside. Reading "On Being Brought . . ." in this manner brings to this text a new and unifying order in which all parts flow into one another.

Wheatley expresses in this poem her earliest written acknowledgment of the rude lesson taught her by the white world's "severe Schoolmaster." This Janus-like world speaks, even preaches, one message yet clearly practices a contradictory one (see earlier discussion of this complex poem in chaps. 1 and 3). But the important point to recognize here is that, unlike her Black poet contemporary Jupiter Hammon, who resigned himself to a temporal existence of inequality and postponed his hope for equality to the spiritual realm, this young Black poet challenges, blatantly, white insidiousness evident in the Boston public she knew and then rebukes those same authors of deceit with an unmistakable assertion of equality.

Surely such courage and forthrightness could only have proved to bigoted whites that this blooming poet was nothing but an "uppity" slave—one who was better silenced than allowed to exercise the freedom of a literate pen. As this title was among those in her first 1772 "Proposals" for a volume that was rejected by the Boston public, it is possible that some Bostonians knew of Wheatley's "uppity" notions and refused to support her first volume's publication because of them. "On Being Brought from Africa to America" is an extremely important poem to this poet's evolving liberation poetics; perhaps the fact that this piece enjoys a reputation among recent readers as one of her most controversial poems signals its importance. I submit, moreover, that, although in these 1772 "Proposals," Wheatley gives 1768 as the year of composition for "Thoughts on Being Brought from Africa to America," by the time of the 1773 *Poems,* she has revised the earlier "Thoughts . . . ," omitting this noun and producing a masterpiece of subversion and rebuke.

In addition to challenging the injustice of the status quo, Wheatley is here in the act of determining her role as poet. Not at all content with resignation, she steadfastly, even at this early moment, confronts those who would condemn her and her race, and challenges their tyranny over her and hers. Having been in New England for only seven years, perhaps she is recalling in this poem traditional African folk songs as she delivers to an unsympathetic audience this highly moral warning, replete with a tone of entreaty, perhaps even of flattery, yet which at the same moment conveys an attitude of defiance, command, and repulsion.

Another performance by Wheatley that suggests recollection of an African musical setting occurs in her companion pieces, "An Hymn to the Morning" and "An Hymn to the Evening." Despite claims that Milton's "L'Allegro" and "Il Penseroso" inspired these companion poems, neither piece is given to analysis of cheerful or thoughtful men. Rather each constitutes a paean to the sun, recalling her mother's solar worship and in addition restating the general classical origin of the paean as a literary genre first devoted to the celebration of Apollo, Greek god of the sun. Discounting for the moment the subject of these poems, let us examine their structure. The first two lines of "An Hymn to the Morning" present an invocation to the muse: "Attend my lays, ye ever honour'd nine, / Assist my labours, and my strains refine" (56), serves both poems; note the plural "lays." Minus this invocation, each piece is exactly eighteen lines in length. Both poems celebrate the sun's inestimable contribution to the soft, purling streams, gentle gales and singing birds of spring; then each concludes abruptly. Whereas the morning piece cites the poet's musical intention in the line, "In smoothest numbers pour the notes [not beats or stresses] along," the evening piece absorbs the music within this "auditory image," "the birds renew their notes, / And through the air their mingled music floats." This renewal of the birds' song suggests the relationship of statement, or call, and response which obtains between these poems. As the sun reaches its noon zenith in the morning hymn, its complementary descending motion is recorded in the evening hymn. Even use of the word "hymn" in each title signals the musical structure of a sort of antiphonal anthem.

In his discussion of African poetry in the *Princeton Encyclopedia of Poetry and Poetics* (2nd ed.), Lyndon Harries asserts that lyric is "probably the most common genre of oral poetry in Africa" and "has a great variety of forms." Then he defines the genre as "basically . . . a short poem sung or recited either antiphonally or by an individual." He next describes the subjects of African lyric as "about every conceivable topic in the African experience. Songs about or attributed to birds are very common, but the main interest is human life and conduct" (910). These two poems, among Wheatley's shortest, place great emphasis on the songs of birds, on antiphonal structure, or call-and-response so common among African American spirituals, and on the moral lesson to be learned from proper appreciation of the sun as God's gift: "Fill'd with praise of him who gives the light; / And draws the sable curtains of the night, / Let placid slumbers sooth each weary mind, / At morn to wake more heav'nly, more refin'd" (58–59).

In the chapter "Lyric" from her *Oral Literature in Africa*, Ruth Finnegan offers two more details that suggest an affinity between these two lyrics by Wheatley and the praxis of lyric in Africa. She declares, for example, that the soloist of antiphonal songs in Africa often "has complete scope to improvise his part of verse as he chooses (apart perhaps from the very first line)" (259). Wheatley's demonstrated fondness for the invocation to the muse suggests a parallel to the African practice of frequently accepting the first line of a lyric (within the soloist's contribution, which frequently opens the entire song) as *donnée*. Finnegan goes on to detail another parallel practice: "Sometimes the end is abrupt, and the leader simply stops" (260). Wheatley's own morning hymn ends: "And scarce begun, concludes th' abortive song." She uses this sort of abortive conclusion in "On Imagination" and in "Niobe in Distress . . ." (if one considers this poem to conclude at line 212).

One additional way in which the musical quality of Wheatley's poetry may be said to recollect her African origins is the underlying rhythm of her lines. Although this manifestation of her African heritage is perhaps the most tendentious, it is also the most provocative. In *The Black Mind*, Dathorne presents a description of the rhythmic pattern of African oral poetry, one "to which the trained African audience could respond, a rhythm that they and the poet had inherited" (62). After noting that trying to impose principles of classical or Western prosody on African oral poetry simply will not work, he describes the typical poetic line of African oral poetry as comprising "commonly regular speech units which are marked by breath-pauses (or breath-groups of words) and which together constitute a line" (63). Usually two such breath-pauses, in each of which one or more syllables is stressed, complete a line and may be separated by a caesura. In *The Epic in Africa: Toward a Poetics of Oral Performance*, Isidore Okpewho observes of the "metrical requirement" of these breath-groups "that the singer keep in rhythm with his instrumental accompaniment" (142). As Wheatley has no obvious instrumental accompaniment for her lines, we may say her steady iambic pentameters provide a musical accompaniment of sorts.

It requires only a glance at a few of Wheatley's evenly measured meters to determine an almost implacable allegiance to the ten-syllable count requisite for each line of the heroic couplet, this poet's most often chosen metrical pattern. Such "glances" have prompted commentator after commentator to conclude of Wheatley that her verse slavishly imitates that of Alexander Pope and that it consequently lacks originality.[12] Comparison between a short passage from Wheatley and one of the same length from Pope, requiring more than a mere glance, is in order, along with a synoptic discussion of how each poet's lines compare to patterns of African verse. This effort will remain brief because I do not wish to press beyond reason a demonstration from which one may draw only a speculative conclusion; even so, this demonstration suggests yet another instance of Wheatley's persistent African heritage and erodes the "myth" of her dependence on Pope.

Although I have chosen the passage from Pope at random,[13] I selected the Wheatley lines because of their powerful plea for the freedom of her race from oppression. Pope's is from his popular "An Epistle to Bathurst," while Wheatley's is from one of her unfortunately less well-known poems, only recently found and printed, "On the Death of General Wooster."[14] Below I quote each passage, scanning Pope's lines according to standard rules of classical or Western prosody and Wheatley's in accord with the marking of African verse described above, following which is an attempt to distinguish significant differences between the rhythms of each.

> Ténants with sīghs the smoákless tōw'rs survéy,
> And túrn th' unwílling steéds anoťher wáy:
> Benighted wanderers, the Fŏrest o'ěr,
> Cúrse the sav'd candle, and unóp'ning door:
> While the gaunt mastiff growling at the gate,
> Affrights the beggar whom he longs to eat.
>
> (fr. "An Epistle to Bathurst," ll. 193–98)

> "But how presumptuous shall we hope to find
> Divine acceptance with th' Almighty mind
> While yet, (O deed Ungenerous!) they disgrace
> And hold in bondage Afric's blameless race?
> Let Virtue reign—And thou accord our prayers
> Be victory our's, and generous freedom theirs."
>
> (fr. "On the Death of General Wooster," 149–50)

Since all twelve lines may be scanned with little trouble as regular iambic pentameters, with the exception of Pope's initial trochees in the first, fourth, and fifth lines and spondee in the second foot of lines four and five, I have not taken the space to diagram this easily perceived pattern. Rather I have moved a step beyond ordinary scansion and have represented what I see (others may discern a different schema) as the underlying, wholly distinctive rhythmic pattern obtaining within each passage. I have marked only those syllables receiving primary [or medial] stress. Note that each of Pope's lines contains only four primary stresses, though in each, one foot has a medial stress which may be said to be "promoted" to the status of primary stress in order to complete the schema of five stresses required in a pentameter line. In "The Native Rhythm of English Meters," Joseph Malof, among such others as Northrop Frye and Paul Fussell, has described this frequently occurring phenomenon in English-language poetry as "a significant tendency in the line to lead a double life, to qualify for strict iambic pentameter, through such devices as 'promotion' of a medial stress to the rank of a full one, and yet to assert beneath the surface the four strong beats of our native meter (i.e., of Anglo-Saxon poetry)."[15]

I make this point simply because, try as I may, I cannot hear such a pattern in the Wheatley passage—with the exception of the third foot of the second line, "with th' Al-," in which one could make a case for the preposition's receiving medial stress and thereby claim this line carries only four stresses with one promoted stress. But I actually hear even fewer than four primary stresses per line. Rather each line appears to carry two primary stresses, wherein three medial stresses are promoted to primary stresses to accord with the adopted metrical pattern. What may be traced in the young woman's lines, therefore, easily accommodates the sort of rhythmic pattern Dathorne and Okpewho describe of African oral poetry, where the caesurae mark the end of a speech unit in each of which is contained at least one primary stress. Also note the enjambment of lines one and three which, in each case, smoothly conveys the rhetorical sense and fits neatly into the rhythm of a single speech unit carrying two primary stresses. Wheatley's lines do not appear to recall the memory of native English, but rather to echo the rhythm of her native African tongue. It may be said that she writes in English but that she still hears and reproduces the rhythms repeated to her countless times by poets of her African homeland.

Another manifestation of her African poetic heritage appears in her repeated practice of the panegyric, which is, according to Finnegan, "one of the most developed and elaborate poetic genres in Africa" (111). She further points out that "cultivation of panegyric poetry . . . [gives] rise to poetry of profound political significance as a means of political propaganda, pressure, or communication" (83). Such poems as "To Samuel Quincy, Esq; a Panegyrick," "To the King's Most Excellent Majesty," "To the Rt. Hon. William, Earl of Darthmouth," "To His Excellency George Washington," and "Liberty and Peace" all eulogize political events and figures, each of which in itself dramatizes decisive moments in America's struggle for independence. It is appropriate here to make two observations. First, the political praise poem is a genre of no small significance to Wheatley. Second, her boldness in composing such political commentaries, while functioning under the disadvantages either of being a slave when they were written or of being relegated to the status of Black female domestic even after having been freed, suggests strong roots in an African tradition which taught her that political praise poems were at the very center of one's responsibility as poet.

Wheatley's panegyrics, however, were not limited to politics. In such poems as "Thoughts on the Works of Providence," "To S.M. a Young African Painter, on Seeing His Works," and "An Hymn to Humanity," she offers praises to her conceptions of God, individual artistic achievement, and mankind. Each of these poems celebrates some manifestation of freedom. While the verses on "Providence" exalt God in his works of nature and "To S.M." enthusiastically describes the artistic accomplishment of a fellow African, "An Hymn to Humanity" first extols "Divine *Humanity*" and then sounds the ideal of the Age of Reason, tolerance, in these poignant lines spoken by God to His son, "my heav'nly fair":

> "Descend to earth, there place thy throne:
> To succour man's afflicted son
> Each human heart inspire
> To act in bounties unconfin'd:
> Enlarge the close contracted mind,
> And fill it with thy fire."
>
> (96)

The son of man (or sons of man) is "afflicted" because he is not tolerant, that is, because of his "close contracted mind." "To act in bounties unconfin'd" is to give the gift of freedom decreed as a gesture of largesse. Written for the 1773 *Poems,* this poem predicts the more direct plea for racial equality in "On the Death of General Wooster" (1777). "An Hymn to Humanity" does indeed celebrate the human spirit, not for what it has done but for what it promises to do. To be sure, expression of some sort of hope is an attendant *donnée* among examples of the African genre; it is surely no accident then that this same critical but hopeful attitude characterizes much of the literature by Black Americans from the time of Wheatley to the present day.

In addition to the objects of praise already noted in the African panegyric are "a stress on royal or aristocratic power and an admiration for military achievement" (Finnegan 111). Certainly such poems as "To the King's Most Excellent Majesty" stress royal power, and others such as "To His Excellency George Washington" show much approval for military prowess. But Wheatley's debt to the African panegyric is not limited to subject matter alone. Still another way in which her panegyrics recall her African heritage is in their form. According to Finnegan, typical of the African form is a "loose ordering of stanzas by which a series of pictures of a man's qualities and deeds is conveyed" (135). Since Wheatley best exhibits this sort of structure in certain of her elegies, a genre of African oral poetry that is integrally related to the panegyric, an examination of her elegy on the Voice of the Great Awakening, George Whitefield, provides a vivid illustration. In order to demonstrate how the structure Wheatley employs differs from the expected English form, a brief comparison of her "On the Death of the Rev. George Whitefield" with two other elegies on the same subject but by white authors, the Colonial poet Benjamin Church and the English hymnodist Charles Wesley, proves instructive.

Wheatley's elegy opens with this arresting image: "Hail, happy saint, on thine immortal throne" (22). In the English elegy of the late eighteenth century, this sort of apotheosis ordinarily occurs, if it occurs at all, in the closing lines. Neither Church's nor Wesley's elegy contains an apotheosis. Church's "An Elegy to the Memory of that Pious and Eminent Servant of Jesus Christ the Reverend Mr. George Whitefield" begins with a complaint against death's "poison," announces Whitefield's departure, moves to an *ubi sunt* lament, then progresses into a general treatment of his subject's evangelical career, which he intersperses with maudlin expressions of grief such as the following: "Forgive the tempest, should our sorrows rave, / While o'er thy moldering dust our heads decline" (Walker 213). This poem closes with a stanza asking that some fitting marble monument be erected to Whitefield's glory. The Wesley memorial, entitled "An Elegy on the Late Reverend George Whitefield," is, at 536 lines, over five times the length of Church's. Wesley's elegy is by far the most reflective and measured of the three. After starting with a lament over Whitefield's passing, the poem moves into a lengthy and detailed rehearsal of the principal spiritual events of Whitefield's life and ministry, including the author's first meeting with his subject. The last part of this elegy is in the best Protestant tradition a general plea to the unregenerate to become moved by Whitefield's example to seek forgiveness for their sins through conversion.

Wheatley's poem contrasts markedly with these two elegies. Both Church and Wesley have clearly composed laments. The Black poet, however, has constructed an encomium, whose prevailing tone of praise is established in the first line, "Hail, happy saint, on thine immortal throne." Unlike Church and Wesley, Wheatley has written her poem with great economy; whereas Church's is 97 lines long and Wesley's more than five times as long, the Black poet's is a mere 47 lines.[16] Church's elegy follows somewhat the typical structure of the so-called Puritan elegy,[17] wherein a portrait of the deceased's biography, broken down into details of vocation or conversion, evidence of good works (justification), and treatment of the deceased's joyous reception into heavenly reward (sanctification), is then followed by an exhortation to the listeners to put off mourning and to concentrate on earning for themselves a reward similar to that of the deceased. Church does not detail Whitefield's conversion, probably because such information simply was unknown to him, nor does he include an exhortation to the living. This well-known Colonial poet does, however, speak of Whitefield's work with orphans, of his many ocean voyages (seven to be precise) to the colonies on missions of evangelism and of his great success in bringing about converts, as well as his own achievement of heavenly reward.

Perhaps surprising is Wesley's faithfulness to the Puritan elegy. Wesley's portraiture is one of the most elaborate I have encountered among elegists writing in English before 1800. It is obvious from the great number of details in the life of Whitefield that Wesley records, including his subject's conversion, that Wesley knew Whitefield intimately. Indeed, at one point in the careers of John and Charles Wesley and Whitefield, while they were at Oxford, these three practiced in concert an inchoate form of Methodism. Charles Wesley assures his readers that Whitefield has earned his heavenly reward, an inevitable conclusion he adduces from the overwhelming evidence of this evangel's good deeds; additionally, this poet's emphasis on exhortation has already been noted. We observe, then, that Wesley brings out fully the structure of the Puritan elegy.

While Wheatley's celebration of Whitefield does assuredly show familiarity with the Puritan elegy as do most of her elegies, at the same time, however, she does not appear in this elegy, as in many others, to derive her form exclusively from the Puritan genre. With its "series of pictures" and its "laconic and often staccato sentences," descriptions Finnegan gives of the African panegyric praising a specific individual (135), this poem establishes a pattern that her childhood internalization of African panegyric may well have suggested to her. Confining the motif of lament to such expressions as "we the setting sun deplore" (22) and to drawing a picture of orphans mourning "Their more than father [who] will return no more" (24), Wheatley concentrates on Whitefield's power to "Inflame the heart, and captivate the mind" (22)—two objectives, by the way, of her own poetry—on her subject's longing "to see America excell," and especially on the universality of Whitefield's message to new converts.

In one extant version of this elegy, apparently printed in London and carelessly edited by another hand than the poet's, "An Ode of Verses on the Much-Lamented Death of the Rev. Mr. George Whitefield" dramatizes a portion of one of Whitefield's sermons in these affective, though noticeably rebellious, lines:

> "Take him, ye Africans, he longs for you,
> Impartial Saviour is his Title due.
> If you will walk in Grace's heavenly Road
> He'll make you free, and Kings, and Priests to God."
>
> (210)

In the versions printed in America, the last couplet is muted to read, "'Wash'd in the fountain of redeeming blood, / You shall be sons, and Kings, and priests to God" (23). Wheatley's insistence on the equalizing result of conversion echoes her sentiments in "On Being Brought from Africa." In any event the short, staccato effect of the pictures the poet has drawn here of the deceased, along with her loosely organized and vivid portraiture contrast markedly with the more calculated and larger portraits of Church and Wesley. Even her recording of Whitefield's conversion is reduced from Wesley's nearly one hundred lines to a single clause subordinated to the subject of his ministry: "That Saviour, which his soul did first receive" (23).

One may argue that such a lack of detail bespeaks merely a parallel lack of the poet's familiarity with her subject. It must be observed, however, that Whitefield was in Boston only a week before his death in Newburyport, Massachusetts, on September 30, 1770; and that he had visited Boston during his sixth trip to America between 1763 and 1765, some two years after Phillis had become a member of the Wheatley household. Given the considerable extant correspondence between Wheatley's mistress Susannah and Selina Hastings, Countess of Huntingdon, whose privy chaplain was Whitefield himself, it is probable that Whitefield was offered accommodations in the Wheatley mansion when visiting Boston. Phillis and Whitefield, therefore, may well have met twice and talked socially while under the same roof. In any case, it is most probable that Wheatley had heard Whitefield preach on at least two occasions prior to composition of her eulogistic elegy. Certainly, her elegy preceded that by Wesley by several months, a factor that may have contributed to its popularity in England. The Black poet's elegy, having come to England probably aboard the same ship that brought the news of Whitefield's death, appeared at a most opportune moment.

It was not merely timeliness that contributed to the success of Wheatley's elegy; there were also such practical factors as the poem's brevity which allowed it to be issued in broadside, hence making it cheaper to purchase and easier to circulate than Wesley's 536 lines, requiring a more cumbersome, more expensive pamphlet for distribution. But particularly attractive to readers must have been Wheatley's economy of form. Whitefield's immense popularity in America, but especially in England, demanded some sort of acceptable tribute; surely concerned readers found Wheatley's brief but pithy tribute both consoling and appropriate. The Black poet's African heritage served her well, for it quite probably assisted her in constructing a public statement with "little stress on personal emotions," another characteristic of panegyric described by Finnegan (recall that even her plea for equality is not a personal one), but which conveyed a succinct and recognizable portrait of a well-known figure in "laconic and often rather staccato sentences" (135). I underscore the significance of her success with the Whitefield poem because it most definitely assured the patronage of the Countess of Huntingdon and the subsequent appearance of her 1773 *Poems,* a project that may never have materialized had Wheatley not come to the attention of the countess during the time of her grief over the loss of her chaplain. Another way of putting this point is that Wheatley's African heritage may quite simply have been crucial to her success as a poet.

Such heritage may even have helped prepare her for the composition of her two experiments with the short epic, "Goliath of Gath" and "Niobe in Distress." Lyndon Harries has asserted that panegyrics "have been described as intermediary between epic and ode, a combination of exclamatory narrative and laudatory apostrophisizing" (909). Certainly the biblical story of David's confrontation with the Giant contributes to praise of the young boy's fitness for kingship, while the Niobe episode warns against too much self-praise. Both Wheatley's experiments, then, deal with the praise motif, the one emphasizing the positive and the other the negative side of the subject. As these two poems are her longest, running to 222 and 212 lines, Ruth Finnegan's observation about long praise poems is relevant:

"Many of the lengthy praise poems... do contain some epic elements and provide the nearest common parallel to this form in Africa."[18]

More recent scholarship has considerably modified Finnegan's conclusions regarding the epic in Africa. Certainly Okpewho's *The Epic in Africa* and Stephen Belcher's *Epic Traditions of Africa* (which has a long chapter on epic among the Fula) help to set the record straight. In the radically revised third edition of *The Princeton Encyclopedia,* now called *The New Princeton Encyclopedia of Poetry and Poetics,* Lyndon Harries's article on early African poetry has been replaced by Daniel P. Biebuyck's "In the Indigenous Epic Tradition." Determined, according to his own assertion, to correct Harries's perceived overemphasis on the panegyric, Biebuyck misleadingly promotes the epic tradition at the expense of the panegyric tradition; consequently his otherwise fine essay loses sight of the interrelation between panegyric and epic. To be sure, Wheatley's poetry displays a substantial demonstration of the interplay between epic and panegyric, which even includes a debt to African folklore.

In altering the traditional tale of young David's heroism and Niobe's pride, the Black poet has accomplished a demonstration of what Makouta-Mboukou has called the African folk poet's art. In Makouta-Mboukou's words, "The talent of the African folk poet resides only in the practice of the art of his narrative that he embellishes in accord with his own poetic insight. He always works with an accepted traditional tale" (20). The transplanted Black African has, then, taken two traditional moral tales and embellished each, transformed them by her talent, and created them anew as short epics.

Although Wheatley's handling of the gods in each of these epyllia may quite simply be the result of the Old Testament's early henotheism and the classical world's religious perspective, it may as well be indebted to the manner by which a much younger Wheatley heard African oral poets render their (and then, her) gods. In his discussion of spoken African mythic literature, O. R. Dathorne notes as especially significant that "the gods... are frequently humanized or, rather more than that, they are not thought of as being any different from human beings."[19] Perhaps her memory of African oral poets at least complemented and made more feasible to her literary imagination (the subject of her religious consciousness I will take up in the next chapter) the characters of Samuel's Jehovah and Ovid's Apollo. In Wheatley's epyllia, as in their traditional sources, "gods" are enraged by challenges to their authority and subsequently carry out concrete measures to destroy the objects of those challenges; Jehovah sends a messenger who gives Goliath an ultimatum, and Apollo looses arrows from his bow which eliminate the fourteen expressions of Niobe's pride, all her children. In other words, the gods of Wheatley's epyllia act in predictable, anthropomorphic ways as they do in their sources and as African deities acted in moral tales of the gods.

Before leaving the subject of Wheatley's debt to African epic, we would do well to examine more closely several additional particulars, especially about "Niobe. . . ." Noting, for example, that African "epic song is hardly a clear, mellifluous stream" (43), Okpewho remarks that epics frequently employ "an interchange, whether we call it interpolation or interflow" (42). In "Niobe . . ." and in "Goliath" Wheatley frequently interjects into the flow of narrative several lines not present in her sources (Samuel and Ovid). The Black poet conveys considerable empathy for Niobe, twice describing her, for example, as "all beautiful in woe." While Ovid refers to his Niobe once as beautiful in "anger," pointing out the extremity of her presumption toward the gods, Wheatley twice insists Niobe moves "all beautiful in woe," choosing not to address her sin of offense but rather to empathize with her egregious loss, her fourteen children. This condition of identification with the bard's subject Okpewho describes as "the tremendous empathy the bard establishes between himself and the subjects of his tale, particularly the hero" (18).

According to Okpewho, Africans believe that "the gods are responsible for evil as well as good" (9). In "Niobe," Wheatley has her heroine assert in her own words, "the case of 'my goddesship'" (184), thereby characterizing Okpewho's insistence that "the hero's world is somewhat more than human" (111); at the same time, moreover, Wheatley's heroine clearly commits the major sin of pride, which, by the way, carries just as much severity in the classical world as in the Judeo-Christian. Among the Fula, as Belcher points out, the themes of Fulani epics "involve easily presented notions such as self-worth and pride" (162).

Quoting A. B. Lord, Okpewho applies the following judgment to African epic: referencing orality Lord states that "'the roots of oral tradition are not artistic but religious in the broadest sense'" (153). I make this point because we are going to take up the issue of orality in the next paragraph and because the broadening dimensions of the oral epic tradition, with which Wheatley would certainly have had some familiarity, help to explain the tendency in her work toward religious syncretism. In other words, given this African perspective regarding the development of religious consciousness, we may more readily be prepared to grasp how it is that this talented poet presents us with a highly complex religious outlook; for when she has Niobe's children's eyes flash "living splendors" (102) and when she describes

Niobe's bid for "goddesship," Wheatley does indeed participate in a species of theological rendering. We will take up in chapter 5 this complex religious syncretism so evident in Wheatley.

The property of orality figures prominently in the poetry of Wheatley. Perhaps this quality appears most obviously in her penchant for the dramatic; for example, her elegies contain numerous examples of the deceased giving counsel to the living. One way in which Wheatley may incorporate the orality of her African heritage within her own poetic oeuvre may be suggested by an observation Okpewho makes about the early Gilgamesh epic. Noting that Gilgamesh "is probably not the record of a performance" but that "it is clearly indebted to the devices of the oral narrative song and copies them faithfully" (151), Okpewho follows this observation with an excursus on repeated lines which signal oral tradition. This practice, evoking characteristics of the oral formulae common in Homeric and other early (oral) epic traditions, may be easily located in Wheatley's repetition of the significant phrase describing Niobe as "all beautiful in woe."

In her depiction of the death of Niobe's last child, Wheatley cleverly adds use of the classical echo device. Pleading with Phoebe that the inhuman goddess leave her her last child, Niobe affectively exclaims, "' . . . ah spare me one.'" This exclamation Wheatley, but not Ovid, immediately follows with the line, "'Ah! Spare me one,' the vocal hills reply'd" (112). I submit that given the context just established, the classical echo device has become complicated by Wheatley's residual African heritage. This sort of appreciation for repetition and for the dramatic strongly suggests in Wheatley a pattern of imaginative movement from the oral to the written.

One other instance that strikingly resonates with Wheatley's African heritage regarding the oral epic occurs in her 1771 elegy on Dr. Samuel Marshall, who served as the Wheatley family physician. While it is so that the chthonic plays an undeniable role in the conception of this elegy, in African epic, according to Biebuyck, the hero of epic usually possesses "certain medicines." Here Dr. Marshall, called Aesculapius, hence assumes the godlike, heroic traits of the Greek god of medicine. As well his unborn child is described in this arresting couplet: "The babe unborn in the dark womb is tost, / And seems in anguish for its father lost" (87). This description closely resembles the unborn hero of African epic, about whom Biebuyck remarks "the unborn hero speaks in the womb" (14).

While the Black poet's embellishment and characterization within her biblical and classical epyllia suggest a positive correlation to her African origins, her praxis of the elegy indicates an even more positive correlation to such origins. The predominance of the elegy in Wheatley's extant verse has already been remarked; the eighteen elegies that number among her poems make up almost a third of the existing canon. So the importance of this genre to Wheatley Studies can hardly be exaggerated. Although this genre held great importance for her, most of the English and American elegies written during her time were by men, as of course was the case with other types of writing. Such was not the standard practice, however, among Black Africans of the day. At several points in her *Oral Literature in Africa,* Ruth Finnegan emphasizes the fact that the saying or singing of elegies was usually the province of women. Characterizing elegiac verse as "more private and normally lacking the political relevance of panegyric poetry," the elegy "tends to be performed by non-professionals (often women) rather than state officials" (147). Since such dirges as sung in Africa "often involve wailing, sobbing, and weeping," Finnegan continues, they are "particularly suitable for women—for in Africa as elsewhere such activities are considered typically female" (148). Among the Akan peoples, for example, "Traditionally all Akan girls were expected to learn how to sing and compose dirges" (166). As for the Fulani per se, Paul Riesman points out in *Freedom in Fulani Social Life* that "women may weep publicly about someone's death, while men must not do so" (202). In recent years, I have been most fortunate to have had in several of my graduate seminars students from Burkina Faso, Ghana, and Chad, all of whom have assured me that, even now, mourning is the office of women.

Given this sort of heritage it should come as little surprise that Wheatley devoted a great deal of her poetic energies to the composition of elegies, for engraved upon her childhood memory was surely the recollection of women performing dirges. The inertia of Wheatley's African heritage regarding the elegy may have suggested more to her than simply the role and responsibility of the elegies; indeed, several characteristics of the genre as practiced in Africa also appear in her elegies. For example, according to Finnegan, the dirge singer is expected to make "frequent references to the wisdom of the dead"; these references are typically to be drawn "by the singer's lamenting that she no longer has anyone to give her advice" (155). In her elegies on Joseph Sewall and Samuel Cooper, Wheatley carries out these specifications. Of Joseph Sewall, who was son of the diarist Samuel Sewall, who was for fifty-six years pastor of the famous Old South Church of Boston, and whose services the poet attended until his death in 1769, Wheatley wrote: "I, too have cause this mighty loss to mourn, / For he my monitor . . . sought the paths of piety and Truth" (21) from his youth. While Sewall apparently served her as spiritual advisor during her adolescent days, Cooper, who baptized her, served her in another capacity. In her 1784 elegy on this latitudinarian minister of Boston's Brattle Street meetinghouse, Wheatley, in the year of her own death, identifies Cooper as one "drawn by rhetoric's commanding laws" (152) who "Encourag'd oft and oft approv'd [my] lays" (153). In addition to remarking his role as counselor to her verse, the poet celebrates his intellectual gifts in this arresting line, "The Sons of learning on thy lessons hung" (152).

While the elegies on Whitefield by Church and Wesley both extol their subject for his knowledge of scripture and spiritual matters, neither describes Whitefield as personal counselor. Such personal acknowledgments as appear in Wheatley's elegies on Cooper and Sewall were in general uncharacteristic of American and English elegies of the time. Also uncharacteristic of the genre was Wheatley's penchant for the dramatic (already remarked) which appears in many of her elegies. Whitefield, for example, speaks five verse couplets in his elegy by the Black poet; a deceased girl of five utters six lines of advice from her heavenly abode in another, while several others among the departed in still other elegies offer suggestions to the living describing how they may imitate in their lives the behavior of him or her received into joyous reward and thus obtain similar reward. In his discussion of the African elegy, Dathorne declares, "funeral dirges frequently are directed at the living" (56). He even goes so far as to say, "Frequently the form of the dirge is itself dramatic."[20] Perhaps Wheatley's own flare for the dramatic and her concentration in the elegy on the conduct of the living are still other manifestations of her African heritage.

Given the present inaccessibility to most details regarding Wheatley's life in Africa, *any investigation of her African origins must, of course, remain somewhat speculative.* At the same time, however, too many points of positive correlation obtain between her poetry and African oral literature to be ignored. The fact that she saw her role as poet to be in large part governed by a responsible moral conviction accords well with African practice. Provocative echoes of African rhythm may be traced in her lines. She so enthusiastically embraces the panegyric, among Africa's most prevalent genres, that even many of her elegies spill into panegyric. Her experiments with the epic demonstrate affinities for African long praise poems and for characterization of African gods. And most substantially her praxis of the elegy harmonizes so well with the African that we travel full circle, back to definition of her function as poet: for in Africa, elegies are overwhelmingly sung by women. Wheatley's biological origin in Africa is incontestable: now we can begin to speak of her literary origins also as having come from Africa. But two other worlds exercised formidable influences on the development of her poetics: both of these are less speculative and may be more accessibly traced in her writings. These are her post-African religious and intellectual development.

CHAPTER FIVE

Post-African Religious Development

Having delineated her African origins, we are now prepared to investigate Phillis Wheatley's post-African religious and intellectual growth. Because her African origins play such a pervasive role in her evolving religious and intellectual development, we will of necessity frequently touch base with the inertia of her African heritage. As our poet's religious and intellectual development is so integrally intertwined, this and the next few paragraphs serve as a preamble to our investigation of both these concerns.

Avenues of religious development with which Wheatley was confronted after her arrival in Boston included Christianity, embracing its secularizing forays, particularly for Wheatley, into the realm of the religious sublime; classical paganism, which offered her a ready opportunity to make syncretistic connections to her African solar worship, animism, and Islam; and the Renaissance's and the Age of Reason's preoccupation with the search for wisdom. Because Wheatley so deftly and pervasively interweaves elements of classical paganism within the tapestry of her evolving religious consciousness, we will examine these classical elements as they arise within her responses to Christianity and her quest for wisdom.

The course of her intellectual maturation traveled a parallel journey, albeit this course involved a largely secular program of reading the works of several authors outside the Holy Circle (Peter Gay's term), such as Homer's *Iliad* and *Odyssey*, Vergil's works, Horace's *Ars Poetica*, Longinus's *Peri Houpsos* (*On the Sublime*), Shakespeare's works, Shaftsbury's *Characteristics*, Akenside's *Pleasures of Imagination*, Pope's poetry, Edward Young's *Night Thoughts,* James Thompson's *The Seasons*, and William Collins's poems. Of course, Wheatley also knew the poetry of John Milton, the King James Bible, and the lesser-known (today) poets like John Phillips and William Shenstone. As well, she very likely read the prose works of other British thinkers including those of Henry Home, Lord Kames, John Dennis, William Duff, Thomas Burnet, and perhaps even of Edmund Burke (his *A Philosophical Enquiry into the Origin of Our Ideas of the Sublime and Beautiful*).

In the realm of politics, Wheatley would have known the numerous American pamphlets which preceded the Revolutionary War written by such authors as Jonathan Meyhew, James Otis, Benjamin Church (who eventually became a Loyalist), Joseph Warren, and John Hancock. She would, moreover, certainly have heard of treatises by the Brits Thomas Hobbes (*Leviathan*), John Locke (*Essay Concerning Human Understanding*, 1696; and *Two Treatises on Government*), the German Samuel Pufendorf (*The Whole Duty of Man, According to the Law of Nature*, trans. into English, 1735), the Frenchman the Baron de Montesquieu (*Spirit of the Laws*, trans. by the 1750s), and the Swiss Emmerick de Vattel (*The Law of Nations*, trans. 1760). All these European political theorists place emphasis on the notion that the laws of mankind derive (or should derive) from the laws of nature, and their works exercised a major influence on the evolving American thought preceding the Revolutionary War. As all the works just named were cited by the pamphleteers listed, it is unlikely that Wheatley was unfamiliar with these authors and/or their works.

We may draw two conclusions from this litany of resources: first that Wheatley, like all literate American colonists, had access to the major eighteenth-century texts produced in Great Britain and the Continent; and, given the fact that all indications are that little actual work (cleaning, dusting, etc.) was exacted from Wheatley, she should have had ample time to study and then to contemplate the results of her study. To this juncture in our investigation, there should be no surprise at all.

When we explore further the sources available to Wheatley in Colonial America, however, we do encounter what for most of today's literary critics must surely be unexpected resources for her spiritual and intellectual growth. What adds substantially to the surprise inherent within an investigation of these American resources is the simple fact that these homespun authors and thinkers, actually much more sophisticated and knowledgeable than has been recognized, were appreciatively more determinative upon Wheatley's evolving liberation poetics than were the Brits and the Continentals. While Wheatley does indeed sound verbal echoes to Pope, Akenside, Thompson, and Young, for example, she displays remarkable affinities for the American authors Joseph Seccombe, Samuel Cooper, William Billings (America's first native-born composer, whose preface to his *New England*

Psalm-Singer bears comparison to Wheatley's treatment of imagination), and especially Mather Byles.

According to Phillis Wheatley's principal biographer, Margaretta Oddell, Mary Wheatley, one of the two children (twins) of John and Susannah Wheatley, "undertook to learn [sic] her to read and write" (12). Because of her astonishing mastery of the English language, the young Phillis was soon diverting her attentions away from the usual tasks befalling a servant; as Oddell puts it, Phillis "was not devoted to menial occupations, as was at first intended" (12). While I suspect Phillis came to feel that she was on display because of her precocity (not unlike a circus sideshow), this immensely talented and gifted child came to surpass all members of the Wheatley family in her retention of knowledge, evidencing an apparently unlimited capacity for absorbing new learning.

Oddell is clear on this point, for Wheatley "soon attracted the attention of the literati of the day, many of whom furnished her with books" (13–14). Her principal biographer continues by noting that Wheatley "was now frequently visited by clergymen, and other individuals of high standing in society" (14). As the congregational minister and Harvard graduate, Mather Byles, lived across the street from the Wheatley mansion, he was certainly among the clergy who called on the prodigy; Byles had inherited what was for the times a huge library (one of the largest in the Colonies, containing well over two thousand volumes) of his uncle, Cotton Mather, for whom he was named, and was therefore well equipped to loan her books and to offer her intellectual and spiritual counsel.

Also living close to the Wheatleys was Thomas Hutchinson, governor of Massachusetts Bay, whose library rivaled that of Byles. We know Hutchinson was well acquainted with Wheatley because he joined Mather Byles and others as a signatory of the famous letter of attestation to the authenticity of Wheatley's authorship of the 1773 *Poems on Various Subjects, Religious and Moral*. This letter was published as part of the prefatory matter of *Poems*. A third, large library to which Wheatley had ready access was that of Thomas Prince (1687–1758), who bequeathed his famous library of books (over fifteen hundred), manuscripts, and maps collected over a lifetime to the Old South Church, the congregation Prince served as minister. As Prince was a classmate (at Harvard College) and intimate friend of Joseph Sewall, Wheatley's first spiritual "monitor," as she phrased it, it is certain Wheatley was well aware of this collection and would have been encouraged to use it. So we see that Wheatley had easy access to three of the largest libraries in

Colonial America. We will conclude that she made excellent use of these resources.

Among the gatherers of these three libraries, Prince had expired in 1758, before Wheatley arrived in Boston on July 11, 1761. Hutchinson and Byles were, nevertheless, alive and available to her. For that matter, Byles's proximity to Wheatley, his youthful experience as a poet, and his reputation as a champion of budding, new poets strongly qualify this poet, scholar, and minister as a probable tutor to Wheatley. The simple truth is that Byles was one of the most prolific poets of the first half of the eighteenth century in America. We will soon learn that his 1744 *Poems on Several Occasions* served Wheatley as a paradigm for her 1773 *Poems on Various Subjects*.

As he was so well equipped to do, Byles probably served Wheatley in another capacity, that of tutoring her in Latin language and literature. Oddell notes that the young student of English was soon "endeavoring to master the Latin language" (14). Having looked into the possibility that some member or members of the Wheatley family would have been able to instruct the eager student in Latin, I discovered that no member of the Wheatley family ever matriculated at Boston Latin, much less at Harvard College. So unless the Wheatley children, six years Phillis's senior, received private tutoring, neither twin could have instructed her in Latin. To be sure, it is unlikely that John Wheatley would have paid for private tutoring for one of his slaves. We should therefore look across the street for the most likely person who was well prepared and perhaps even concerned to assist such a fine mind as Wheatley possessed.

While Byles probably did serve as Wheatley's intellectual tutor, it is unlikely that he often gave her serious spiritual counsel, for the Wheatleys (John and Susannah) did not attend Byles's Hollis Street Church. They did, however, attend Joseph Sewall's Old South Church, site of Thomas Prince's library. In her elegy, "On the Death of the Rev. Dr. Sewell [sic], 1769," Wheatley identifies Sewall as her most trusted spiritual counselor, "my monitor" (21). Wheatley's ascription of "monitor" to Sewall's role is worth examining.

In our analysis of "On Being Brought from Africa," we learned that Phillis Wheatley was, early on in her poetic career, perfectly capable of registering an ironic use of words or of situation. Wheatley applies the word "monitor" to the departed Sewall in a spoken, dramatic couplet which forms a part of her concluding epitaph composed on Sewall's behalf; as she has it: "I, too have cause this mighty loss to mourn, / For he my monitor will not return" (21). Two years later, Edmund Burke penned the ironic observation: "Strict and faithful monitors . . . keep watch on every action of my life" (*O.E.D.*). I suspect that Wheatley has made a similar usage in her Sewall elegy for several reasons. To be sure, she obviously wants her readers to believe she intends to identify Sewall as her spiritual guardian; she was, nonetheless, aware that "monitor" could be used to describe one who surveils "every action" of her life, most likely for the purpose of determining whether the young girl, some seven or eight years out of Africa, could possibly make a "good" Christian.

Significantly, Sewall did not baptize Wheatley before his death; she was forced to wait for this gesture until Samuel Cooper, one of the most liberal ministers of Boston (whose theological position approached Unitarianism) and soon to become a much valued spiritual *and* literary advisor to her, performed this ritual on August 18, 1771. It should not go unremarked that it was soon after this event that Wheatley's poetry began to articulate her first period of maturity, this period demonstrating a distinctive turn inward toward a use of her power over words essentially to discover freedom within her poetic compositions.

It would appear then, that Wheatley had not quite convinced the orthodox Sewall that she would make a "good" Christian. A glance at two of her earliest poems may well reveal whence came Sewall's reluctance. As "Atheism" and "An Address to the Deist," both from 1767 when Wheatley was but thirteen or fourteen, have the "look" of exercises in catechism, each strongly suggests an effort on the poet's part to convince her "monitor" that she was fit for baptism. These poems are indeed most indicative of a catechumen, one studying to join the faith (in this case that of Congregationalism).

The first couplet of "Atheism," for example, reads more like a threat delivered to a somewhat confused petitioner than a celebration of an established believer: "Where now shall I begin this spacious Field / To tell what curses unbelief doth yield" (129). More than "curses" may be visited on the disbeliever, however, as the next couplet admonishes: "Thou that dost daily feel his hand and rod / And dare deny the essence of a god" (129). Although the "hand and rod" are probably figurative, the temptation to view the "Thou" of this couplet as Wheatley herself, one who is vulnerable to the "curses" of the first couplet, is indeed strong.

"Atheism" contains other suggestions that this poem serves as an exercise in catechism. The phrase "Thy Ignorance" seems to be a thin veneer for Wheatley's own lack of knowledge regarding Christian dogma and history. For just a few lines below we have another grave threat: "Thy heart in unbelief will harder grow" (130). As well, so continues the speaker (Sewall?), "Thy unbelief disturbs the peaceful mind" (130). In another, perhaps earlier version the poet has used "distroys [sic] thy" (198), instead of "disturbs the." Perhaps this change reflects an attempt to redirect attention away from Wheatley herself. In other words, the poet may be responding in "Atheism" to the severe censure of a spiritual advisor that she must expunge all thoughts that her former, African religious consciousness could ever be acceptable in Christian Boston—even though the truth is *all* of Boston was probably never completely Christian.

Indeed in this time frame, especially, not to be Christian was to be an atheist. Recall that Tom Paine was frequently accused of being an atheist and that he wrote the *Age of Reason* with an eye toward disproving this charge. Wheatley at thirteen or fourteen could have hardly been expected to respond with such a treatise (Paine convinced few) to the charge that her African religious consciousness was nothing but an atheistic approach to religion. In an important early article, "The Religion of the American Negro Slave: His Attitude Toward Life and Death" (1923), Gold Refined Wilson observes that "American missionaries reported that it was harder to teach the slaves [the Christian religion] who were born in Africa than those born in this country" (44). Wilson later concludes that "what was religion in Africa was generally regarded by the American slaves themselves as mere superstition" (45).

This attitude goes a long way toward explaining why Wheatley remained so very solicitous of Obour Tanner's adopted Christianity; Tanner, Wheatley's most frequent correspondent that we know of, was several years older than Phillis but was probably not her intellectual equal. Tanner's age, birth in Africa, and her proximity (she lived in Providence, RI), combined with our knowledge that Phillis visited her, suggests a powerful relationship obtained between these two women. Robinson calls Obour Wheatley's "soul mate" (*Phillis Wheatley and Her Writings* 314). I will venture that these two women both arrived in Boston on the same slaver, *The Phillis,* and that Obour may well have kept alive the younger and weaker Phillis during the horrific Middle Passage.

Even years after she modified her own idea of God with a syncretized combination of classical paganism, Islam, animism, solar worship, and Christianity, Wheatley respectfully and with great affection wrote Obour that, "Your reflection on the sufferings of the Son of God, and the inestimable price of our immortal souls, plainly demonstrate the sensations of a soul united to Jesus" (171). Note that Wheatley does not assert that she believes herself to be so united.

In 1767, nevertheless, Wheatley was more or less at the mercy of so-called benevolent white folks whose intolerance toward any observed inertia evidently deriving from her African heritage could only have added to the trepidation Wheatley doubtlessly felt whenever she found herself "examined" by her *alleged* superiors. My "reading" is that Wheatley was herself moving rapidly on a road toward an intellectual, moral, and spiritual superiority to all persons about her, irrespective of race or background.

Toward the end of "Atheism" Wheatley takes special pains to disavow the forcefulness of classical deities in comparison with the one Christian God. Apollo can not save the soul from "deepest hell." Minerva's wisdom is insufficient to gain heaven. Cupid can only inspire physical pleasure, not brotherly love. And Pluto can only fail to reveal to the student of classicism that perdition is the reward "for thy learning made" (131).

All this time Wheatley gives to a denial of the eternal effectiveness of these pagan deities (seven lines) bespeaks a subtext, wherein Wheatley's obvious devotion to all things classical (of which she was aware) surely caused her to earn the disapproval of many white Christians. Even Jupiter Hammon, an African American poet born in America who was Wheatley's contemporary, cautioned the younger poet, in his "An Address to Miss Phillis Wheatly [sic]," published in 1778, to "leave the things of time" and reject the "thousands [who] muse with earthly toys" (O'Neale, *Jupiter Hammon* 78). Hammon here appears not to be totally convinced that Wheatley has reliably chosen the path toward the Christian idea of God; perhaps Hammon was responding to the classicism that pervades her 1773 *Poems*. It is certain that she herself later refused to follow the counsel she advanced in "Atheism."

The way Wheatley concludes "Atheism" predicts her later affection for classicism. And this conclusion would most certainly have displeased Sewall, for just after having, apparently, condemned a too-emphatic dependence on classical paganism, Wheatley closes this poem with these fine lines, which unabashedly celebrate classicism:

> Mark rising Phoebus when he spreads his ray
> And his commission for to guide the day
> At night keep watch, and see a Cynthia bright
> And her commission for to guide the night
> See how the stars when they do sing his praise
> Witness his [God's] essence in celestial Lays.

(131)

Trying hard to relegate Phoebus to a simple sun and Cynthia to the moon, why does she insist on giving these bodies classical names? While the concluding couplet may at first appear to echo Miltonic astronomy, it as well suggests a modicum of Islam and its emphasis on the heavens. We may, then, make a case that these three couplets blend classicism and Islam with Christianity, thereby predicting what becomes a normative praxis in Wheatley's oeuvre.

However disconcerting "Atheism" may have been to the dogmatic Joseph Sewall, "An Address to the Deist" would have probably been more convincing, though its subtext more clearly reveals a catechumen trying to please a spiritual "monitor." In this poem, about fifteen lines shorter than "Atheism's" fifty-eight lines, the poet, for the most part, sustains a Christian posture. Making a strong if repetitive, declaration of the Christian Jesus' power over evil, at one point Wheatley inserts this diverting line: God "Sees thy vain arg'ments to divide the three" (132).

This articulation of the heresy of tritheism, which holds that the Father, Son, and Holy Ghost are three separate beings (gods if you will), rings all too much like a misstep made by a student of the Congregational faith. In other words, this line suggests that Wheatley herself confused the doctrine of the unity of the trinity with the possibility for multiple deities, as in the henotheistic constructs within animism and the first half of the Old Testament. If so, then she would have found herself in the most uncomfortable position of being forced to suffer severe rebuke from her "monitor."

The remainder of this poem rehearses various points of orthodoxy, even pausing to put the question common to Christian typology, "Who trod the wine-press of Jehovah's wrath?" (131). This query refers to the sixty-third chapter of Isaiah, which Christians standardly treat as a prediction of the power of Jesus as the Christ. Wheatley later wrote a thirty-line paraphrase of the first eight lines of this biblical chapter, which she published in *Poems*.

Try as she might to reassure Sewall of her readiness to join the Christian faith, she did not enjoy baptism until 1771, as we have observed. Perhaps it was this lack of acceptance that motivated Wheatley to explore self-consciously other avenues of religious consciousness. In any event it is certain she did so. Application of the three orders—body, mind, and charity—delineated by the Roman Catholic mathematician, philosopher, and theologian Blaise Pascal (1623–1662), in his famous *Pensées*, which Wheatley may have seen, proves instructive toward discovering with some precision how Wheatley's religious consciousness evolved.

Body (flesh) included, according to Pascal, the realm of the physical, the sensations which closely lessoned the imagination. The order of the mind fell most positively within the province of the power of genius, whose great accomplishment does not depend on the flesh. Finally, charity, the third order, has no dependence at all on either of the other two orders but derives exclusively from a heart made right for God. Pascal has here somewhat revised Augustine's trinity of memory (embracing the senses, appetites, and the imagination), understanding or reason, and will, these three corresponding to God the Father, Son, and Holy Ghost. Augustine, who was early in his adult life a rhetor at Rome, drew his interpretation of memory, understanding, and will from classical rhetoric, wherein this triune construct of the mind usually served as a philosophical exercise to be applied in preparation for oratorical performance. I make much of Augustinian meditation because Wheatley's "Thoughts on the Works of Providence" demonstrates the process of the *meditatio* (meditation) and because poetic meditation was much in vogue during the seventeenth and eighteenth centuries on both sides of the Atlantic. Examples of this vogue may be readily found in the *Holy Sonnets* of John Donne and in the poetry of Francis Quarrels, George Herbert, and Andrew Marvel in Britain, and in the poetry of Anne Bradstreet, Philip Pain, Edward Taylor, and Roger Walcott in America.

Augustine explicated his radical revision of the classical meditative process or *meditatio* in his extended *De Trinitate,* whose principles became absorbed by contemplative, philosophical meditation characterizing the monastic life. In the Augustinian philosophical process of the *meditatio,* the practitioner (say a monastic monk) contemplates a particular biblical passage (a locus) by employing the imagination/senses, which then instruct the understanding or reason which weighs the import of the passage to the committed believer; when properly performed, this process helps to prepare the practitioner to bring about a resolve of the will or an act of the mind, which under the most ideal circumstances can lead the contemplative to move from philosophical contemplation to mystical contemplation or union with the Deity. In its most emphatic expression within the contemplative life, the meditative process leads to a profound manifestation of love or charity. As Mary T. Clarke explains it, "Under the influence of Paul, Augustine cited charity as the fundamental end of the contemplative life" (285).[1]

So we see how easily Pascal would have become acquainted with the *meditatio*. But his revision of this process refigures Augustine's revision of the classical rhetorical exercise. Indeed, in Pascal's reconception, his triune construct of body, mind, and charity no longer describes an ascending process of mind in action but a wholly discontinuous mode of human behavior, each stage or order of which differs in kind, not in degree. For that matter, says Martin Price in *To the Palace of Wisdom: Studies in Order and Energy from Dryden to Blake*, "There is no gradation by which one moves easily from one to another, nor does one order prepare [one] for the next above it" (19); in Augustine, of course, mastery of each stage (order) prepares for the next.

"The order of charity," so Price continues, "is based upon a hatred of selfhood" (19). It is at this juncture that Wheatley rejects (or never embraces) Pascal's notion of charity. For before one can achieve the highest order, that of charity, Pascal demands one must, in Price's words, "surrender the self-determination that is inevitable illusion" (20). To Wheatley the principle of self-determination is, as we found in the poetics of liberation chapter, absolutely necessary to her feeling of dignity as a thinking, sentient being. And it is precisely at this point that Wheatley departs from Jupiter Hammon's belief, which is somewhat closer to Pascal, that, even if all does not appear to be fair and balanced in this world, God/Jesus has assured the faithful that all will be fair and balanced in the next.

In his analysis of Pascal, Price maintains that, "Power stimulates imagination, and imagination creates happiness" (20), or more directly imagination constructs an illusion of happiness. Yet, in Wheatley, her power over words creates, or better reifies, an alternative world, in "On Imagination," for example, which here and now provides a temporary realization of liberation—not a projected promise of freedom. While, as Price declares, "Pascal resists any Stoical deification of mind" (22), Wheatley moves surprisingly close to such a position. For example, her "Thoughts on the Works of Providence," perhaps her most philosophical poem, may be read, as observed earlier, as a *meditatio*—hence ascertaining that this poet is thoroughly familiar with poetry as an act of the mind.

Price acknowledges that, in the order of mind, "The greater [one's] confidence in [her] rational power, the greater [her] sense of freedom"; moreover, such a one "can choose for [herself]" and her "choices have authority," representing a "proper fulfillment of [her] nature" (24). But of course Pascal rejects such a "mental fantasy," as he might have called it, and instead opts for a "radical separation between Christ and culture" (Price 25). Price recognizes as Wheatley would have, however, that, while Pascal's third order "has its sublimity," it also "sets so abrupt a chasm between the orders as to imperil all aspiration" (25). On the one hand, Wheatley is, to be sure, a victim of this world; on the other, Pascal moved in a culture that respected and celebrated his achievement. Wheatley found herself celebrated, but as a sort of carnival act, hardly occupying a place of genuine respect. While Wheatley can say that God is "incomprehensible, unknown / By sense" (20), she can also insist that it is sense and mind which serve her as a means toward freedom, hence effecting a break of sorts between her need to be free and the restrictions white folks' Christianity would impose upon her. To her "to imperil all aspiration" would be tantamount to living a death; for as she so affectively described herself, "an intrinsic ardor prompts [me] to write" (15). We should recall this poet spent an immoderate amount of time exploring the *power* of poetic afflatus; indeed, this poet aspired.

While Wheatley certainly did not, then, reject Christianity outright (though she appears to have summarily rejected certain Christian behavior), she just as certainly did refuse to embrace so severe a Christianity as Pascal's, whose idea of charity sounded all too tellingly like "a purity that looks very much like irrelevance" (Price 26). What was relevant to this brave young poet was that she find a way to mitigate her victimization and thereby gain a measure of dignity. This onerous task she accomplished through her adoption of a mask of innocuousness which she constructed because of her brilliant mastery of language—that is, her power over words.

What comparing Wheatley's approach to Christianity with Pascal's three orders accomplishes is to demonstrate that Wheatley's Christianity was probably never "pure" but was even becoming, as she grew older, more and more liberal, in an emphatic way. One touchstone for this liberalizing or secularizing effect on her work was this poet's handling of what David Morris has called the religious sublime. In *The Religious Sublime: Christian Poetry and Critical Tradition in Eighteenth-Century England*, Morris describes the biblical paraphrase as perhaps the most popular genre used to express the religious sublime, which entails an articulation of the enthusiastic passions (i.e., the sublime) in predominantly Christian language and images.

These biblical paraphrases, Morris maintains, can be "either an original poem which relies strongly upon scripture for imagery, style, situation or subject . . . or a reasonably close reworking of specific biblical passages" (107–8). Wheatley's biblical paraphrase, "Isaiah lxiii, 1–8," fits this description fairly well, with the exception that the style Wheatley adopts is not biblical but is wholly her own. This poem represents her most concerted effort to create highly compressed and elevated verse. Her choice of scripture is of great consequence. One of the principal editors of *The Interpreter's Bible* (1st ed.), James Muilenburn, has observed about this biblical passage:

Church fathers like Tertullian, Origen, Jerome and their successors have interpreted it [63:1–8] messianically. Theology and poetry have joined in recasting and reinterpreting the thought in ways which, while foreign to the original meaning, have nevertheless done some justice to its sublimity. (5:726)

Wheatley's own interpretation falls into the same pattern established by the church fathers named by Muilenburn. The poem opens with this arresting couplet: "Say, heav'nly muse, what King, or mighty God, / That moves sublime from *Idumea's* road?" (60). The couplet is arresting because of its invocation (none in Isaiah, or for that matter anywhere in the Bible) and because of Wheatley's way of deifying this figure who in the biblical passage remains a traveler, albeit a traveler with a definite agenda, one that includes wreaking vengeance upon the enemies of Zion. Given the fact that Milton (and many others) was fond of using the phrase "heav'nly muse" (appearing four times in his English poetry) and that Christian typology clearly saw this passage as a prediction of the coming of the Christ (as Muilenburn states), the reader may at first find nothing amiss here.

Closer inspection of this couplet in the context of the entire poem, however, leads us to a more complex reading. The phrase "heav'nly muse" is by itself not of particular concern. The wedding of "King" and "God," however, may raise an eyebrow. Although Wheatley does later in the poem identify the traveler as "th' Almighty Saviour" (60), in keeping with typological interpretation, the phrase "What King or mighty God" resonates with the descriptions of such classical semi-divine figures as Herakles, and even with henotheistic deities like the Jehovah of the first half of the Old Testament and like similar divine/semi-divine figures in the African epic. If the concerns raised here were only these, we would probably be wise to drop the matter.

These details, however, do not stand alone. They are modified in this piece by two additional details. While we may be tempted to call the "heav'nly muse" somewhat syncretistic, temptation becomes tantamount to certainty when we observe that Wheatley's "Almighty Saviour" first spoke and then "shook the dazzling glories of his head" (60). There is nothing like this description in the Bible; where we do find such descriptions is in classical epics. Later in "Isaiah," her "Great God" possesses eyes which flash lightening: "what light'ning flashes from thine eyes?" (61). This Vergilian description which portrays flashing lightening emanating from the eyes of the immortal gods (Pope is fond of using such a description) Wheatley uses to characterize Niobe's children in the epyllion or short epic, "Niobe in Distress . . .": "From their bright eyes the living splenders play, / Nor can beholders bear the flashing ray" (102). As well we have pointed out Wheatley's attempt to make her heroine a deity closely resembles a parallel practice with African epic. So we see that Wheatley knew full well she was not drawing on biblical tradition for the additions she has made in her poem about the biblical Isaiah. Clearly then the poet has syncretized biblical and Christian imagery with that from the ancient classical world, mixed with a modicum of her African heritage, to attempt to enhance an attitude of sublimity within this passage from Isaiah. Having done so she demonstrates how this syncretistic process imparts to her poetry an intensifying, secularizing effect, not completely classical or African but also not wholly Christian.

While other poets of Wheatley's era, like Milton[2] for example, do indeed employ an occasional nod toward the classical world, few, however, carry this process as far as does Wheatley—hence the concern of a Joseph Sewall or a Jupiter Hammon. For even though she sets herself the task of composing a Christian biblical paraphrase on an especially sublime passage, she cannot refrain, or better she chooses not to refrain, from interpolating obviously classical/pagan and even African elements within a biblical paraphrase; finally then her "Isaiah" is not biblical nor classical nor African but is a syncretization, and more to the point "Isaiah" is simply "pure" Wheatley.

We may also conclude from this discourse that Phillis Wheatley's peculiar brand of Christianity blended with classicism, along with a bit of the African, became instrumental toward giving this poet the freedom she required to express her personal liberation poetics. As we have already observed, her fondness for classicism, especially, greatly assisted her quest for expressive space. I suspect the reason she found classical myth so friendly to her had much to do with the obvious fact that the classical deities could be easily adapted to her African heritage. Aurora, for example, must surely have reminded her of her beloved mother who *"poured out water at [the sun's] rising."*

Because Aurora was of course a feminine principle, we do not have to travel far to see this goddess as an affectionate characterization of her mother. In "On Imagination," for example, her second construction of a heterocosm tells the tale of Aurora and Tithonus. According to William King, author of the widely distributed and widely used *An Historical Account of the Heathen Gods and Heroes* (1710; ten London editions by 1761), Aurora "became Mother to the Stars, and the Winds" (33–34); and with Tithonus, her lover, she was mother to the Black Memnon, called by Hesiod, the Greek author of *Works and Days*, the king of Ethiopia. As there can be little doubt that Wheatley knew *Heathen Gods and Heroes* well, she would have had no difficulty thinking of herself as sister to Memnon, perhaps explaining why Wheatley refers to herself as "An Ethiop" in the early 1767 "To the University of Cambridge in New-England" (16). King's identification of Aurora as mother of the stars resonates interesting with Islam's emphasis on astronomy and with Wheatley's study of this science.

Given Aurora heralded the coming of the sun whose arrival Wheatley's mother celebrated, the fact that solar imagery is the most frequently recurring image-pattern in her extant oeuvre should come as no great wonder. We should expect, as well, to find that Wheatley often employs the eighteenth century's fondness for punning on Son/sun. In the case of Wheatley, however, what we observe is a conscious blending or syncretization of these two ideas. In "Thoughts on the Works of Providence," for example, the poet declares "That *Wisdom*, which attends *Jehovah's* ways, / Shines most conspicuous in the solar rays" (44). Here the inertia of Wheatley's African heritage serves her well as she creates an effective syncretization of the Old Testament's Jehovah and a vestige of her parents' hierophantic solar worship with the seventeenth and eighteenth centuries' preoccupations with the quest for wisdom.

The earliest known expression of interest in the pursuit of wisdom in Wheatley occurs in "On Virtue" which the poet composed in 1766 when only about twelve years old. At this early point, Wheatley declares that "Wisdom is higher than a fool can reach" (13). Whether or not Wheatley saw herself self-deprecatingly as "a fool," she certainly continued to search for wisdom, this quest punctuated by an occasional encounter with a two-hundred-year-old evolving theoretics of imagination, several texts of which we will explore in the next chapter. This early use of wisdom appears to come from Proverbs 1:7: "The fear of the Lord is the beginning of knowledge: but fools despise wisdom and instruction." For Wheatley's part, her early observation about wisdom would surely have pleased her "monitor," Joseph Sewall; "On Virtue," in fact, reads like yet another exercise in Wheatley's desire for Christian acceptance. So it is ironic that the orthodox Sewall very likely served as a conduit to the early-sixteenth-century skeptic, Pierre Charron.

The connection to Charron Joseph Sewall enabled for Phillis Wheatley was bridged by Joseph Seccombe who has the distinction of authoring the first tract on sport published in America, as a sermon on the value of fishing, especially on the sabbath. Sewall had delivered Seccombe's ordination sermon, in which Seccombe and two other young clergy were commissioned to minister to Native Americans.

After three years of service, which white folks judged to be distinguished, Seccombe accepted a call to the church at Kingston, New Hampshire. He assumed the duties of minister in October 1737, after which Seccombe settled down (having married in January 1738) to the relatively quiet life of a prosperous parson.

Seccombe was not always well fixed, however; for, having humble origins, Joseph found himself, because of his evident intelligence and genteel disposition, well supported in his grammar school days and throughout his college tenure at Harvard (A.B. 1731). This financial support came from the generosity of Old South Church, which he had joined, following his mother, in 1723. As his ties with Old South Church were, then, almost from the beginning quite strong, and all his publications appeared first in Boston, it is reasonably certain that this thinking man's works were available to the young and eager student, Phillis Wheatley. Seccombe died in 1760, just a year before Wheatley's arrival in Boston. Given Sewall's role as spiritual counselor to Wheatley and his association with Seccombe, it is likely that Sewall directed Wheatley's attention to this man's well-known works.

When we examine his output, we discover that Seccombe may not have been as "safe" a writer as Sewall probably thought him to be. In his *Some Occasional Thoughts* (1742), for example, we encounter the name of the famous skeptic, Pierre Charron, and a quote in a footnote from his *de la Sagesse* (*Concerning Wisdom*). According to Eugene F. Rice Jr., in his *The Renaissance Idea of Wisdom,* Charron's *de la Sagesse* marks "the triumph of wisdom as a naturally acquired moral virtue"—not a gift of God's grace (179). In other words, in his widely circulated Renaissance work, Charron constructed "a purely human wisdom" (179), recalling the ancient, classical understanding of the term. Seccombe's subject in *Some Occasional Thoughts* is the recent spate of enthusiasm brought on by George Whitefield's emotional preaching. Whitefield, about whom Wheatley would later write an internationally published and famous elegy, was chaplain to Selina Hastings, Countess of Huntingdon, but was also much hailed as the dramatic "voice" of the Great Awakening. Even Jonathan Edwards, spearhead of the Great Awakening, had lamented that Whitefield's provocation of trances, visions, and such enthusiastic responses had too often become manifestations of hypocrisy.

As Seccombe opens *Some Occasional Thoughts* with a quote from Edwards, one would expect these two to be in accord. Such is certainly *not* the case. Whereas Edwards in his *Treatise on the Religious Affections* holds firmly that the imagination is the means through which Satan invades the human soul, Seccombe argues that "The Divine Spirit, striving with Man, would operate on the *Imagination.*" Even though Seccombe acknowledges that the imagination is "a lower Power of human Nature" (Wheatley later elevates imagination to the highest level of the mind), he declares that, "Yet under Conduct of Understanding, it's a very useful and powerful Faculty" (9).

What provokes further interest here is that, in a footnote to this passage, Seccombe quotes the following from Charron's *de la Sagesse:* "'Imagination . . . is a loud, a blustering and restless Faculty [which] seems perfectly bound up in the profoundest Sleep, but is continually buzzing at the brain, like a boiling Pot'" (9). What we notice here is that, although Seccombe appears to cite Charron as an authority on imagination, what he has actually done amounts to an extension of Charron's thought in which he somewhat elevates imagination by giving it more "favorable press" than even Charron had ventured. We find here that Seccombe is assuredly opposed to Edwards's vilification of imagination. Seccombe concludes his discussion of imagination by maintaining that, "Though the Divine Spirit makes Use of the Imagination, it can never be serviceable without the Understanding" (9).

So although we have not moved to the position to which Wheatley later came, we have certainly departed from Edwards's Calvinistic point of view. It is worth noting that Seccombe quotes Charron from George Stanhope's 1707 translation of Charron's French *Sagesse,* thereby ascertaining that Charron was alive and well in Massachusetts Bay; as well, when Seccombe died, he left a library of five hundred volumes. So the copy of *Concerning Wisdom* Seccombe used could well have been his own and thereby have come into the hands of Phillis Wheatley. Seccombe's attitude toward imagination, then, becomes a suitable "theoretical" framework for Samuel Cooper's 1761 assertion that "Imagination! [is a] heav'n-born maid" (*Pietas* 45).

Another author Seccombe cites who did not enjoy universal approval among New England's clergy, but who probably did contribute to Wheatley's religious evolution, is Thomas Burnet, this reference appearing in Seccombe's *Business and Diversion . . . in the Fishing Season.* Burnet's *Sacred Theory of the Earth* presents an interpretation of the earth as an infallible sign that the planet itself argues for mankind's fallen state (post–original sin). Cotton Mather condemns Burnet's theoretics as unsound and not acceptable in his *Christian Philosopher* (103).

As Wheatley probably took her estimate in "Thoughts on the Works of Providence" that the distance from the earth to the sun is "twice forty millions" (44) from Mather's *Christian Philosopher* (48), and given that Mather Byles certainly did have a copy of his uncle's tome, we can calculate that Wheatley came across C. Mather's disapproval of Burnet. But soon we will discover that Mather Byles himself found Burnet's *Sacred Theory* diverting enough to devote most of a poem, "The Conflagration," to Burnet's prediction of the final days. We can, therefore, conclude from Seccombe's use of Charron and Burnet that Wheatley's local exposure to some of the major theological arguments of her day proved to have been instructive and formative to her own religious development, especially as suggested by her search for wisdom.

Seccombe's own search for wisdom would certainly have piqued her curiosity. From looking through Seccombe's published works, one could well reckon that the pursuit of wisdom is Seccombe's central subject. In all his works, his attitude toward wisdom resembles that of a mundane, cultured gentleman; indeed, the figure suggested by Seccombe's works comes uncannily close to describing Samuel Cooper, Wheatley's close advisor following the death of Sewall. To be sure, Seccombe devotes an entire homily to an argument that wisdom and happiness are, or should be considered to be, wholly compatible, this tract entitled, *A Specimen* [sic] *of the Harmony of Wisdom and Felicity*.

The foregoing title states Seccombe's thesis: that wisdom and "felicity" combine to create a harmony. Seccombe defines the achievement of wisdom as the means by which "a Man knows himself and is humble, acquaints himself with Men and pays Defference [sic] to every one according to Desent [sic]." The idea of humility is apropos of all considerations of wisdom among all cultures. What is peculiar to Seccombe here, and perhaps also to Wheatley, is the idea that the seeker after wisdom must be accompanied by "Felicity." The men he seeks to instruct his quest are not necessarily, according to the time, his neighbors, but rather hail from history, such classical authors as Livy, Scipio, Herodotus, and more recently the French Charron and the British John Locke.

What I find diverting in the word "felicity" is that this word bears connotations of secularity; it bespeaks how one may obtain satisfaction in this world. As he does not actually recommend that one should postpone her desire for bliss to the next world, clearly Seccombe focuses in *Harmony* on a search for bliss firmly grounded here and now. Note that the figures he names are all essentially secular in their orientation. Seccombe's approach to achieve happiness/wisdom now, by living a gentleman's life of the cultivation of culture, but always with a character of humility, not only resonates with secularity but parallels the kind of life Phillis Wheatley came to prefer—a life of comfortable, contemplative study. When we couple Seccombe's penchant for a theoretics of the imagination with his quest for wisdom, we discover in this man a well-informed and surprisingly secular aesthetic and spiritual guide and source for a young genius who gives every indication that she profited either from his direct example or at least from the flow of thought which came to typify the secular age of American classicism (see *The American Aeneas*, passim).

As we examine closely her "Thoughts on the Works of Providence," we quickly recover all parts of the *meditatio*, a self-conscious exploration of wisdom, and an inchoate analysis of the operation of the imaginative faculty. Taken together these three factors characterize the spiritual and aesthetic development not of a puritanical Christian, but of a brilliant child of the Enlightenment (in the *best sense* of this term). For example, "Thoughts" opens with a ten-line invocation to the "Celestial muse" (43); the length here is certainly unusual, if not virtually unique. While this invocation is indeed her longest, Wheatley opens both her epyllia, "Goliath of Gath" and "Niobe in Distress," with eight-line invocations; as the muse is never far removed in Wheatley's poetry, we may readily conclude that she is preoccupied with the phenomenon of poetic afflatus to such an extent that her reliable repetition of this preoccupation assumes the power of religious ritual. Always in her poetry a concomitant to the muses' ritual is the notion of flight, of an attempt to achieve celestial height—as she puts it, to "raise my mind to a seraphic strain" (43). This pattern of mental movement or action of the mind characterizes Wheatley's first period of poetic maturity. The ultimate object of this 131-line *meditatio* is, of course, to understand Providence or God, the better by means of contemplating His works, especially those of the sun and the human race, the two loci or images on which, in this particular mental exercise, the mind of this meditator fastens. Calling God "Providence" here furthers this contemplative exercise because this word already refers to God as that entity functions within the universe. This observation goes far toward explaining why Benjamin Franklin and George Washington were so fond, during this same period, of frequently evoking the favor of Providence.

Wheatley makes clear that she does not see the sun, "The peerless monarch of th' ethereal train" (43), in and of itself as the object of her focus. Indeed in sun hierophanies, devotees view the sun as a symbol, as here, of a much greater controlling power. Noting the great span of space, 80 million miles (a la C. Mather), but known today to average 93 million miles, separating "Sol" and earth, the poet points out that this body drives "ev'ry flow'ry birth" and "dazzles mortal sight." The thrust of her meditation soon becomes apparent as she poses the query whether mankind, who avidly pursues the study of astronomy, actually grasps, or cares to grasp, the wisdom and power behind the creation of sun and earth. In her words, "are thy wonders, Lord, by men explor'd, / And yet creating glory unador'd?" (44). In her calculated interest in nature and her finding that nature declares the power and wisdom of the Deity, Wheatley begins to sound like Charron. For as Rice observes of the French skeptic, to Charron "the law of nature is a shining ray of divinity, an emanation and dependence of eternal divine law" (192).

At this juncture, Wheatley completes her evocation of memory, the first step in the meditative process and subsequently moves on to the second stage, that of attempting to grasp the meaning of these loci, Sol's and man's relation to the Deity. She opens this investigation of her own understanding by asserting: "that *Wisdom*, which attends *Jehovah's* Ways, / Shines most conspicuous in the solar rays" (44). Note that here the poet summons "*Jehovah's* Ways," not those of Jesus or of a clearly Christian God. Throughout this poem, Wheatley refers to God as "Almighty Providence," "Lord" as we have remarked above, and as "the Eternal," but never as "Jesus" or "Christ." The words she chooses to refer to God are simply too general to be identifiable references to Christianity. This generality appears to be no accident; quite the contrary, this generality signals her spiritual journey away from an orthodox Christianity toward a syncretized religious consciousness that characterizes her mature period as a poet.

Her idea of the "great God" describes a Being who extends "his love" to all earthly creatures; "His *Wisdom* rules them, and his *Pow'r* defends." As the poet comes repeatedly to appreciate this "love" her God manifests, her recognition, remembering the ultimate goal of Augustinian meditation, leads her repeatedly to exhort mankind to follow her in her appreciation. When describing the coming of her mother's dawn, for example, she urges mankind to "salute the smiling morn" with "grateful strains" "before its beams the eastern hills adorn!" (46). Here the poet moves beyond Christian adulation of the natural world by encouraging all about her to engage the ritual worship of "the sun at his rising." A bold move to press an African ritual upon her New England audience of white folks!

Quoting Genesis, "'Let there be light,'" Wheatley contends that the power which "forms a ray of light" is the same "That call'd creation from eternal night" (47). From this final and sublime citation of cosmic infinity, apparently taking her cue from "eternal night,"

Wheatley moves abruptly to a remarkably interior analysis of the human mind in the state of sleep. And of course the real mind in action here is the poet's own. This identical movement of mind, from contemplation of the cosmos to an interiorization of the human mind, Wheatley later traces with even greater economy in her important "On Imagination." This turn inward as an opportunity to discover wisdom parallels Charron in *de la Sagesse* wherein, as Rice observes, "Finally, the object of wisdom became man himself, and its fundamental command [became] self-knowledge" (212).

Calling upon the power of reason or understanding, Wheatley insists that the entity which controls reason or understanding is, of course, the Deity. As Wheatley explores an analysis of sleep here that she had earlier taken up in "On Recollection," she fascinatingly predicts in both poems Freudian dream analysis. As we may expect, Wheatley's principal interest in the realm of sleep is first its liberating power and then the role of dreams in the poetic process. To her, dreams provide a world wherein, while physical "action ceases," nonetheless, "ideas range / Licentious and unbounded o'er the plains." Note the rare instance in Wheatley of enjambment between these two lines. The poet appears to be on the verge of ecstasy; for as she continues, dreams enable not only her release from the chains of slavery but as well a momentary repose "Where *Fancy's* queen in giddy triumph reigns" (47).

In her conception, dreams then become a repository of images with which the mind of the poet may become engaged. In "On Recollection" she is more specific when she holds that the memory's "ample treasure" presents "in her pomp of images display's" considerable assistance "To the high-raptur'd poet" (62). With little effort we may conclude that Wheatley has constructed here an inchoate theoretics she improves upon in "On Imagination." Even at this moment in "Thoughts," nevertheless, she has recognized that the mind can be a source of profound liberation. Of even greater significance, however, is her observation that this realm of the mind, with its capacity for delivering the space of release, is ruled by a feminine queen (God has receded into the background) who triumphs in her manipulation of subordinate "*Fancy.*" Clearly in "Thoughts" Wheatley pursues a poetics that she will more or less perfect in "On Imagination." So we may reasonably date "Thoughts" as having come after the late 1771 "On Recollection" but before "On Imagination."

Wheatley then extends this experimental mode into which she has induced the meditative process to incorporate a dialogue which she asserts arises "Among the mental pow'rs" (48). This dialogue is to take place "(so let *Fancy* rove)" (48; the parentheses are Wheatley's) between "*Reason*" and "*Love.*" As these two debate the query, "'What most the image of th' Eternal shows?'" the character, Love, evoking Augustinian meditation, maintains that the question should be referred "to *Recollection's* shrine / Who loud proclaims my origin divine" (48).

This dialogue so clearly resembles Augustine's analysis of wisdom in *de Trinitate* that one may well think Wheatley had the text on her writing table during composition of this passage. In *de Trinitate*, for example, Augustine declares that the trinity of memory, understanding, and love of God, attained by an act of the will (the ultimate goal of philosophical meditation) leads, by means of correct application, to true wisdom. "In so doing," in the words of Augustine, the mind "is made wise itself" (*de Trinitate* 191).

Curiously, however, Wheatley brings her dialogue between Reason and Love to a conclusion by having Reason, convinced by Love's assertion, embrace Love; as the poet puts it " . . . kindling at her charms / She clasp'd the blooming goddess in her arms" (49). Augustine has no goddesses who instruct or inform Christian thought anywhere in his works. This description is more redolent of classical/African mythology than of Augustine. In *The Renaissance Idea of Wisdom*, Rice points out that, during the late sixteenth century, just proceeding the publication of *de la Sagesse,*

> "Wisdom [became] no longer necessarily Christian and a gift of grace; it is purely human and a perfection of the natural man, naturally derived from the dictates of the autonomous human reason, experience, contemporary ideals and practice, and the Greek and Roman moralists"—Plato and Seneca, *e.g.* (177)

Charron of course continues to promulgate such an approach to his quest for wisdom. This wisdom, recovered in the secular world of the human, "finally, is no longer a solitary, contemplative [monastic] blessedness but mundane happiness [directed toward] a good and successful life" (177). Such a state of being appears to be desiderata for both Joseph Seccombe and Phillis Wheatley.

Wheatley's investigation of memory, understanding, and will (as love), elements of the *meditatio;* of an analysis of wisdom; and of an incipient poetics finally do not lead her to an articulated faith in Augustine's Christian idea of God but rather to a syncretized, finely tuned religious consciousness. This intensely personal religious consciousness, moreover, is so firmly held by this poet that she is emboldened to chide her readers who "ungrateful" pay their God "But little homage, and but little praise," to set aside their pettiness and raise jubilant songs to His power and wisdom.

Yet another indication that Wheatley developed what we may term a relaxed Christianity is the appearance in several of her elegies of a chthonic interpretation of the afterlife. This interest in the chthonic, referring to the gods, goddesses, and other figures in the ancient underworld, begins to appear in the middle of 1771, with Wheatley's publication of "To Mrs. Leonard, on the Death of Her Husband." Opening with the stark phrase, "Grim Monarch!" (205), Wheatley stridently signals her shift from voicing self-conscious, Christian allusions to Jesus or Christ—as her poetic mentor Mather Byles was vigilant to make, particularly in his elegies—toward her first period of maturity during which she seldom draws in her works definitely Christian connections.

In six of her elegies composed between June 1771 and August 6, 1773, the date of the London publication of *Poems,* Wheatley adopts a predominantly chthonic perspective. "On the Death of Dr. Samuel Marshall. 1771," first published on October 14, 1771, and reprinted in *Poems,* serves as an example of her chthonic approach; as we saw earlier, this elegy bears connections to Wheatley's Africa. Here Wheatley has the deceased looking back, "Through thickest glooms" of the underworld, as an "immortal shade" (86), upon "that confusion which thy death has made." Or, as the poet continues, the departed physician may as well look down "from *Olympus'* height" (86). Note the radical shift from the depths of the underworld to the heights of Olympus, echoing the mind's movement in "Thoughts" from the cosmos to the interior seat of contemplation. Of course the mental traveling here in no way duplicates or references anything Christian.

As Marshall was a relative of Susanna Wheatley, he had probably attended the Wheatley family, including Phillis—hence the line, "In him *we* find the father and the friend" (87; italics added). While she does call the Doctor Apollo and Aesculapius, she never in the poem addresses him by his Christian name, just as she never calls on any figures from the Christian faith. The naming of Aesculapius and Apollo is of special note, because according to King's *Heathen Gods and Heroes,* both Apollo and his son Aesculapius were gods of physic. As the caduceus was their symbol, the fact that King identifies "the Serpent twining about it [as] an Emblem of Wisdom" (111) only reinforces the argument that Wheatley searched for wisdom outside the Holy Circle.[3] Indeed, within a puritanical Christian context, the serpent can only call up the "evil" reptile of Eden, certainly not a power of healing.

In her first of three extant letters to John Thornton, renowned British philanthropist and acquaintance of Selina Hastings, Countess of

Huntingdon, Wheatley observes in December 1773 that, in spite of her manumission, she has found that both she and her African American brothers and sisters, as well as Native Americans, are "despised on earth on account of our colour" (174). This bleak observation she later embellishes in her third letter to Thornton when she declares: "The world is a severe schoolmaster, for its frowns are less dang'rous than its smiles and flatteries, and it is a difficult task to keep in the path of Wisdom" (183). Even so by the end of 1783 Wheatley tells us she has continued to search for wisdom with the help of her recently deceased spiritual mentor Samuel Cooper, the gentleman who baptized her.

Her elegy on Cooper's death reveals that Wheatley believed all "The Virtuous lov'd Thee" and "the wise admir'd" him (152). For that matter, Wheatley attests that "The Sons of Learning" hung "on thy lessons" (152). In what is perhaps the most personal remark about another person in her extant oeuvre, the poet states that, "as The hapless Muse," herself, mourns "her loss in COOPER," "she sits, she writes, and weeps, by turns"; for Cooper was to her "A Friend sincere, whose mild indulgent rays / Encourag'd oft and oft approv'd her lays" (153). Like Sewall before him, he too shone as the sun, but not like Sewall, this man appreciated and commented on her poetry. His counsel regarding her poems came from one who was himself considered to be a poet of no small repute, as his contributions to *Pietas et Gratulatio* ably attest.

Perhaps of greatest interest in this poem is how vastly different is her treatment of Cooper as a minister from that she gave to Sewall fifteen years earlier. While Sewall was "redeem'd by *Jesus'* blood," has in death become "a saint with God" (20), and has now "arriv'd th' immortal shore," Cooper has in death achieved no sainthood, nor does the poet make any mention of Jesus, of rebirth in the blood or of the miracles of Christ. What she has written bespeaks the career of a mundane, latitudinarian clergyman who participated actively in the search for knowledge and wisdom; the compatibility between the poet, Phillis Wheatley, and this spiritual and poetic counselor should at this juncture become obvious.

The most revealing elegy Wheatley ever composed, however, is the one she wrote upon her own impending death. In the powerful and affecting "An Elegy on Leaving———," we see not a whit of Christianity. As the persona of this poem bids farewell to a thoroughly pastoral world of "friendly bow'rs," a "sequester'd seat," and groves that offer a "kind retreat" from "noon-tide rays" (156), she laments the coming loss not of a heaven of Christian bliss, but of a realm wholly devoted to the ideal of Vergilian poetic creativity; indeed the world this poet regrets to lose is the world of poetry.

Has Wheatley in the last years of her life, then, become a devotee of pure literary aesthetics? Jupiter Hammon appears to have recognized that she could very well have engaged such a path. For in the 1778 poem addressed to Wheatley, he admonishes the younger poet:

> Thou has left the heathen shore,
> Thro' mercy of the Lord;
> Among the heathen live no more,
> Come magnify thy God.
>
> (77)

Hammon too appears to have been unconvinced by Wheatley's "On Being Brought from Africa to America." Or a more likely source for Hammon's admonishment, other than the inertia of her African heritage (recall Hammon was born in 1711 in the American colonies), may well be her non-Christian, chthonic display appearing in several of her published elegies.

It is, nevertheless, a certainty that, whether or not Wheatley actually saw "An Address..." (there was, after all, a most distracting War of Independence going on), she did not "benefit" from its warning. Quite the contrary, not even the practice of Augustinian meditation could dissuade her from her syncretized religious consciousness. As this young woman's religious perspective evolved, she first, of course, embraced the ancestor worship/animism, hierophantic solar worship, and Islam of her parents, in the process already learning how to blend religious ideas.

After being brought to America, and desiring to become an acceptable member of her newly imposed home, she attempted to accommodate the allegedly superior Christianity. Not finding herself either accepted or acceptable, she sought an interiorized peace of mind in which all components of her religious heritage, now extending to her beloved classicism, could in her brilliant mind be resolved. Rejecting an external insistence that she abandon all thought of her African religious heritage and then later that her poetry waxed all too pagan, Wheatley discovered the ecstatic liberating force available to her within the interior space of her own poetry, for her power over words enabled her to achieve a life-saving measure of self-determination. It must be added that in no way does this recording of her complex, developing religious consciousness even begin to suggest that this sensitive, keenly intelligent soul was either insincere or anything but seriously committed to her personal idea of the Divine.

CHAPTER 6

Intellectual Development

JUST AS WHEATLEY'S POST-AFRICAN RELIGIOUS CONSCIOUSNESS EVOLVED FROM A PERIOD OF RESTRAINT AND CONFINEMENT INTO A PERHAPS SURPRISINGLY UNRESTRAINED AND UNCONFINED THEOLogy of liberation, the journey of her intellectual progress followed a similar liberating path. The direction of influence upon her intellectual education came principally from four cultural areas, those of ancient classicism, the Continent, Great Britain, and her adoptive America.

We have already noted how Wheatley demonstrated an almost instantaneous agility for intellectual pursuits, following her purchase by John and Susannah Wheatley on July 11, 1761. In the prefatory letter to her 1773 *Poems*, her then master, John Wheatley, states that, within sixteen months of her arrival in Boston, Wheatley could "read, any, the most difficult Parts of the Sacred Writings [KJV], to the great Astonishment of all who heard her" (6). Note the unmistakable imputation that she "performed," doubtlessly for white folks, much like a denigrating circus act. He also took this opportunity to point out that "She has a great Inclination to learn the Latin Tongue, and has made some Progress in it" (6). Judging from her excellent translation of Ovid's *Metamorphoses*, book 6, the Niobe episode, she made much more than "some Progress" in Latin; she mastered this classical "Tongue."

This mastery doubtless brought her into contact with such additional classical authors as Horace and Vergil. As Mather Byles had years before (during the 1730s) acquired from Alexander Pope himself autographed copies of his famous translations of the *Iliad* and *Odyssey*, we can be certain that she was familiar with these two Greek epics. Recall that in "To Maecenas," which opens the 1773 *Poems* and serves as its introduction, the poet paraphrases the first lines of Pope's translation of the *Iliad*, book 16, the passage in which Patroclus pleas to Achilles that he be allowed to wear his warrior lover's armor as an incentive to the Greeks to intensify their ferocity against the Trojans.

Wheatley gives ample evidence throughout her oeuvre that she had great appreciation for Vergil, "the *Mantuan* Sage," as she describes him in "To Maecenas." She also suffuses her poems with elements of pastoral, showing an unmistakable knowledge of Vergil's *Eclogues*. About both Homer and Vergil, Wheatley declares in "To Maecenas," "O could I rival thine [Homer's] and *Virgil's* page" (10), and thereby announces to her readers her intention to explore the epic genre after having received instruction and inspiration from the ancient world's best practitioners. In her repeated use of the Horatian ode in such poems as "To Maecenas," "On Recollection," "On Imagination," and "Thoughts on the Works of Providence," this African American poet attests her command of this subgenre of the ode or lyric. In contrast to the brilliance and boldness of the Pindaric ode, the Horatian ode affects a solemn and meditative tone and displays a generally regular stanzaic pattern, but not strictly so. Wheatley's interiorized contemplative poems from her first period of maturity, which are made up of regular heroic couplets arranged into stanzas of four to sixteen lines, capture the mood and form of the Horatian ode.[1] In fact, she demonstrates in "On Imagination" how she can adapt the Horatian ode to her own needs by blending the classical form with African call-and-response.

For in this, perhaps her most important poem, stanzas on the imagination "call" to those on fancy which give answer, back and forth, setting up an intricate pattern of call-and-response, thereby contributing to the interiorized separation of these two faculties into the imagination as leader (that which calls) and the fancy as follower (that which takes instruction from imagination). This pattern enables Wheatley's readers to grasp the relation between these two mental forces in which the fancy, as subordinate, serves the imagination. As we have observed in "Thoughts," Wheatley describes their association as one wherein "*Fancy's* queen in giddy triumph reigns" (47), albeit by the time Wheatley composes "On Imagination," her interpretation of these two faculties has shifted a bit; now imagination has become the poet's reason and the fancy acts as a subordinate manifestation of the more powerful and encompassing imagination—not unlike the relationship in most African American churches between the minister (caller) and his or her congregation (respondents).

As Wheatley is so fond of exploring the connection between poetry and painting, she may well have found in Horace's famous *Ars Poetica* encouragement for pursuing this interest. Therein the poet would have encountered Horace's proverbial dictum that "Ut pictura poesis" (1. 361; as the painting, so the poem). To be sure, even though

Wheatley's knowledge of the contiguities between poetry and painting may well have reflected an intrinsic recognition, the Roman's observation could only have reinforced and given authority to this recognition. Horace's pronouncement that "Scribendi recte sapere est et principium et fons" ("in order to write correctly, the origin and fountain is to be wise";1. 309) surely as well compelled this maturing poet the further as she pursued her search for wisdom. For that matter, given Wheatley's determination to be a serious poet and knowing her to have intense regard for the authors, history, and mythologies of the ancient Western world, Wheatley could easily have found in Horace the principal impetus for her wisdom quest.

Another great aesthetic theorist of the ancient world whose thought surely did influence Wheatley, and virtually all the poets and aesthetic theorists of the eighteenth century, was the Greek Longinus. His *Peri Hupsous* (*On the Sublime*), written between the first and third centuries A.D., appears to have been unknown during the Middle Ages and was not paid much attention during the Renaissance, though there were Greek versions available. Not until Boileau's 1674 French translation did Longinus's treatise burst on the aesthetic scene. As Samuel Holt Monk, the author of the authoritative *The Sublime: A Study of Critical Theories in XVIII-Century England,* insists, Longinus's *Peri Hupsous* was "On everyone's tongue" (24). The fact that in "Thoughts" Wheatley uses the "Let there be light" passage from Genesis may well reflect Longinus's identification of the Genesis reference as one of the most sublime expressions ever made in literature.

Now let us turn our attention to the British critics and aesthetic theorists of the seventeenth and eighteenth centuries who collectively fueled the flow of thought that informed Wheatley's intellectual world. We have already demonstrated the presence in Wheatley's poetry of the religious sublime. But more often her interpretation of the feelings of the sublime or the enthusiastic passions resembles the theories expressed by several of the sublime's eighteenth-century commentators, such as John Dennis, Joseph Addison, Edmund Burke, and Henry Home, Lord Kames. As I will demonstrate in my next book on Phillis Wheatley, *Phillis Wheatley and the Romantics,* in many respects, Wheatley's treatment of this aesthetic category even anticipates Immanuel Kant's "Analytic of the Sublime."

Before we examine the impact of British aestheticism, we would do well to touch base with the philosophical perspective of the times. Two British philosophers of almost universal impact on Wheatley's century were Thomas Hobbes and John Locke. Hobbes's *Leviathan* (1651), although its major political concerns defend absolutism in government, places great importance on the function of imagination and its instruction of reason. At the outset of *Leviathan,* Hobbes declares he will examine "the Thoughts of man, *Singly* and afterwards in *Trayne,* or dependance upon one another" (85). In "On Imagination," Wheatley speaks of the faculties of the mind in terms of a "mental train." According to Hobbes, however, "All Fancies [equal here to imagination] are Motions within us, reliques of those made in the Sense" (94); therefore, to Hobbes, the creation of new worlds is virtually impossible. Not so to Wheatley, who would "with new worlds amaze th' unbounded soul" (66)!

Hobbes's explanation of the "Infinite" is arresting because it so clearly foreshadows the general eighteenth-century conception. To Hobbes, "When we say anything is inifinite, we signifie only that we are not able to conceive the ends, and bounds of the thing named." Given this condition of perception, or the lack of it, we evoke the Deity "not to make us conceive him; (for he is *Incomprehensible;* and his greatnesse, and power are unconceivable)" (99). Thus Wheatley can hold that the "Great God" is "incomprehensible, unknown / By sense" (20). The enjambment between these lines registers the poet's ecstatic recognition. Wheatley nevertheless departs from Hobbes's unshakable opinion that "Fancy, without the help of Judgement, is not commended as a Vertue" (135). To her, imagination, Hobbes's "Fancy," becomes the indisputable "leader of the mental train" (67).

We should note that Wheatley's interpretation of imagination evolved and was certainly not self-evident to her when she first became enamored of this somewhat mysterious faculty. What is to be observed here is how close she comes to Hobbes at certain points but also how summarily she disagrees with him at others. So we may well predict that she is not going to find palatable John Locke's take on the enthusiastic passions. In Locke's chapter, "[Of Enthusiasm]," added to the fourth (1700) edition of *An Essay Concerning Human Understanding,* Locke speaks disparagingly about fancy or imagination:

> And what readier way can there be to run ourselves into the most extravagant errors and miscarriages, than this to set up fancy for our supreme and sole guide, and to believe any proposition to be true, any action to be right, only because we believe it to be so? (II 437)

Much like Jonathan Edwards, who was remarkably influenced by Locke's strong endorsement of reason ruled by judgment, would later conclude in his 1746 *Treatise Concerning the Religious Affections,* Locke condemns enthusiasm as conducive of delusions and as a means by which "the power of the Prince of Darkness" confuses the human soul and reason (2:438–39).

While Wheatley herself did not to my knowledge in any way ever find delusional behavior the least bit appealing or reliable, she just as definitely did not embrace Locke's emphatic distrust of fancy or his almost paranoid (delusional?) insistence that the imagination was an evil faculty. We should at this juncture acknowledge, nevertheless, that Locke's hostility toward the imaginative faculty came from a broad context of such hostility. As early as 1526 when he published his translation of the Pentateuch, William Tyndale rendered into Early Modern English these passages from Genesis 6:5: "every imagination of the thoughts of [mankind's] heart was only evil continually"; and from Genesis 8:21, "the imagination of man's heart is evil from his youth." Both the Geneva Bible (1564) and the King James Version (1611) take the lead from Tyndale and duplicate his translation.

So the biblical text used by the Calvinists and Puritans (i.e., the Geneva Bible) repeated Tyndale's translation. As the ministers of Calvinistic Puritanism all had comparable training in Hebrew, Greek, and Latin, any of them should have known that the proper translation of the Hebrew *yeçer* was "inclination" rather than Tyndale's "imagination" (See *Interpreter's Bible* [1952] I 536–39 and 547; and *New Interpreter's Bible* [1994] I 384–94). Even so, probably because their parishioners had no knowledge of any of the biblical languages (maybe some had a bit of Latin), the ministers were pressed to endorse the English text before them. Hence we can explain why William Perkins, one of the fathers of British Puritanism, in *A Treatise of Man's Imaginations. Showing His Naturall Euill Thoughts: His Want of Good Thoughts: The Way to Reforme Them* (1607), penned these condemnatory lines in reference to how adults may dissuade children from depending too much on their imaginative faculty: " . . . the imaginations of mans heart are evill from his youth [fr. Genesis 8:21], therefore, they [i.e., parents, masters, and tutors] must all joyne hand in hand betime to stop up or at least to lessen this corrupt fountain" (164–65).

I cannot resist observing that Perkins's "corrupt fountain" reveals just how actively and even creatively this Puritan's imagination functions. Perkins further admonishes that " . . . the cause of naturall Imagination in them [children], . . . without the special grace of God, will bring eternall condemnation both to souls and bodie" (167). Jonathan Edwards, over a century later, occupied essentially the same position. For that matter, the conservative Christian attitude toward the imaginative faculty has not budged, even down to recent times. This position holds that, in order for the imagination to function "safely," only one who possesses the gift of God's grace can properly deploy this faculty.[2] Given the fact that one does not know for certain whether the Deity has bequeathed the gift of grace until after death, how is it, then, that one may ever rely on one's imagination?

Unquestionably, Phillis Wheatley subscribed to no such austere prescription. In fact, looking at Jerome's *Biblia Sacra Latina*, commonly known as the Vulgate, we may well wonder why it was that Tyndale registered his negative, anti-imagination translation in these two Genesis passages. Jerome's paraphrase of the Hebrew for Genesis 6:5 was as follows: "Videns Deus et cuncta cogitatio intenta cordis esset ad malum omni tempora" ("and the whole conception of the heart [of mankind] was inclined toward evil all the time"); and for Genesis 8:21: "sensus enim et cogitatio humani cordis in malum prona sunt ab adolescentia sua" ("for the understanding and reasoning of the human heart are inclined toward evil, from his youth").

Here we look in vain for any reference to imagination, much less for a negative position. We are left to conclude that Tyndale must have had a powerful distrust of imagination and probably a thoroughly positive regard for the understanding/reason. In any case, the biblical scholars who constructed the Geneva and KJV Bibles either trusted Tyndale's capacity to render the scriptures into English or they agreed with Tyndale's hostility toward the imaginative faculty. One factor is tantamount to a certainty; these later biblical scholars did not even attempt to correct Tyndale's willful error. Consequently, all who read the Geneva or the KJV (or both) Bible(s) who did or could not read the Bible in Jerome's Latin version were taught, religiously, that the imagination was an evil faculty. One other possible explanation for a failure to accept Jerome's Vulgate, as far as Puritans were concerned, could very well have been their fanatical hatred of anything Roman Catholic.

I should point out that all English-speaking Christian clergy, Roman Catholic or Protestant, throughout the seventeenth and eighteenth centuries assuredly did know Jerome's close Latin paraphrase of the Hebrew, Aramaic, and Greek portions of the Bible. As far as Wheatley's Boston is concerned, not only could the clergy of her time, as earlier, handle Jerome's Latin, but they could as well move with some ease among the three languages of the original biblical text. For that matter, Wheatley herself could have read Jerome's Latin text, which was often used in the early forms of the Latin grammar schools (because it was thought to have been translated into fairly easy Latin, in comparison to Vergil or Horace).

Given its use in the Latin grammar schools, the Vulgate would have been readily available to her; indeed, Sewall or Cooper or Byles could have provided her this text if she had requested it. The point to be made here is simply that she probably did discover the willful "error" Tyndale and others made regarding imagination; therefore, she would have learned that the imagination was in fact *not*, in and of itself, an evil faculty. For example, had she asked Cooper's opinion about imagination or seen his strong endorsement of it in the *Pietas* line, "Imagination! Heav'n born maid," she would have been reassured that the imagination was even a good faculty, this despite Pope's condemnatory lines in *Essay on Man*, "Imagination plies her dangerous art / And pours it all upon the peccant part" (Epistle II,11.143–44).

From a macrocosmic perspective among English-speaking peoples, Tyndale's substitution of imagination for reason, understanding, and/or inclination could only have exacerbated the period's grasp of Augustine's (and before him Aristotle's, in *de Anima*) negative interpretation of the imaginative faculty. As orthodoxy underwent a gradual but general liberating shift regarding use of imagination, particularly during the late eighteenth century in Britain and America, the intellectual elite, although several among this body had always manifested a rebellious temper, increasingly promoted both the imagination and the sublime, two aesthetic categories many considered to be coterminous. Next we will examine, briefly, several of these rebels and movers of thought: Pierre Charron (now in a nonreligious context) in France; John Hobbes (briefly revisited), John Dryden, John Dennis, Shaftsbury, Joseph Addison, Edmund Burke, Kames, and William Duff in Britain; and Joseph Seccombe, Charles Chauncy, Samuel Cooper, William Billings, and Mather Byles, who requires extensive investigation, in the American colonies.

Charron, whom we have met before, makes several additional and provocative observations regarding the imaginative faculty. According to Charron, the imagination is an essential and highly charged faculty which "keeps all [the other parts of the mind] about it awake and sets the other Faculties on *work*" (Stanhope trans. 119). Gendering imagination as female, the French skeptic imparts to the feminine faculty great power and responsibility: " . . . the Acts of Recollection, representing to the Intellectual Faculty, laying up in the Memory, and drawing out those Stores again for Use, are all of them Operations of the Imaginative Faculty" (119). Wheatley's own "On Recollection" speaks of the memory in similar terms as that mental power whose "secret stores . . . to the high-raptur'd poet gives her aid" (62).

Significantly, Charron maintains further that memory and "Fancy, come within the compass of This [imagination], and are not (as some pretend) Powers of the Mind, distinct and separate from it" (119–20).

So we observe that, to this important aesthetic theorist, both Fancy and Memory serve the Imagination and are therefore subordinate to it. I have been unable to discover another such theorist who insists upon this actually quite specific description of the operation of imagination, until of course we come to Phillis Wheatley. It may be then that this authoritative theorist may well have served Wheatley in a pivotal capacity. I should point out that, in his *Creative Imagination,* James Engell makes no mention of Charron or his *de la Sagesse*.

Charron exuberantly holds that the imagination "is *Hot*" which causes poets to indulge "in bold and lofty Flights of Fancy" (116). Here we view a powerful, influential theorist assert that imagination is clearly associated, as in Wheatley, with the condition of high rapture or intense enthusiasm and with the notion of apparently boundless flight. No less a figure than Francis Bacon in 1605 appears to have taken instruction from Charron when the British philosopher describes imagination as an "extremely licensed" mental power which can "make unlawful matches and divorses of things" (1:5). Both these thinkers point directly to Wheatley's "Thoughts" wherein she speaks of a realm residing in the dreaming mind where "ideas range / Licentious and unbounded" and "Where *Fancy's* queen in giddy triumph reigns" (47).

Virtually none of the eighteenth-century British aestheticists pick up on Charron's effort to distinguish imagination and fancy, although they appear to agree with Charron, and many others from Plato and Aristotle to thinkers of the Renaissance, that the imagination is the poet's faculty. Beyond his remarks in *Leviathan,* however, Hobbes, in his 1650 "Answer to Davenant's Preface to *Gondibert,*" makes no distinction between fancy and imagination, genders fancy as a feminine principle, identifies fancy as a faculty of flight which can "fly from one Indies to the other, and from Heaven to Earth" (2:59), and notes that "Poets are Painters" (2:61). John Dryden, just fourteen years later, puts on the breaks regarding the imagination when he admonishes that "imagination in a poet is a faculty so wild and lawless, that like a high-ranging spaniel, it must have clogs tied to it, lest it outrun judgement" (Engell 35).

Mather Byles, writing in America almost eighty years later, appears to indulge his "wild imagination" with impunity, as Wheatley would do over a hundred years after Dryden. To return to Britain, John Dennis, called by some the greatest critic of his age, in remarkable disagreement with Locke, celebrates the enthusiastic passions. In the fourth chapter of *The Grounds of Criticism* (1704), entitled "What the Greate Poetry Is, What Enthusiasm Is," Dennis identifies the

"Enthusiastick Passions" as "those emotions which excite great poetry. Contemplation and meditation give rise to these emotions" (338), the strongest of which "must be rais'd by religious Ideas; that is, by Ideas which either shew the Attributes of the Divinity, or relate to his worship" (339). David Morris interprets Dennis's perspective as having moved a significant step, beyond Longinus. In Morris's words: "For Longinus, the interaction of passion and imagination contributed to the sublime; for Dennis it created the sublime" (66).

Anthony Ashley Cooper, Third Earl of Shaftsbury, who, according to Douglas Den Uyl, author of the contemporary "Foreword" to Shaftsbury's *Characteristics,* "wrote one of the most important and influential books of the eighteenth century" (Shaftsbury 1:vii), remarks in a 1708 "Letter Concerning Enthusiasm" that, regarding poetic afflatus, "*Inspiration* may be justly call'd *Divine* ENTHUSIASM: For the Word it-self signifies *Divine Presence,* and was made use of . . . to express whatever was sublime in human Passions" (Shaftsbury 1:34). Perhaps Wheatley actually saw this tract; it is certain that her enthusiastic pursuit of poetic afflatus constitutes a dominant pattern in her poetry.

Sounding much like a paraphrase of Charron, Shaftsbury holds that appetites and desires reside in the imagination, that the imaginative faculty is "a Business which can never stand still" (Shaftsbury 1:199), and that this faculty becomes manifested in "*Giddiness* and *Dream*" (1:201). Shaftsbury even goes so far as to recommend writing as an invaluable "*self-examining* Practice and Method of *inward* Colloquy" (1:202). To be sure, here Shaftsbury draws on the introspective tradition of meditation, a tradition that Wheatley clearly inherited. But like Dryden, Shaftsbury strongly advises that fancy (not here made distinct from imagination) and enthusiasm require "some Controuler or Manager" (1:198); in order to guard against "mere Imagination or the Exorbitancy of Fancy" (2:90), one must acknowledge that what he insists on here is a healthy moderation, summoning up the classical Greek cultural ideal of *sophrosyne*— nothing in excess, sanity in all things, the golden mean.

While Shaftsbury's sentiments on inspiration could have provided Wheatley useful instruction, Dennis's welding of imagination and the feeling of the sublime of course predicts Wheatley's combination of these two aesthetic categories in "On Imagination." Her work, nevertheless, demonstrates that, once again, she did not agree with Shaftsbury's notion of a manager for imagination, or for that matter for the sublime. Indeed, the principle of order in her liberated poetics was the imagination itself! Joseph Addison, Edmund Burke, and Henry Home, Lord Kames proved to be more favorable, more compatible theorists regarding imagination, and therefore more in line with Wheatley's interpretation than Shaftsbury, although these later British thinkers indicate contiguities of thought no more remarkable than the parallels between the African American poet and the French Charron or the British Dennis.

Joseph Addison, who was one of the most enthusiastic early advocates for imagination and whose *Spectator* was the most widely read of the gentleman's magazines of eighteenth-century England, expressed in language designed to edify English gentlemen some of the most lofty but clearly stated ideas about the sublime working in concert with the imagination. In *Spectator* 412, for example, he writes:

> Our imagination loves to be filled with an Object, or to grasp at anything that is too big for its Capacity. We are flung into a pleasing Astonishment at such unbounded Views, and feel a delightful Stillness and Amazement in the Soul at the Apprehension of them. (3:540)

This passage identifies the imagination as the faculty of one who desires intensely to grasp the infinite and the ineffable. Samuel Holt Monk holds that what Addison describes here is "essentially the sublime experience from Addison to Kant" (*Sublime* 58). Wheatley's "On Imagination" articulates the power Addison extols, but with a significant difference:

> From star to star the mental optics rove,
> Measure the skies, and range the realms above,
> There in one view we grasp the mighty whole,
> Or with new worlds amaze th'e unbounded soul.
> (66)

Wheatley's words, "view," "grasp," "amaze," "unbounded," and "soul," echo Addison. Like Addison, Wheatley specifies a limitless vision, but she adds the idea of "new worlds." While Addison's description speaks of views in created nature, Wheatley's "new worlds" introduces the poet's conception of myth making. Indeed, Wheatley proceeds to build not one but two heterocosmic worlds in remarkable anticipation of the apocalyptic Romantics.

In his extremely popular *Philosophical Enquiry into the Origin of Our Ideas of the Sublime and Beautiful* (1757), Edmund Burke concentrates on a sensationalist view (which holds that all knowledge originates in sensation) regarding the psychology of the imagination/sublime. Sounding a perception of divine wisdom that parallels Wheatley's, Burke declares:

> Whenever the wisdom of our Creator intended that we should be affected with anything, he did not confide the execution of his design to the languid and precarious operation of our reason; but he endued it with powers and properties that prevent [precede] the understanding, and even the will, which seizing upon the senses and imagination, captivate the soul before the understanding is ready either to join with them or to oppose them. (107)

As expected from a psychology of sensation, Burke's center of interest here is directed not toward God and devotion but toward an analysis of response. In Wheatley's work she too is driven to an analysis of how the power of imagination and its attendants—memory, fancy, the senses, and the appetites—interplay in her construction of a poetic world.

In Wheatley's analysis, however, these powers usurp reason at that moment that she elevates the imagination, having finally absorbed all its attendant parts, to the position of reason as leader of the mental train or as the poet's reason. In "On Imagination," then, the poet pictures the mind's eye—that is, the fancy—as seizing upon "some lov'd object" which "all the senses bind, / And soft captivity involves the mind" (65). But in her determination to carve out an idea of infinite space, she opts to ascribe to the unbounded and even at selected moments licentious imagination the power(s) of enabling her to launch sorties into the infinite realm of freedom, thence bypassing the less free, less licensed, understanding or reason.

As Phillis Wheatley was certainly, if regrettably, no stranger to pain and this world's vicissitudes, she may well have found Edmund Burke's aesthetic analysis of pain in the *Enquiry* to be useful to her own management of pain, especially in her poetry. Burke affirms, for perhaps the first time, that pleasure serves as the source for the idea of the beautiful and pain, for the sublime. In anticipation of Kant's "Analytic of the Sublime," as well as Keats's oxymoronic figures of "sad joy," Burke bases his theory of the sublime upon "Whatever is fitted in any sort to excite the ideas of pain, and danger, that is to say, whatever is in any sort terrible, or is conversant about terrible objects, or operates in a manner analogous to terror" (39). Monk states that " . . . in introducing pain as the basis of sublimity, he [Burke] opens the way for the inclusion of ideas and images in art that had hitherto been considered as lying outside the sphere of aesthetic pleasure" (91). Wheatley derives the emotions of pain and danger which evoke the sublime from three sources within her own experience: first, from the desire to escape temporal "woes, a painful endless train" (152); second, from depicting the wrath of an angry god as in "Goliath," "Isaiah," and "Niobe"; and third, from an aching reluctance to surrender her poetic world.

Henry Home, Lord Kames, in his *Elements of Criticism* (1762), focuses not on pain, but on the pleasure obtainable from imaginative literature. Having settled on Addison's earlier description of grandeur or greatness as the sublime, Kames asserts that the enthusiastic passions "commonly signify the quality or circumstance in objects by which the emotions of grandeur and sublimity are produced; sometimes the emotions themselves" (1:211). In this last phrase Kames foreshadows Kant, who will later insist that the sublime does not reside "in any of the things of nature, but only in our own mind" (Kant, *Aesthetic* 114). To Kant, the feeling of the sublime never occurs "in objects" but always results from a mental response to their contemplation. Like Kant, Wheatley, as we have seen, considers the sublime to be a mental response and thereby avoids Kames's tendency to confuse object and response.

In his examination of the sublime, Kames emphasizes height, but he studiously avoids identifying the sublime as an elevated distance above the contemplating person. He does, nevertheless, maintain that "Ascent is pleasant because it elevates us" (1:220) and that "an expression or sentiment that raises the mind" is "great or elevated" (1:223). "The effect of motion and force *in conjunction* [emphasis mine] provokes the most sublime response, which," continues Kames, "the image of the planetary system most successfully stimulates." In close anticipation of Wheatley's descriptions, Kames even goes so far as to declare: "But if we could comprehend the whole system at one view, the activity and irresistible force of these immediate bodies would fill us with amazement: nature cannot furnish another scene so grand" (1:256). Three lines from Wheatley's "Thoughts on the Works of Providence" amply display Kames's combined motion and force:

> Ador'd the God that whirls surrounding spheres,
> Which first ordain'd that mighty Sol should reign
> The peerless monarch of th' ethereal train.
>
> (43)

As we have observed in "On Imagination," the poet and her readers "comprehend the whole system at one view." The mind's eye takes in this view while at the same time enjoying the celestial motion in these lines:

> From star to star the mental optics rove,
> Measure the skies, and range the realms above,
> There in one view we grasp the mighty whole.
>
> (66)

The similarities here are striking. Clearly Wheatley registers contiguities of thought with the Brits. At the same time, however, she departs from them when she elevates imagination to the poet's reason and when she constructs new worlds.

Just at a moment when British aesthetic theory would appear to have been warming to Wheatley's use of imagination and the sublime, a reactionary response is levied. In *The Creative Imagination,* James Engell misses this reactionary response when he remarks of William Duff's 1767 *Essay on Original Genius* that Duff "attains a view of the imagination as a broad and natural power whose scope in poetry is 'absolute and unconfined'" (84). Three years after the *Essay,* however, Duff appears to countermand his earlier position. Indeed, in the 1770 *Critical Observations on the Writings of the Most Celebrated Original Geniuses in Poetry,* which Engell does not mention, Duff, toward the end of this later work, finds in the poetry of the Italian Ludovico Ariosto, especially in his *Orlando Furioso,* abundant evidence that, characteristic of original genius, is "an irregular greatness, wildness, and enthusiasm of imagination" (296–97). So Duff's radical shift to a decidedly negative position toward the imagination assuredly comes as a surprise in the last pages of *Critical Observations* when he admonishes that "There is indeed at the same time great danger of being betrayed into error, from the unrestrained indulgence of imagination on religious subjects" (353). If it is true that all great geniuses of letters pursue a nondenominational theology in their work, a process that Wheatley, as we saw in the preceding section on her religious development, most assuredly does embrace, then all literary geniuses must err with stubborn alarm. As for Wheatley's experimentation with heterocosms, Duff maintains that "This tendency to contrive visionary schemes, it is obvious, arises from imagination irregular and unchastised" (356). Such a dangerous imagination must be tamed "by the chastening power of the reasoning faculty" (356). So Duff's final pronouncement against imagination has moved, most disappointingly, not a dust mot away from the positions of William Tyndale, William Perkins, or Jonathan Edwards!

While the British aesthetes at several points appear to be providing Wheatley useful instruction in her intellectual shaping of her own poetics, they finally give her less than courageous and/or liberal assistance. For the most formative sources of what we may now call Wheatley's rebellious spirit within the realm of literary aesthetics, an aesthetics that clearly points toward Romanticism, we must turn, perhaps surprisingly, to Colonial Americans. All these potential teachers resided in or near Wheatley's own Boston, among whom numbered Joseph Seccombe, Charles Chauncy, some of the poets of the 1761 *Pietas et Gratulatio* (including Samuel Cooper), William Billings, and her principal literary model, Mather Byles.

In his attempt to construct an intellectual history of the imagination in his *Creative Imagination,* James Engell not only neglects to investigate the contribution of Charron's *de la Sagesse* or of William Duff's *Critical Observations;* he fails to give any attention to Seccombe, Cooper, Chauncy, Billings, or Byles. For that matter, neither does he make mention of Phillis Wheatley. While he suggests that Philip Freneau initiates an analytical examination of the fancy in "The Power of Fancy" (1770; it is unlikely that Wheatley knew this poem, at least not before her 1773 *Poems*), Engell finds that no really penetrating pursuit of the imaginative faculty occurred in America before Poe and Emerson (188–96).[3] Perhaps this volume will serve, among a myriad of other functions, as a necessary correction for Engell's lack of knowledge.

Joseph Seccombe, Wheatley's fellow traveler on the path toward wisdom who cited Charron in the Stanhope translation of *de la Sagesse,* and Charles Chauncy, who signed Wheatley's "To the Public," her letter of attestation regarding the authenticity of her authorship, each commented on the imagination and enthusiasm prompted by the voice of the Great Awakening, George Whitefield. We have already examined Seccombe's endorsement of the imagination. Chauncy, however, despite his identity as an Old Light liberal minister, expressed an opposing attitude toward imagination. For in the same year (1742) as Seccombe's endorsement, Chauncy, in *Enthusiasm Described and Cautioned Against,* declares, in rhetoric predicting the hostility Edwards would show in the later *Affections,* that his purpose in this published sermon is to guard the people "against the wilds of a heated imagination" (i).

Equating the terms "enthusiasm" and "imagination" throughout this sermon, Chauncy claims with an exaggeration betraying the passion of his own imagination: "*Enthusiastic wildness has slain its thousands*" (iii, italics in original). At one point Chauncy even calls imagination "meer pretense" (2). Despite the fact that he acknowledges the etymology of imagination "carries in it a good meaning, as signifying inspiration from God" (3), he stubbornly insists, "But the word is more commonly used in a bad sense, as intending an *imagi-*

nary, not a *real* inspiration" (3). Toward the sermon's end, Chauncy holds, "Next to the Scripture, there is no greater enemy to *enthusiasm*, than *reason*" (18).

Here this minister displays the conservative position of a New Light Calvinist, a contradictory posture for one whose career has been judged to have been that of a liberal. Chauncy's assertions are, nevertheless, the more interesting for two reasons. First, if he is to be believed, that imagination is "more commonly used in a bad sense," then Seccombe's position toward this faculty assumes the character of rebellion. And second, Chauncy's equation of imagination and the enthusiastic passions or the feeling of the sublime only reinforces the argument that by 1742 in Wheatley's Boston these two aesthetic categories were thought to blend or to operate inseparably. Although Chauncy viewed that the operation of these two faculties in concert could only lead to perdition (in accord with Edwards's *Affections*), Seccombe assuredly did not; in his opinion the path from imagination to the divine is direct and unobstructed. As well, of course, all this attention given to the imagination/sublime attests irrefutably that this faculty enjoyed considerable public impact, hence underscoring Engell's unfortunate ignorance but Early Americans' growing aesthetic sophistication. This contextualization of Wheatley's own experimentation with imagination can only raise our expectations that her experimentation was not only credible but may well have been, given her obvious predilection for aesthetics, inevitable.

Samuel Cooper, who was old enough (1725–1783) to have read these tracts by Seccombe and Chauncy when published, demonstrates in the thirteenth poem of the 1761 *Pietas et Gratulatio* that he has not merely agreed with Seccombe, but that he has extended his analysis of imagination. Because this book had great political and aesthetic importance for Wheatley, *Pietas et Gratulatio* (Devotion and Gratitude) deserves some concentrated treatment. This quarto volume, replete with rubrication and the use of a font for Greek characters, was the most elaborately produced single publication in America before 1800, thereby increasing the probability that Wheatley perused it. This elaborate production, assembled to celebrate the death of George II and the ascension of George III, comprised thirty-one poems by several unnamed authors, among which three poems were in Greek, twelve English, and sixteen Latin.

Of great interest to the political panorama of the times is the volume's twelve-page epistolary dedication to the new monarch. This "dedication," however, merely has the "look" of a dedication; for, upon examination, the prose epistle masks a thinly veiled statement to the young monarch of a litany of expectations. Echoing Lockean political theory, the author, whom I strongly suspect to have been Cooper, observes that "Other Empires have generally been formed by the infringement of the Liberties and the destruction of the Lives of mankind," but then he hastily adds "that, which will owe to your Majesty its firm establishment, will be founded upon the maintenance of the Freedom of the people—the security of their Possessions and the Encrease of their numbers" (*Pietas* vi). The principles of life, liberty, and the pursuit of happiness are alive in these words.

After the impassioned declaration that Great Britain "is erected the Temple of Liberty" (*Pietas* viii) for all the nations of the world, the author unabashedly claims the American colonies to be

> a Retreat for the wretched inhabitants of [Europe]; an Asylum to which they may retire from the reach of Wars and set themselves down in Peace, sure to reap the fruits of their Industry, secure in the enjoyment of their civil and religious Liberties, and exempt from the miseries which distress most other Countries. (*Pietas* ix–x)

Once again the ideals of life, liberty, and the pursuit of happiness ring throughout these phrases, and Crevecoeur's emphasis on the rewards of industry in *Letters from an American Farmer* is firmly predicted. In the words of Charles W. Akers, Cooper's principal biographer, "By praising English Kings [in *Pietas*] for what they were not or were assumed to be, Cooper and his countrymen also established what monarchs must be" (Akers, *Divine* 38).

In the first of the two English poems, the thirteenth and the twenty-eighth, thought by the most reliable authorities to be by Cooper (Akers, *Divine* 376–77n40), the poet repeats his intense desire for liberty so evident in the "dedicatory" essay. For example, Cooper disperses throughout this elegy on George II's death such phrases as "liberty, bright goddess," "every patriot [with] virtue crown'd" and a "grand design . . . Sacred to liberty and law" (*Pietas* 46, 47). Cooper closes the poem with an image of the new young monarch, George III, "Stretching each nerve to freedom's goal . . . For Heaven and Earth delight in Patriot Kings" (*Pietas* 51–52). The language here closely resembles that of Wheatley, especially in "To George Washington" and "Liberty and Peace."

It is in the following stanza lamenting the death of George II, however, that Cooper states his grasp of imagination as an aesthetic category:

> Imagination! Heaven-born maid!
> Descend and dissipate the cloud,
> The black'ning cloud, which soils the mind
> Too deeply tinctur'd with its grief:
> Oh! Speak the virtues of the godlike man.
>
> (*Pietas* 45)

Without qualification (no necessary manager), Cooper identifies imagination as the divine maiden, Minerva or Athena, personification of wisdom.[4] In this stanza, imagination does not merely work in association with the divine; she is herself divine and is asked to descend from her sublime abode to "dissipate" Cooper's "black'ning cloud" of grief by speaking or narrating the deceased's accomplishment.

With this poem, Phillis Wheatley as a student of poésis may well have been guided by her "Friend sincere . . . [who] Encourag'd oft, and oft approv'd her lays" (153), to consider imagination to be the *unqualified* poet's understanding or reason, the principle of order, the arranger, organizer, or creator. At the same time Cooper here portrays imagination as possible mediator between the divine and man. It is very likely this last function and the association of that function with the act of poésis which most appealed to the young Black slave woman become poet. Beyond these obvious connections between Cooper and Wheatley are his application of imagination to the elegiac mode and his insistence that imagination and wisdom are inseparable. Having already established Wheatley's eager acceptance of Cooper as a paragon of wisdom, we need not rehearse that relationship.

As for her own application of imagination's controlling function to her elegies, the poem which immediately follows "On Imagination" in *Poems*, "A Funeral Poem on the Death of C.E. an Infant of Twelve Months," displays unmistakable ties to Wheatley's preceding analysis of the poet's reason. In her elegy, for example, the departed "wings his instant flight" through "airy roads" "To purer regions of celestial light" (69), much like imagination's swift course through the cosmos to discover "Th' empyreal palace of the thund'ring God" (66). As well, Wheatley's deceased subject, echoing Kames's most profound expression of the sublime, takes in "the universal whole" wherein "Planets on planets run their destin'd round" (69). Just three pages earlier, "On Imagination" describes a parallel moment in which we as empathic readers may "in one view . . . grasp the mighty whole" (66). The thought in Cooper's (*Pietas*) elegy, then, bespeaks strong connections to Wheatley's own poetic praxis.

Several other links between Wheatley's oeuvre and the *Pietas* volume should be pointed out. In the twenty-eighth poem of the volume, also by Cooper, for example, appears the statements "fan the sacred fire" (86) and "fan the sacred flame" (89). These declarations of poetic afflatus do not occur in Pope, Milton, or Shakespeare, but do closely resemble Wheatley's line in "Hymn to the Morning" about the muses: Calliope's "fair sisters fan the pleasing fire" (56).[5] Cooper's celebration in this poem of the accession of George III is punctuated throughout with elements of pastoral as he narrates this new opportunity for "The Graces and the Virtues [to] join / T'adorn the Royal Train." Here we find "sequester'd bowers" which echo Philomela's "thrilling musick," causing "each soft passion of the grove / To charm the royal ear" (87, 88, 89).

As well the *Pietas* volume in general makes much of "patriot— virtue[s]" (35, etc.), "silken thought[s]" (16), pointing to Wheatley's "silken fetters" (65), and occasions when "glorious liberty her pinions spread" (23). Throughout the collection the attributive "celestial" recurs with frequency, perhaps encouraging Wheatley's frequent use of this modifier.

William Billings, Wheatley's next close mentor in the evolution of her intellectual identity, was America's first native-born composer. His *New-England Psalm-Singer* (1770), a collection of church anthems and songs, enjoyed considerable fame well into the nineteenth century. It has been observed by a mid-nineteenth-century American historian of music that Billings's "Chester," a hymn of intense patriotism, "did more to inspire a spirit of freedom than any one thing that occurred at this critical moment [the American Revolution]" (Gould 44). This hymn's first lyric stanza reads:

> Let Tyrants shake their iron Rod,
> And Slav'ry clank her galling Chains;
> We fear them not, we trust in God,
> New England's God forever reigns!
>
> (Billings 321)

With its rhetoric concerning "Tyrants" who enslave, and its clanking, "galling Chains," along with its declaration of strong belief in the Deity, this hymn cannot but have exercised a major influence on the young Wheatley.

These two, William Billings and Phillis Wheatley, definitely knew one another. Indeed, Billings collaborated with Wheatley in their shared effort to commemorate the death of Samuel Cooper, who died on December 29, 1783. On the second of January, there appeared an eight-page pamphlet that was prepared for the occasion of Cooper's well-attended funeral. This pamphlet included Wheatley's elegy on Cooper, which we have examined; Wheatley's "Elegy . . . [on the] Learned Dr. Samuel Cooper" was followed by a two-page "Anthem" by Billings. Wheatley and Billings probably met as early as 1769. In October of this year, Billings entered a notice in the *Boston Gazette:*

> "John Barry [then Billings's associate] and William Billings Begs [*sic*] Leave to inform the Publick, that they propose to open a Singing School THIS NIGHT, near the Old South Meeting-House, where any Person inclining to learn to Sing may be attended upon at said School with Fidelity and Dispatch." (McKay and Crawford 36)

These Singing Schools were ordinarily attended, "for the duration of three months . . . mostly [by] young adults and teenagers" (McKay and Crawford 37). Wheatley, about sixteen at the time and given the assurance that "*any Person* inclining to learn to sing [emphasis mine]" would be welcome to attend, would have been an ideal candidate for Billings's Singing School. As the "Old South Meeting-House" was the church which the Wheatley family attended and was under the ministry of Wheatley's "monitor," Joseph Sewall (who had died June 27 of the same year), it is most likely that Susannah Wheatley and Phillis herself would have taken an interest in this notice. The fact that Billings includes in *The New-England Psalm-Singer* an anthem entitled "Africa," which speaks of "Fears, / Suspicions and complaints," evoking the possibility that Billings herein delivers Wheatley an embedded message regarding her difficulty with Boston's racial prejudice, when combined with the other factors above, multiplies the probability that Wheatley attended Billings's Singing School.

Certainly, the patriotic rhetoric of Billings's anthem, "America," with its sentiments that the American colonies are a land bereft of "Persecution's Iron claws," indeed a country where "Liberty erects her Throne" and "Freedom lift[s] her cheerful Head," would have greatly appealed to Wheatley's identical sentiments, which she expresses in her numerous political, but always patriotic, poems. Given all these indications just enumerated, the probability that Wheatley knew Billings's *New-England Psalm-Singer* is all but irrefutable. Particularly of interest to this ambitious young poet would have been Billings's brief prefatory essay, "To all Musical Practitioners," wherein Billings makes several provocative observations regarding the "Rules for Composition" (Billings 1:32).

Billings prescribes that *"Nature is the best Dictator"* [italics in original]. "Nature must lay the Foundation," so Billings continues. Indeed, "Nature must inspire the Thought." " . . . the more Art is display'd, the more Nature is decorated." Billings interestingly exacts no qualifying intervention of judgment or reason, no "manager." When Wheatley remarks in "On Imagination" that "*Fancy* dresses to delight the Muse" (68), she appears to be in agreement with Billings's position that "Art," the artificial creator of the anthem or of a poem, decorates nature herself.

Billings further refines his analytical understanding of the creative process by declaring, "Fancy goes first, and strikes out the Work roughly, and Art comes after, and polishes it over." We have here an inchoate grasp of how the piece of music, or the poem, comes into being, except that in Wheatley, "Art" has become the "imperial queen," imagination. I do not mean to suggest that Billings here draws a clear distinction between fancy and imagination. What he does describe, however, is a line of thought that begins to separate elements of the poetic process into identifiable compartments of responsibility, a responsibility that owes little or nothing to reason or judgment per se.

Billings moves on to state daringly that " . . . if I am not allow'd to transgress the Rules of Composition, I shall certainly spoil the Air, and Cross the Strain, that fancy dictated" (32). To a young, but maturing poet, such a liberalizing of the creative process could only have encouraged Wheatley in her personal quest for liberation. Billings expands upon the creative process for poets when he says that he has "felt the disagreeable and slavish Effects" of exterior restraints imposed upon the artist; such restraints have been felt, so Billings holds, by "every composer of Poetry, as well as Musick." Billings reinforces what he sees as a close alliance between poetry and music when he declares that "Poetry and Music are in close connection, and nearly allied, besides they are often assistants to each other and like true friends often hide each others [*sic*] failings" (32).

One additional pronouncement of Billings that Wheatley would have found compelling is as follows: "I don't think myself confin'd to any Rules for composition laid down by any that went before me" (32). Using Billings as an authority for composition, whether of music or poetry (and after all Billings did compose most of his own lyrics), Wheatley could have, taking up Billings's lead, found herself liberated all the more, if not in her actual adaptation of form, definitely in her internal choice and handling of subject. When we add to what we have already pulled together about Billings and Wheatley, first that the text of Billings's "America" is actually that of Mather Byles's famous "New-England Hymn" and that Billings eventually became a communicant of Byles's Hollis Street Congregational Church, the relationship between Wheatley and Billings becomes solidified.

For it is certain that Byles's *Poems on Several Occasions* (1744) served Wheatley as the model for her arrangement and choice of subject matter for her own *Poems on Various Subjects, Religious and Moral*. Not only did Byles sign Wheatley's letter of attestation that she, in fact, wrote *Poems*; he lived across the street from the Wheatley mansion. Hence there can be no doubt that these two knew each other, and all indications are that they knew one another quite well. Additionally, that Wheatley was thoroughly acquainted with Byles's 1744 *Poems on Several Occasions* cannot be doubted. Both poets employ in their volumes similar poetic forms, meters, and conventions, such as the elegy and hymn stanza, heroic and blank verse, and the invocation to the muse; both exhibit specific likenesses in their choice of language, more often resembling each other than such popular British poets of the day as Milton, Thomson, and Pope; and both develop notably parallel theories of poetry.

The notion that Byles's literary theory directly influenced the development of Wheatley's educated, creative imagination becomes more than mere suggestion when one observes the number of specific parallels that obtain among the literary forms, language, and overall structure of her 1773 volume and his 1744 *Poems on Several Occasions*. Each poet includes a biblical poem treating David's defeat of Goliath, though Wheatley's treatment is much more extensive than that of Byles. His seventy-eight-line version of 1 Samuel 17 remains largely paraphrase. He entitles his piece "Goliath's Defeat" and promises in a headnote to render the incident "In the Manner of Lucan." If by this promise Byles intends to imitate the exaggerated style of Lucan's epic *Bellum Civile* (or the *Pharsalia*, as it is popularly known), then he does indeed meet the challenge; he distends the intense, biblical description of Goliath's armor by using extreme rhetoric like that in the following depiction of the giant's helmet: "His helmet like a fiery Meteor shone / Blaz'd high amidst the Heav'ns; another Sun" (Byles, *Poems* 21).

In her poem entitled "Goliath of Gath," Wheatley avoids such extremity of expression, bordering on bombast, and instead expands the same biblical incident to 222 lines. She interpolates into her version an 8-line invocation to the muse (no invocation in Byles), a 30-line dialogue between Goliath and "A radiant cherub" (37) in which the angelic messenger admonishes Goliath for the futility of his rebellion against the God Jehovah (much after the fashion of Homer's messenger gods in the *Iliad*), and a final 12-line description of the havoc and gore of destruction among the Philistine army following David's slaying of Goliath. As may be expected, these three interpolations do indeed intensify the drama of the well-known story, and the poem that results from their inclusion closely resembles the classical epyllia of Callimachus and Ovid. Byles embarks upon no such venture into the short epic or epyllion in any of his poems, but Wheatley constructs a second epyllion in her "Niobe in Distress. . . ."

Wheatley, like Byles, devotes the middle section of her volume to a careful consideration of the function and design of her art. Byles's "To an Ingenious Young Gentleman . . ." expresses his adoration of Pope and his extravagant aspiration to "Soar sublime" on the wings of poesy; Wheatley's "On Recollection" and "On Imagination" explicate the core of her poetics. In the last half of each volume there appears a poem on the sea, Byles "Hymn at Sea" and Wheatley's "Ode to Neptune," as well as a poem about a specific artist, Byles's "To Pictorio, on the Sight of His Pictures" and Wheatley's "To S.M.: A Young African Painter, on Seeing His Works."

The similarities between Byles and Wheatley merely begin to surface from an overview of the arrangement of their volumes. An examination of the content of the poems in these two volumes reveals closer likenesses. Both favor overwhelmingly the use of heroic verse except when writing the hymn stanza or the ode. Byles uses blank verse only once, and there it is entirely fitting, in "Written in Milton's *Paradise Lost.*" Wheatley adopts blank verse twice, in the early poems "On Virtue" and "To the University of Cambridge in New England."

Both poets are quite fond of invoking the inspiration of the muse. Byles either invokes the muse at the opening of his poems or makes concrete allusions to the muse intermittently throughout the poem, hence presenting the appearance of strict conformity to convention. Wheatley's invocations are less conventional. When she calls upon the muse, she distends the conventional formality, creating a solemn prayer for divine, though not necessarily Christian, inspiration and guidance. The invocations in her two epyllia, for example, run eight lines in "Goliath of Gath" and expand to ten in "Niobe in Distress . . ." Another curious distinction between Byles's and Wheatley's employment of this convention is that, whereas Byles summons the muse in each of his elegies, Wheatley avoids doing so in any of hers. Death alone appears to be sufficient inspiration to set her creativity into motion because of her powerful belief in celestial ascension of the deserving spirit. That is, the deceased about whom she is writing has already achieved unity with her idea of God; invocation to the muse as a force of temporary union with divine inspiration becomes in Wheatley superfluous when the subject of the poem has itself already accomplished eternal union with the Deity.

A commonly reoccurring eighteenth-century poetic form that both poets employ is the hymn stanza. This conventional form was particularly popular with Byles; he includes ten hymns patterned after the English master hymnodist Isaac Watts (he even dedicates two of his hymns specifically to Watts). Wheatley's volume contains only two poems written in hymn stanza, although the author calls two other poems hymns which are actually written in heroic verse; these are the companion pieces, "An Hymn to the Morning" and "An Hymn to the Evening." But, to be sure, both poems embody the spirit of the hymn and may be called prayerful anthems in celebration of classical/African deities.

Although the parallels between the two poets' uses of the hymn stanza are slim, such is not the case in the adoption of the elegy. In fact, Wheatley appears to have patterned many of her elegies directly after Byles's. The elder poet includes six elegies in his collection, whose total selection is about two-thirds the size of Wheatley's. She appears to be even more attracted to the genre and gathers seventeen into her volume. Both poets intersperse their elegies in small clusters among their other poems. Each poet includes in his or her collection one elegy which closes with an epitaph. Byles liked the genre of the epitaph well enough to have written five separate ones. Wheatley ventures into this genre only one time. The basic elegiac form of both poets appears to be that prescribed by Byles in his elegy, "To a Friend, on the Death of a Relative":

> But sacred is the Muse; by Heav'n she's led
> T'instruct the Living, not to blanch the Dead.
> Ye Living, hear her tuneful Lips rehearse
> No trifling Themes, nor in ignoble Verse.
>
> (45)

Wheatley follows this directive closely; her elegies never represent attempts to whitewash the deceased. Quite the contrary, she confines her attention almost wholly to instruction of the living. She goes so far as to have the departed spirits in four of her elegies speak aloud, giving dramatized comfort to the living and assuring them of the deceased's attainment of the promised raptures in heavenly life. The deceased spirit of one poem, "To a Clergyman on the Death of His Lady," directly addresses the husband:

> Thy spouse leans downward from th' empyreal sky:
> "O come away," her longing spirit cries,
> "And Share with me the raptures of the skies."
>
> (53–54)

Byles has no such dialogue in any of his elegies; rather the dead soul " . . . visits now no more this dull Abode / But talks with Angels, and beholds his God" (43). Wheatley, then, clearly exceeds her predecessor in her dramatic representation.[6]

Another departure from Byles, this one radical, is Wheatley's repeated use of the chthonic in six of her elegies (see discussion in preceding chapter). Although Byles had stated in his "Preface" to *Poems on Several Occasions* that he had composed these poems as "Amusements of looser Hours" in the spirit of "Entertainments" and was now, with their printing, giving up "these lighter Productions" and bidding "adieu to the airy Muse," he does later occasionally publish poems, like the "New-England Hymn," for example; unlike Wheatley, however, and despite Byles's intermittent use of classical allusions, even when he does refer to ancient classicism, he *never* delves into the chthonic in *any* of his poems, whether elegies or not.

But the similarities in the poetic vocabularies of these two poets assert the probability of a literary relationship more urgently than do parallels of poetic forms. The phrase "round the central sun," for example, occurs in Byles's "To Pictorio" (89) and in Wheatley's "On Recollection" (63). This expression is not to be found in Pope, Milton, Shakespeare, Thompson, nor in the King James Bible.

When Byes and Wheatley write of providence and eternity, they employ like terms. In "Eternity," Byles describes a "System" which "own'd the central Sun" and was ruled by chaos before the existence of order; then he renders the motion of this ordered System in the rhetoric of mechanical, not mythological, machinery: "Through all the Worlds of Light his Axil rung, / And rolling Wheels resistless smok'd along" (108). In much the same fashion in her poem, "Thoughts on the Works of Providence," Wheatley talks of " . . . the God unseen, / Which round the sun revolves this vast machine" (43); she avoids Byles's awkward smoking wheels and achieves the sensation of restlessness by not attempting to be as specific as Byles. But it is in this same poem that she, like Byles, records that "Old Chaos heard, and trembled at the sound" of God prior to the moment of creation.

As one can easily recognize, both poets are dealing in these poems with subjects of lofty grandeur or sublimity. In these same pieces Byles and Wheatley both speak of the overwhelmingly sublime image which is, according to Boileau, pioneer translator of Longinus's *On the Sublime*,[7] the first light of creation as presented in Genesis 1:3: "And God said, Let there be light, and there was light." Byles renders this sublime image in the following manner: "Anon Creation rose in instant Bloom, / And smiling Light dispel'd the horrid Gloom" (107). Wheatley's persona is even more dazzled by this sublime moment:

> "Let there be light," he said: From his profound
> Old Chaos heard, and trembled at the sound;
> Swift as the word, inspir'd by pow'r divine,
> Behold the light around its maker shine,
> The first fair product of the omnific God,
> And now through all his works diffus'd abroad.
>
> (47)

In Wheatley's conception the experience of first light becomes synaesthetic; that is, both the senses of sight and sound are evoked, not the sense of sight alone, as in Byles.

Wheatley's construction of a more dramatic and intense image suggests an expansive awareness of the possibilities of the sublime as a manifestation of the enthusiastic powers—not merely as an image of grandeur. Byles uses the word "sublime" seven times in his volume; Wheatley uses the word four times in a body of poems which is far more extensive than that of Byles. But each time Byles uses this word, he always does so as a reference either to the sublime style or to height. He speaks of the language of Milton's *Paradise Lost* as an example of "the true Sublime" (25), and he describes the new home of the deceased Daniel Oliver as "your sublime Abode" (42). Wheatley, however, uses the word *sublime* first to indicate height or loftiness and second to suggest majesty or awe. In "Isaiah LXIII" she characterizes God-like motion as sublime: "Say, heav'nly muse, what king, or mighty God, / That moves sublime from Idumea's road?" (60). Here "sublime" is used not simply as an adverb of place or height but also as an adjective describing the manner of majesty.[8]

Another similarity of language obtains in Byles's apostrophe to God, "O fathomless Profound!" (15) and in Wheatley's juvenile poem "On Virtue," where she captures an attitude of astonished reverence in the phrase, "fathom thy [i.e., virtue's] profound" (13). Two observations are pertinent here. First Wheatley's use of "fathom" as a verb represents a more dramatic application and hence indicates an improvement upon Byles's adjectival "fathomless." Second, nothing like this combination of words occurs in Pope, Milton, Thomson, Shakespeare, or the King James Bible.

Both Wheatley and Byles also make frequent use of sun imagery. In one instance, Wheatley directly echoes her predecessor in the phrase "gay *Phoebus*" (46), although Byles had represented the image simply as "the gay sun." (38). Wheatley demonstrates here her preference for classical allusions; some two hundred appear in her volume as compared to only forty-two in Byles's. But Wheatley's use of Phoebus in place of the sun suggests more than just a preference for classical allusions. Wheatley's sun is never a simple figure of nature; rather in her poetry, as we have found, it usually assumes religious significance, often recalling her mother's daily ritual of pouring out "water before the sun at his rising." In her meditative poem "Thoughts on the Works of Providence," for example, the power of the sun, which she names variously Sol and Phoebus, directly emanates the goodness and the wisdom of "the Almighty Sire" (46).[9]

Other vocabulary parallels include Byles's "Fancy rove perpetual" (33) and Wheatley's "the roving Fancy flies" (65); the rendering by both poets of the eyes of celestial beings flashing preternatural light (such light imagery ultimately derives in each case most likely from Dante's *Paradiso*); and Byles's "the frozen Floods"[10] and Wheatley's "The frozen deeps" (66). Echoes of Byles's vocabulary in Wheatley are too numerous to be accidental. But if they do indicate that Wheatley found Byles's choice of language appealing, they also illustrate that she was an inventive student—one who was generally capable of improving upon her example.

Nevertheless, the most substantial parallel which argues that Wheatley took instruction from Byles's poetry remains to be investigated. Both poets build in their works a poetics in which an enthusiastic persona desires ardently to soar, by means of poesy, toward God. In the poem "To an Ingenious Young Gentleman on His Dedicating a Poem to the Author,"[11] which appeared first in a magazine in 1727 and later in his 1744 volume, Byles employs a rhetoric of ecstasy in which his persona appears to want to unite with God above. The poem's speaker first claims to dare "Soar sublime" (52); then he states:

> Ravish'd my Ear receives the heav'nly Guest,
> My heart high-leaping, beats my panting Brest:
> Thro' all my Mind incessant Rapture reigns,
> And joys immortal revel in my Veins.
>
> (52)

Later in the poem, the thinly veiled persona becomes "Convinc'd, I own Eternity a NOW" (56). Byles concludes this finally abortive attempt at ecstatic unity with God by offering the following, somewhat pompous advice to the "ingenious" young man:

> Thus let your Poesy refine, improve,
> And match the Musick of the Choirs above;
> Still from your Lips let such soft Notes arise,
> And songs of Seraphs sound beneath the Skies,
> Till as your Muse, your Soul expands her Wings,
> And to their bright Abodes, exulting, springs.
>
> (56–57)

Byles's prescription of a poetics which matches "the Musick of the Choirs above" suggested to Wheatley an approach to the composition of poetry which offered her temporary relief from a hostile world where she found herself confined as a slave. At an early point in his *Occasions,* Byles has a "Hymn to Christ" which speaks of "ev'ry Sense" (17) and subsequently cites Pascal's triad of memory, reason, and Love: "To Thee my Reason I submit, / My Love, my Mem'ry, Lord" (18). As we have observed Wheatley too treats memory, understanding, and love in "Thoughts on the Works of Providence"; whereas Byles embraces Pascal's austere triad adapted from Augustinian meditation, Wheatley's loyalty to her struggle to determine her own vocation as poet and to be free prevents her from surrendering, according to Price's description of Pascal, "the self-determination that is inevitable illusion." Byles can make a declaration of such a commitment, though I doubt this declaration ever became actualized; Wheatley cannot even bring herself to register a written aspiration to achieve Pascal's Love or Charity.

In Wheatley's hands this poetics becomes adapted to her personal predicament and serves her as a source of freedom, a momentary means of escape from harsh reality into the imaginary, happy world of the poem. "On Imagination" demonstrates the power Wheatley attributes to the world of the poem in words which echo Byles:

> Soaring through the air to find the bright abode,
> Th' empyreal palace of the thund'ring God,
> We on thy pinions can surpass the wind,
> And leave the rolling universe behind.
>
> (66)

Like Byles's, Wheatley's objective is to reach God, but the younger poet strikes a different note in this picture. She maintains that the poem permits the imagination full range; so powerful is the imagination in her poem that it can permit the mind to absent itself from "the rolling universe." While the older Byles had in his poetry extolled "my wild imagination" (26), the same author, in one of his prose ventures into literary criticism, "Bombastic and Grubstreet Style: A Satire" (appeared first in the *New England Weekly Journal,* April 17, 1727) complained of an "Extravagance of Imagination" (Miller and Johnson 2:691), predicting Dr. Johnson's exact phrasing later in the century. As well in the same poem in which he had conjured his "wild imagination," he insists in this poem's conclusion that what his imagination has summoned is merely a congeries of "ideal Dreams, / Imaginary Trances! vain Illusions!" (34). Byles, then, like most before him, demanded imagination be restrained or managed. At another point, the poet soon to become minister remarks the "busy Fancy" (42), once again calling up Pierre Charron. Finally, to Wheatley, however, the power of imagination can even "with new worlds amaze th' unbounded soul" (66). Byles too claimed in "To Pictorio" that "at our Word, new Worlds arise" (93). But he does *not,* as Wheatley *does,* move on to construct new worlds. Wheatley's poetics, then, moves into a realm distinct from that of Byles. He had advanced the aspiration that human poetry could strive toward imitation of angelic song (the music of the spheres).

But Wheatley emphasizes the capacity of poetry, not merely to levy a claim to reach Pascal's love or to serve the pious duty of angelic imitation, but to build new, reified worlds. Wheatley sees poetry, then, not merely as an imitative activity, but as a potentially mythic, recreative one. The remainder of "On Imagination" constitutes an attempt to create not one but two new worlds in the face of an unsatisfactory one:

> Though *Winter* frowns to *Fancy's* raptur'd eyes
> The fields may flourish, and gay scenes arise;
> The frozen deeps may break their iron bands,
> And bid their waters murmur o'er the sands.
>
> (66)

In the midst of *"Winter* austere" (66), the power of imagination enables the poet to construct an opposing world of warm spring and, a bit later, another world celebrating the warm sun. But these imaginary worlds can only bring temporary escape; for "northern tempests damp the rising fire; / They chill the tides of *Fancy's* flowing sea" (68). Wheatley's recognition of the power of the imagination to conjure up a new world and of its inevitable failure to sustain this new world anticipates Keats's "Ode to a Nightingale" where the English poet discovers, like she already has, that the wings of poesy provide an escape which is all too brief.

Surely Wheatley's bondage urged upon her this essentially romantic approach to the writing of poetry; certainly her use of "iron bands" as a metaphor for ice can not be construed as accidental. Here as in every other instance, Wheatley demonstrates that she surpasses Byles in forcefulness and in imagination. Unlike Byles who had bade "adieu to the airy Muse,"[12] Wheatley pursued the art of poetry as a serious commitment throughout her short adult life. Yet another indication of that seriousness is the way she alters Byles's enthusiastic response to Milton's grand or sublime style in *Paradise Lost*. In a blank verse poem of 184 lines, one of Byles's longest, "Written in Milton's *Paradise Lost*" concludes its 14-line introduction, resembling a sonnet, in which Byles details his heated response to Milton's "true Sublime" (25), with the attestation that, if he had the skill, " . . . with ambitious Hand, / I'd boldly snatch / A spreading Branch from his [Milton's] immortal Laurels" (25).

To seize the laurel was, to ancient classical poets, to achieve success as a mature poet. Of course in Byles's version, the implication is that Byles lacks the skill, which causes the taking of the laurel to elude him. In Wheatley's hands, this exercise of the laurel brings quite a different result. For she intends this ritual to be fully successful. In the Horatian ode, "To Maecenas," which opens *Poems*, Wheatley states in the only triplet (used for emphasis) in the poem that:

> While blooming wreaths around they [Maecenas's] temples spread,
> I'll snatch a laurel from thine honor'd head,
> While you indulgent smile upon the deed.
> (12)

Note that Byles's contrary-to-fact subjunctive has become a declarative statement of clear intention. Wheatley even goes so far as to command in a closing imperative couplet, approaching insolence, that Maecenas "grant . . . they paternal rays, / Hear me propitious, and defend my lays" (12). The young, though now by her own estimation, fully mature, poet commands, not once, not twice, but three times, that Maecenas, her patron (the white folks who collectively purchase her volume) "grant," "Hear" and finally "defend" her achievement in verse. Wheatley had not yet been manumitted. What courage!

This entire poem, "To Maecenas," sounds a wholly different opening than Byles's first poem of *Occasions*. Entitled "The Almighty Conqueror," Byles declares in the first of this hymn's thirteen stanzas: "To thee, my God, I sing" (1). In the third stanza Byles disavows the muses, along with their classical associations:

"Your tuneful Aids, fictitious Nine [i.e., the Muses], / No more shall tempt my Eyes" (2). While Byles certainly does breech this disclaimer several times throughout *Occasions* by citing the muses and applying classical allusions, Jesus or Christ or such phrases as "Omnipotent Redeemer-Lord" (1) do appear on almost every page.

In stark contrast to Byles, her mentor, whose book on the surface, at least, served her as a model, Wheatley's "To Maecenas" captures the essence of the ancient classical world. The only reference Wheatley makes in this poem to her idea of the Deity occurs toward the poem's end when she resolves to sing the virtues or manifestations of the moral behavior of "great *Maecenas!*" and to sing, as well, "In praise of him, from whom those virtues sprung" (11). Also unlike Byles, Wheatley seldom names Jesus; such namings have a habit of turning up, usually, in poems written before late 1771, marking the beginning of her first period of poetic maturity.

Byles uses his first poem to wax ministerial; Wheatley constructs "To Maecenas" to serve as an introduction to her entire volume. In the first stanza, this one of six lines, the poet announces that she will elaborate upon the world of pastoral: "Maecenas, you beneath the myrtle shade, / Read o'er what poets sung, and shepherds play'd" (9). Myrtle, shade, poets, and singing and playing (on their oaten pipes) shepherds all evoke the realm of Vergilian pastoral. As Wheatley will apply this world subversively, as she does here, her evocation of pastoral is necessary to her intense need to achieve freedom. The next line, "What felt those poets but you feel the same?"(9), is also most telling, because it is to the universal human feeling to be free that she fervently hopes to appeal. As well, such an emphasis on feeling points directly to the feeling of the sublime and to Wordsworth's "spontaneous overflow of powerful feeling."

The poet next queries, "Does not your soul possess the sacred flame?" (9). Here, Wheatley asserts that she expects first Maecenas, who was himself an infrequent poet, and then second the largely white audience who she hopes will purchase her volume (therefore providing her the patronage, for which Maecenas was famous), to empathize or even to identify with the flame of inspiration which is itself sacred to her. Not only has Wheatley not counterfeited Pope; neither has she imitated Byles. Indeed, comparison of the works of Wheatley and Byles affirms that this young Black woman has surpassed her predecessor in originality and creative achievement.

Next, Wheatley, in a fourteen-line stanza which we may call an embedded sonnet,[13] celebrates Homer, whom she names "Great Sire of verse" (10); his *Iliad* appears to have been favorite reading for her.

Indeed, she paraphrases the opening lines of book 16, the affecting passage in which Patroclus pleas to his warrior-lover that he, Achilles, allow him to wear his armor to incite the Greeks to great ferocity. The poet subsequently offers equal praise to Vergil, whose *Eclogues* taught her how to render pastoral. "O could I rival thine [Homer's] and *Virgil*'s page / Or claim the *Muses* with the *Mantuan* [Vergil] Sage" (10), so Wheatley asserts she could, then, bring her soul to soar on the sacred wings of poetry. Here Wheatley reveals several points about her vocation. She has read the best poets of the ancient Western world, and she has found them not just palatable, but a major source of profound inspiration. Her enthusiasm alerts us to the fact that inspiration itself serves as one of her principal concerns. In addition, her great fondness for the two major authors of epic prepares us to find her two epyllia, "Goliath of Gath" and "Niobe in Distress . . . ," and thence to recover throughout her oeuvre, both poetry and prose, a persistent intertextual epic (see chap. 6 of *The American Aeneas*).

Despite Wheatley's discovery of inspirational classical texts and authors, she remains "less happy" than "The happier *Terence*," ancient Roman (African) writer of sophisticated comedy, whose successful pen freed him from slavery; for she has yet to achieve her freedom. Thus, Wheatley introduces the central subject of all her poems and prose—Liberation. At the same moment she suggests, not merely that she may, by use of her pen, follow Terence into freedom, but that, until her actual release, she can use the enthusiasm and energy that the writing of poems imparts to her to enjoy temporary, momentary release.

We come to understand, then, that Wheatley carries with her a far graver burden than Byles, who, as a free white man, would ever be forced to bear. As a woman and a slave, she can not follow Byles into productions of "the airy Muse"; indeed the pleasure she seeks is hardly "airy" but is rather of the highest order—the pleasure, the absolute joy, of liberation. Simply speaking, much more is at stake for this young genius whose regrettable circumstances have thrust her into slavery. Wheatley's intense desire to write comes from within; as she puts it so well, "an intrinsic ardor prompts [me] to write" (15). But it is not this intrinsic ardor alone that motivates her to acquire knowledge and to yearn for wisdom and then to articulate in words what life has taught her. For she, unlike Byles, is not free.

At this same juncture, we can generalize upon our comparison between Byles and Wheatley. Clearly, we have established that Wheatley is the superior poet. Whereas Byles sometimes gestures toward experimentation in his poetry, Wheatley, who has more reason to venture into experimentation, shows more flexibility in her use of the ode, in her constructions of epyllia, and in her much more adventurous poetics. Byles claims to be anticlassical but does allow his classical training to shadow forth on occasion; Wheatley never makes an anticlassical claim but only displays an intense, almost ubiquitous, and even at times religious, use of classicism.

Byles, who is clearly Christian, applies his poetry to the service of evangelism; Wheatley who, perhaps shockingly for some of her readers, displays a demeanor toward Christianity that, finally, we can not call strictly Christian. Rather we discover that her religious perspective embraces a syncretistic amalgam of Christianity, classicism, Islam, animism, and solar worship. In other words, Byles is obviously Christian, but Wheatley's religious perspective approaches secularity.

When we consider how these two express their concerns about imagination, we encounter a radical difference. While Byles at times *appears* to be pro-imagination, he finally characterizes an enthusiastic imagination as delusional. Here Byles actually carries his negative attitude a step or two beyond the many who require a manager for imagination. To charge imagination with providing the source for trances and "idle Dreams" amounts to one of the most hostile attitudes we have come across, resembling the fanaticism of Jonathan Edwards. Wheatley of course chose a diametrically opposed path, one that elevated imagination to the poet's reason.

The final comparison between Byles and Wheatley, which I have reserved for last, focuses on the titles for their volumes. Byles's *Poems on Several Occasions* immediately signals his lack of seriousness, while Wheatley's *Poems on Various Subjects, Religious and Moral* registers her thoroughly serious intentions. At first glance, of course, Wheatley's title looks innocuous and nonthreatening, which is precisely how she wanted to be perceived. Her correspondence with John Thornton, philanthropist, evangelist, and friend of Selina Hastings, corroborates her desire to be thought by white folks not to be a threat or a problem. In three separate, lengthy letters to Thornton, Wheatley manages to come across as a devoted Christian, although she strategically makes this curious statement in her first letter that the promise of eternity (in Christianity) was "Delightful to those who have an interest in the Crucified saviour" (173). Despite her claim to be one of the interested, this is the letter wherein she observes that she, her Black brothers and sisters, and Native Americans are all "despised on earth on account of our colour" (174). In the last of the three letters written on October 30, 1774, just over a year after her manumission, she deftly and even diplomatically informs Thornton, who has been trying to convince her to return to Africa as a Christian evangel, that she will have none of his plan.

Alluding to Thornton's having importuned her to participate in a missionary venture to include her and two "gentlemen" whom she has not met, Wheatley first attempts to cajole Thornton from his proposal by claiming these two gentlemen are "too good for me." Then, however, she states, firmly, "Now to be serious, this undertaking appears too hazardous," that she does not wish to leave her "British and American friends," and that she is "also unacquainted with those Missionaries in Person" (184). Note how quickly she moves to correct her assertion that she is inferior, a maneuver she would have avoided during her first, subversive period of maturity. Having been freed for over a year, Wheatley has clearly entered her second period of maturity in which she has become emboldened to trade subversion for candor.

What I am getting at is the subversive imputation behind the qualifiers "Religious" and "Moral." For well over two hundred years, Wheatley's readers have not even guessed that her very title may indeed participate in the subversive enterprise of her *Poems*. Rather she has always been thought to be an orthodox Christian who liked classicism a bit too much, perhaps. In fact we have learned that Wheatley's idea of Divinity was uniquely her own, not Christian, not pagan, not animistic, not solar worship, and not Muslim—but a syncretization of all, which is finally pure Wheatley.

As for what is "Moral" about her title, to be moral is *not* to live in a world of slavery, not herself to be a slave, not to live in a world where her Black brothers and sisters are slaves, and not to live in a world where they and Native Americans are despised because of their color. In short Wheatley's moral world had no slaves and no racial discrimination. What is so glaringly ironic, to today's readers, is the omnipresence of the American Revolution's rhetoric of freedom, which claimed ad nauseum that all Americans, regardless of color, were slaves to the British monarch. As we know that Wheatley wrote many political poems and that in every one she is solidly and unwaveringly patriotic to America's struggle to be free, such devotion to the American cultural imperative for liberation would have led Wheatley to have found unthinkable that America's freedom struggle would later not extend to *all* persons. Wheatley's suspicions did, however, become aroused; moreover, she did not sit idly by hoping white folks would act responsibly; quite the contrary, she participated aggressively in the quest for freedom for *all* Americans.

Having constructed an analytical investigation of Wheatley's religious and intellectual background, we are prepared to draw several conclusions. First and foremost, we can now know that Wheatley was most definitely no simple imitator, but that she was a well-read, sophisticated, and complex artist who gleaned from her spiritual and intellectual ambience a poetry and a poetics that served her own, distinct needs. Wheatley's syncretized religion has been ascertained and requires no rehearsal. What we do need to give some time to is how the phenomenon of her intellectual background enabled her to discover to herself her poetics—the source of her agency as a self-determining poet.

While British authors[14] and the French Charron were of importance to her, especially Charron's distinction between fancy and imagination, her American mentors—Joseph Seccombe (by way of reputation), Samuel Cooper, William Billings, and Mather Byles—played far more consequential roles in bringing about her intellectual refinement. Interestingly, just as the eighteenth century's preoccupation with how the imagination functioned assumed two tracks, the one aligned with a religious, conservative approach bordering on fanaticism and deriving from the Puritan patriarch William Perkins, moving through John Locke to Jonathan Edwards, and to such personalities as Wheatley's own Joseph Sewall, and the other following the lead of the skeptic Pierre Charron which may subsequently be traced from Seccombe, to Cooper, to Billings, and, for a moment or two, to Byles (to the point at which he condemns imagination as leading to delusions), Wheatley's quest for wisdom follows a similar two-track progress, the one leaning strongly toward Christian orthodoxy and the other promoting a finally secular orientation. Wheatley's choice during her first period of maturity of the rebellious, secular track for her theoretics of imagination and wisdom brought about her spiritual and intellectual interiorization and her concomitant subversive but courageous poetics.

Along with these two lines of development, Wheatley's use of ancient classicism and her closely aligned African heritage exercised a decisive benefit. As we have already observed, Wheatley, with surprising regularity, adapts her African background to her poetic (and even survival) needs. Such an integrative adaptation may be explained by the Fulani cultural practice of ascribing the principal responsibility of preserving Fulani cultural values to women. According to Paul Riesman in his *Freedom in Fulani Social Life,* the province of women falls to the *wuro* or living unit whose center is the hut, built by women. Margaretta Oddell, Wheatley's principal biographer, remarks, most suggestively, that the young girl "was beguiled from the hut of her mother" (13).

Riesman further tells us that, "in Fulani thought, the symbol of human society and culture" resides within the *wuro*. So "it is logical," continues Riesman, "that feminine work tends toward the creation of culture" (64). It is also logical, therefore, to conclude that Wheatley's resolve to make sense of her spiritual and intellectual knowledge, effectively to carve out a cultural space for her personal identity while displaced from her African heritage, originates within the inertia of that African heritage. Another way of putting this resolve is simply to say Wheatley appears to have relied heavily for her self-definition upon the memory of her mother, from whom she drew great strength. As a Fulani woman, then, we should expect that this brilliant young girl would have instantaneously warmed to cultural pursuits offered her by her new land, even if, for a time, forced upon her. Having absorbed a myriad of trans-Atlantic sources, Wheatley built in the "hut" of her poetry a cultural property entirely her own.

CONCLUDING REMARKS

The Dignity of Wheatley's Poems Restored

In a collection of essays originating from a conference held at Emory Elliott's Center for Ideas and Society at the University of California, Riverside, Elliott observes in his forward-looking "Introduction" that "we need to devote as much time and attention to the histories, cultures, languages, and artistic systems of values of the African peoples as we have been doing for hundreds of years to the contributors of cultures of the European peoples" (*Aesthetics* 15). In trying to reclaim at least a modicum of Wheatley's African heritage; in tracing the undulations and parameters of her evolving intellectual and religious career, hence addressing the details of the history of her cultural identity; in delineating her liberation poetics; in establishing the incorrectness and inaccurateness of evaluating her religious consciousness to be that of a close-minded dogmatist; and in providing frequent and recurring evidence that Wheatley was a sophisticated artist, indeed probably among the most sophisticated of her age, I have in this work endeavored to actualize the desideratum Elliott so admirably urges.

Before clearing the way toward attempting to shape a balanced and judicious examination of this fine poet's work, it occurred to me almost immediately that we must first confront the 220 years or so of unfair and unbalanced commentary which has relegated her work to the status of a less than first-rate author. Unpacking this burden of so-called conventional wisdom, we found that such implacable biases as her color, her gender, her obvious debt to classicism, and the fact that she constructed the body of her work before July 4, 1776, all militated toward assigning her this less than first-rate status. Because the sheer weight of so much skewed commentary obfuscates all efforts to make contact with this poet's excellent texts, I have herein devoted what may appear to some to be an inordinate amount of space to this usually imbalanced and unfair commentary. We have learned, nevertheless, that the biases listed all but obliterated Wheatley from view; but in the process of trying to remove her apparently embarrassing presence to slavery/racist sympathizers, commentator after commentator felt the necessity at least to deal with her. Such necessity worked, ironically, against the effort to make her disappear. Indeed, defender after celebrant arose to explain this phenomenon of a sophisticated African American artist, hence ensuring her survival.

As well, we observed that only in the last twenty to thirty years has the tide of critical scrutiny turned in Wheatley's favor. Yet the sad truth remains that even some of this work, which we can with certainty begin to identify as real criticism, those studies which actually deal with her texts, remains occasionally tinctured with racist and cultural biases. As Toni Morrison puts it in her essential *Playing in the Dark: Whiteness and the Literary Imagination*, "Expensively kept, economically unsound, a spurious and useless political asset in election campaigns, racism is as healthy today as it was during the Enlightenment" (63). I think it no exaggeration to assert that Wheatley and Morrison are on the same page here.

Few, if any, it is unfortunate to be forced to say, have examined Phillis Wheatley's poetic career closely enough to note that it somewhat obviously falls into three periods: that of her juvenilia, during which she composed poems apparently designed to allay doubts among white folks that she did indeed merit baptism. As well, in such poems as "Atheism" and "To the Deist," we may justly assert that this sensitive, displaced young girl intensely seeks equality in her "adoptive" Boston.

Not finding this equality but registering such reactions to her and to her Black brothers and sisters as "'Their colour is a diabolic die,'" Wheatley, perhaps inevitably for one so intelligent and passionate, begins to pursue in her poetic texts an interiorization of her quest for freedom and equality, hence marking her first period of poetic maturity. For in such poems as "On Recollection," "To Maecenas," "Thoughts on the Works of Providence," and "On Imagination," all of these among her finest productions, Wheatley develops a contemplative, subversive mode, one that we may call a poetics of liberation. In this world of her own imaginative construction, slavery recedes into the background and freedom ranges "Licentious and unbounded" (47).

Having been manumitted by October 18, 1773, "at the desire of my friends in England" (170), Wheatley subsequently moves in her poetry away from the interior subversive mode toward a more public, but no less liberated, posture, hence characterizing her second and final period of her poetic maturity. Wheatley punctuates this exteriorization of her poetics of liberation brilliantly in her letter to Samson Occom of February 11, 1774, wherein she declares " . . . in every human Breast, God has implanted a Principle, which we call Love of Freedom; it is impatient of Oppression, and pants of Deliverance" (177). Lest she be perceived as not concerned with the freedom of all Black persons, she continues by making the observation that, "by Leave of our Modern Egyptians I will assert, that the same Principle lives in us." But then she blatantly states that the primary motive for slavery is "Avarice" which "impels them [white folks who own slaves] to countenance and help forward the Calamites of their Fellow Creatures" (177). Not content with merely identifying the despised institution of slavery, Wheatley seizes this opportunity (she allowed this letter to be reproduced in a dozen Colonial American newspapers) to rail against its continued practice.

All these concerns elaborated above contribute toward describing Wheatley's poetics of liberation—the preoccupation with freedom, especially her own but never to the exclusion of others not free; her willingness to practice subversion in order to realize freedom within her own poetic constructs; and her eventual, public quest for freedom for all, this public posture avowedly cast within a universal "Cry for Liberty" which nonetheless permits "the reverse Disposition for the Exercise of oppressive Power over others [Black slaves]." This contradiction Wheatley bravely judges hardly requires "the Penetration of a Philosopher to determine" (177).

In the derivation of a Poetics of Liberation, we noted that the burden of critical commentary on Wheatley's life and work would appear to render impossible such a theoretics of freedom. Undeterred, nonetheless, we soon found that Wheatley's poems stand up even to the application of four of Morimer Adler's five kinds of freedom as elaborated in his massive, two-volume *The Idea of Freedom*. Applying his criteria to Wheatley, her work displays many of the characteristics of circumstantial self-realization, or as in Wheatley's case a capacity to act, say in her poems particularly, in such a way as she sees fit so to do, as when she interiorizes her quest to be free; acquired self-perfection as manifested in Wheatley's search for wisdom; natural self-determination, here displayed more in Wheatley's determination to be free, as in her construction of heterocosms in "On Imagination," than in the reality of her intolerable condition as a slave and/or as a wholly marginalized human being; and political liberty once again. As no universal suffrage was permitted for women, much less for Black women, in Wheatley's

Boston, this move toward freedom remained largely a matter of pursuit in her poetics rather than ever becoming fully realized.

Even though these Adlerian types of freedom prove in Wheatley's case to fall short of self-actualization, application of these criteria enables the student of Wheatley to discover Wheatley's choice of vocation as a poet, her motivation for choosing that vocation, her recovery of the intense moral responsibility which she herself determined must characterize her role as poet, and finally her focusing on deliverance as the primary subject of her poems and prose. Throughout this treatment of Wheatley's poetics, we have come to recognize that it is in Wheatley's theoretics of imagination that she most emphatically articulates her determination to be free.

Recovery of this liberation poetics or what we may just as accurately call Wheatley's theoretics of imagination, even takes us back to an attempt to describe this poet's African heritage. As I am convinced, by surprising and disappointing efforts *not* to see anything even remotely African in what too many would hold is a "whitewashed" approach to the composition of poetry, that Wheatley's poetry can never be fairly and justly read until we have journeyed in search of this artist's obvious African background, I have purposefully included a chapter on Wheatley's "African Origins." Having done so has proved instructive. Indeed, we have traced whence came Wheatley's preoccupation with the genre of the elegy; we have found a plausible explanation regarding Wheatley's emphasis upon solar imagery; we have hit upon a possible source for Wheatley's interest in astronomy; we have become cognizant of the probability that some of Wheatley's apparently neoclassical rhythmic patterns may be closer to those patterns which are African in origin; and we have observed that Wheatley's interest in panegyric and epic may have received a cultural reinforcement coming out of Africa.

For those who may still wish to think any or all parts of "African Origins" remains merely speculative (although the notion that the origins of elegy coming from Wheatley's pen are far from merely speculative), I would remind all that I have never claimed the knowledge here is absolute. Far from it, I have challenged any and all to do better, to come at this problem, Wheatley's obvious origins in Africa, from a position of more knowledgeable preparation. As I have stated earlier, I would be enthusiastically pleased to have provoked a more thorough treatment. At minimum, then, I trust I have stimulated interest in this subject, and perhaps I have diminished or rendered untenable any further efforts to ignore, or worse, to deny Wheatley recalled anything of value from the land of her birth.

Shortly after Wheatley's fateful 1761 arrival in Colonial Boston, John and Susanna Wheatley began trying their best to expunge any residual African heritage from this brilliant but certainly vulnerable girl/victim. As we have seen, however, their efforts proved ineffective. For the kind of religious consciousness Wheatley shaped for herself was not exclusively or narrowly that of dogmatic Congregationalism, but became instead an amalgam of her native solar worship, African animism, and Islam almost seamlessly syncretized with Judeo-Christianity and ancient classicism. I am not the first to notice the presence in this poet of African religious elements: I should hope that now it will become more difficult to relegate Wheatley's religious consciousness to the confines of servile dogmatics.

As well, I am not the first to point out the intensity of Wheatley's classicism. Recall Jupiter Hammon's admonishment to Wheatley that she not give too enthusiastic an emphasis to classicism in her poems at the expense of Christian dogmatics. Another testimony by one of her contemporaries should put to rest for good that tenet of conventional wisdom (which always misses the mark) which would, if it could, relegate Wheatley and her works to the realm of a naïve, uncritical religious commitment. Such relegation usage inevitably leads would-be, serious readers of her works to devalue that work. On April 3, 1773, Richard Cary, who had signed as one of Boston's leading citizens the letter of attestation whose object was to authenticate Wheatley's authorship of her poems, wrote the Countess of Huntingdon a letter of introduction for Wheatley which she carried with her to London. The letter is noteworthy because of this arresting claim: "[I] hope she will continue an ornament to the Christian name and profession; as she grows older and has more experience, I doubt not her writings will run more in an Evangelicall Strain" (Mason 1989, 185–86n).

Cary's "hope" is hardly certainty, and his would-be assurance that time and event will correct what now obviously appears to be less than "Evangelicall" invites the countess to share his judgment that Wheatley still has some distance to travel before her work will prove completely acceptable. The point here is simply that, if Wheatley's contemporaries can see that Wheatley's texts, as they stand in the 1773 *Poems*, indicate a falling away from the holy circle, then why can't we?

The above observation that Wheatley incorporated strains of classicism within her religious consciousness (e.g., in her use of the *meditatio*) thrusts our consideration into the arena of this poet's intellectual evolution. As we established a flow of knowledge from Augustine to Pierre Charron, the Earl of Shaftsbury, John Dennis,

Thomas Burnet, Joseph Addison, and Lord Kames, much of this intellectual background displaying a preoccupation with the function of imagination, we came to find it plausible that our fine poet was in touch with a plethora of sources that could have assisted her evolving liberation theoretics. Still more striking, moreover, was our discovery of a strong and surprisingly sophisticated absorption with the imaginative faculty among the intelligentsia of Wheatley's adoptive Boston. Rather than the perhaps expected British writers, the prominent American figures, Mather Byles (Wheatley's tutor in Latin and poetics), Samuel Cooper (who baptized her), and William Billings (with whom she collaborated), decisively impacted the shaping of her theoretics of imagination.

In the midst of all this formidable flow of thought, Wheatley became not merely an independent theorist of a liberation poetics, but as well she made herself into a consummate classicist. In numerous places, I have called attention to this young poet's classical sophistication. Recovery of Wheatley's mental growth, taking place within an unexpectedly stimulating intellectual ambience, enables readers of her work to find thoroughly credible that this intelligent young woman constructed in her oeuvre a poetics of liberation.

The truth is, as I have stated, Wheatley's theoretics of imagination was among the most sophisticated of this era. This complex poetics of liberation/imagination points directly toward the several European romanticisms which were developing in the late eighteenth and early nineteenth centuries. This study ascertains the validity of Emory Elliott's declaration that "We must examine more deeply the ways that structure, form, verbal rhythms, and American English have been permeated and reconstituted by cultural elements from *our* African heritage [emphasis added]" (*Aesthetics* 15). Indeed, reclamation of a substantial amount of backgrounds and sources which instruct the evolution of this poet's liberation poetics helps to teach us how better to read this author.

Given the range of these extensive backgrounds and sources, it is apposite that, as we draw to a close this quest, we return to the most obvious manifestation of Wheatley's sophisticated accomplishment: her consummate classicism. For it is in this superlative achievement that Wheatley most observably restores her own dignity. Emory Elliott points the direction when he reminds us that Toni Morrison "demonstrates how aspects of her literary aesthetic came down to her from the classics and of the European past as well as from the forms of expression and storytelling she learned from her African heritage" (*Aesthetics* 15). We should then find it no accident that, in

Playing in the Dark, Morrison states that "No early American writer is more important to the concept of American Africanism than Poe" (32). For Edgar Allan Poe was, as Wheatley was and Morrison is, a consummate classicist. As a manifestation of intellect and sophistication, the incorporation of and subsequent ownership of classicism as an intellectual property among all peoples, regardless of color, may be viewed as a touchstone of literary artistry. Witness the recent publication of Patrice D. Rankine's *Ulysses in Black: Ralph Ellison, Classicism, and African American Literature* (2006).

I, for one, now find much less troubling Jefferson's misplaced and ill-conceived challenge to Phillis Wheatley's dignity as an artist. His unfortunate remarks now become dimmed by the certainty of Wheatley's observable accomplishment. For now surely there can be no question that we must all hail this valuable poet to be fully worthy of the dignity of close critical scrutiny.

Notes

Introduction

1. From Thomas Jefferson's *Notes on the State of Virginia* and quoted by William H. Robinson in his valuable *Phillis Wheatley: A Bio-Bibliography* (Boston: Hall, 1981) 39. Concerning Jefferson's slave holding, Marcus Cunliffe has opined, "Preaching liberty, he relied on the labor of Negro slaves. His detractors may in some degree have been correct when they alleged that he was at once dogmatic and devious" (from "Thomas Jefferson and the Dangers of the Past," *Wilson Quarterly* 6.1 [Winter 1982]: 107).
2. William H. Robinson, *Black New England Letters: The Uses of Writing in Black New England* (Boston: Trustees of the Public Library of the City of Boston, 1977), 50–52. In these pages, Robinson reproduces the 1772 "Proposals" as they appeared on three occasions in the *Boston Censor*, a short-lived newspaper of the day, in February, March, and April 1772. The author also includes quotations from a letter written by one of Wheatley's Boston contemporaries ascertaining rejection of her volume on racist grounds. A John Andrews, Boston merchant, wrote to his brother-in-law, William Barrell, a businessman from Philadelphia, on February 24, 1773, in regard to the projected London volume that the venture in publication had not originated from a Boston press because "she was blamd by her friends for printg them here" and because her prospective subscribers refused to put up money for the volume "by reason of their not crediting ye [perfo]rmance to be [by] a Negro" (49). In an article, "The First Proposed Edition of *Poems on Various Subjects* and the Phillis Wheatley Canon," *American Literature* 49.1 (March 1977), Mukhtar Ali Isani also reprints the 1772 "Proposals" and includes the letter from Andrews to Barrell. Robinson, however, gives us a quote from an earlier letter by Andrews to Barrell dated May 29, 1772, in which he explains the failure of the Boston "Proposals" in these regrettable terms: "the want of spirit to carry on anything of the kind here prevented it, as they are not yet published" (50).
3. Mukhtar Ali Isani, "The British Reception of Wheatley's *Poems on Various Subjects*," *Journal of Negro History* 66.2 (Summer 1981): 144–49. One of the reviewers, nevertheless, makes this poignant observation: "We are much concerned to find that this ingenious young woman is yet a

slave. The people of Boston boast themselves chiefly on their principles of liberty. One such act as the purchase of her freedom, would, in our opinion, have done them more honor than hanging a thousand trees with ribbons and emblems" (148).
4. Cheryl Walker, *The Nightingale's Burden: Women Poets and American Culture before 1900* (Bloomington: Indiana UP, 1982) 22.
5. Jane Dunlap, *Poems on Several Sermons Preached by the Rev'd . . . George Whitefield* (Boston: 1771) ii.
6. Dunlap, *Poems* 4.
7. See Margaretta Oddell's "Memoir," quoted in full in William H. Robinson's *Phillis Wheatley and Her Writings* (New York: Garland, 1984) 430–50, esp. 439.
8. Mindy Janak and Maurice Duke, "Martha Wadsworth Brewster (fl. 1725–1757)," *American Writers before 1800: A Biographical and Critical Dictionary*, ed. James A. Levernier and Douglas R. Wilmes (Westport, CT: Greenwood, 1983) 1:207.
9. John C. Shields, ed., *The Collected Works of Phillis Wheatley* (New York: Oxford UP, 1988). Hereafter all quotations from Wheatley's works will be taken from this volume and will be indicated in parentheses following the quotes.
10. For example, in "Wheatley, Phillis," *Dictionary of the American Negro Biography*, ed. Rayford W. Logan and Michael R. Winston (New York: Norton, 1982), J. Saunders Redding asserts, as have so many others, "The Wheatleys were monarchists, and so was Phillis. . . . They [the Wheatleys] were gentlehearted, pious, intelligent Christians, who gave little thought to the political, social, and intellectual problems that were increasingly troubling to many colonists, but gave much benevolent attention to the vicissitudes of family and friends. And so did Phillis" (641). Such implacable misinterpretations motivate the writing of this book.

Chapter 1. A Poetics of Liberation

1. Quoted in an article by Malcome G. Scully, "Endowment Chief Assails State of Humanities on College Campuses," *The Chronicle of Higher Education* 29.11 (November 28, 1984): 16, col. 2.
2. I have derived my understanding in large part from the sensible discussions of Rene Wellek, "Classicism in Literature," in *Dictionary of the History of Ideas*, ed. Philip P. Wiener (New York: Charles Scribner's Sons, 1973) 449–56; M. H. Abrams, *A Glossary of Literary Terms*, 6th ed. (New York: Holt, Rinehart, and Winston, 1993) 125–29; William Harmon and C. Hugh Holman, *A Handbook to Literature*, 8th ed. (Upper Saddle River, NJ: Prentice Hall, 2000) 97–98, 342–44, 441–42; and W. B. Fleischmann and John K. Newman, "Classicism," in *The New Princeton Encyclopedia of Poetry and Poetics*, ed. Alex Preminger, 3rd ed (Princeton, NJ: Princeton UP, 1993) 213–19.

3. Wellek 454.
4. Abbie F. Potts, *The Elegiac Mode: Poetic Form in Wordsworth and Other Elegists* (Ithaca, NY: Cornell UP, 1967) 2.
5. Henry F. May, *The Enlightenment in America* (New York: Oxford UP, 1976) xvi.
6. Emory Elliott, *Revolutionary Writers: Literature and Authority in the New Republic, 1725–1810* (New York: Oxford UP, 1982) 51–52.
7. John Hope Franklin, *From Slavery to Freedom: A History of Negro Americans*, 5th ed. (New York: Alfred A. Knopf, 1980) 106.
8. Mortimer J. Adler, *The Idea of Freedom: A Dialectical Examination of the Conceptions of Freedom*, 2 vols. (Garden City, NY: Doubleday, 1958–61).
9. Adler, see esp. 2:10–11.
10. May 40–41. For a succinct discussion of Montesquieu's influence on the United States' formulation of its restraints on federal power (separation of powers), see Franz Newmann, "Introduction," in *The Spirit of the Laws*, trans. Thomas Nugent (New York: Hafner, 1949) lix–lxiv.
11. Winthrop D. Jordan, *White over Black: American Attitudes toward the Negro, 1550–1812* (Chapel Hill: U of North Carolina P, 1968) 261–62, and esp. 278–79.
12. Adler 2:4–10. On these pages, the author presents a schematic overview of all five freedoms.
13. Paul Lucas, *American Odyssey, 1607–1789* (Englewood Cliffs, NJ: Prentice-Hall, 1984) 155.
14. See Robinson, *Black New England Letters,* and Isani, "The First Proposed Edition of *Poems on Various Subjects* and the Wheatley Canon," cited in notes 2 and 3 of the introduction to this volume.
15. Robinson, *Black New England Letters* 51–52.
16. In their recalling this memory of her mother, critics such as Jordan and Landry do not even hazard a guess as to what this memory may have meant to Wheatley. So in once more (as we have so often viewed) using Wheatley's slender autobiography to make a point in whatever argument they may be pursuing, these critics fail to ask questions that could potentially lead to logical explanations regarding her extensive use of solar imagery, to the importance her use of imagery about Aurora and the dawn may carry to a sensible reading of her poetry, and to how keen recollection of a confluence of solar worship and Islam may have impacted the development of her religious consciousness.
17. Houston A. Baker Jr., *The Journey Back: Issues in Black Literature and Criticism* (Chicago: U of Chicago P, 1980) 9–11. Baker cites the following lines from "On Messrs Hussey and Coffin," her first poem known to appear in print in the *Newport Mercury* of Rhode Island for December 21, 1767: "Had I the Tongue of a Seraphim, how would I exalt thy / Praise; thy Name as Incense to the Heavens should fly" (133). Although these lines may serve the purpose Baker suggests, they most definitely fall into the sort of poetic meditation which Edward Taylor, among other American poets,

had so ardently pursued as a means of philosophic contemplation of the Deity. Note how similar to some of Taylor's *Preparatory Meditations* are the lines which immediately follow those quoted by Baker: "and the / Remembrance of thy Goodness to the shoreless Ocean of Beatitude!—/ Then should the Earth glow with seraphick Ardour." I offer as a parallel point of view the following stanza from Taylor's twentieth meditation, *First Series:*

> View all ye eyes above, this sight which flings
> Seraphick Phancies in Chill Rapture high,
> A Turffe of Clay, and yet bright Glories King
> From dust to Glory Angell-like to fly.
> A Mortall Clod immortalized, behold,
> Flyes through the Skies swifter than Angells could.

I quote from the standard edition, *The Poems of Edward Taylor,* ed. Donald E. Stanford (New Haven, CT: Yale UP, 1960) 34. We can agree that both poets manifest a committed religious consciousness which, even at this early stage in the case of Wheatley's development, tends to transcend the restrictions of dogma.

18. Franklin 91.
19. Lorenzo J. Greene, *The Negro in Colonial New England* (New York: Columbia UP, 1942) 183–84. Although this work made its first appearance over sixty years ago, it continues to be reprinted, and John Hope Franklin calls it "the most important single volume dealing with slavery in the New England colonies" (516).
20. L. Greene 184.
21. L. Greene 190. In *White over Black,* Jordan describes vividly the plight of Black men in the southern states during the Revolution: there "the necessities of war eventually pulled both slave and free Negroes into the armed forces, many of them clutching promises of freedom as their eventual reward for fighting for it." This "participation of Negroes in the struggle for independence seemed to imply that they possessed membership in the new republic. In general, however, Negroes were utilized rather than welcomed." Both quotes are taken from Jordan 302.
22. Montesquieu 235.
23. Franklin 83.
24. L. Greene, 237.
25. Montesquieu 237.
26. George M. Hanfmann and John R. Pollard, "Muses," in *The Oxford Classical Dictionary,* ed. N.G. Hammond and H. H. Scullard (New York: Oxford UP, 1970) 704.
27. Montesquieu 235
28. L. Greene 177.
29. Montesquieu 244.
30. Baker, *Journey Back* 12.

Chapter 2. Wheatley Considered Intellectually Impoverished

1. Franklin goes on to point out that "Before I left the Home, I understood her Master was there and had sent her to me but did not come into the Room himself, and I thought was not pleased with the Visit. I should perhaps have enquired first for him; but I had heard nothing of him" (Willcox 293–94). Wheatley's "Master" on this journey was Nathaniel Wheatley, one of John and Susannah Wheatley's twins (the other was Mary, who had tutored her in English and some writing). Nathaniel, significantly, remained in Britain, for the most part, returning with his London wife, Mary Enderby, only once in September 1774 (Robinson 1981, 28), probably to settle the affairs of the family business with his aging father. My guess is that the problem here for Franklin was a political one. Nathaniel, along with his parents, was a staunch Loyalist and would have probably felt uncomfortable in receiving Franklin. Mary, his sister, however, had by this time married the fiery patriot minister Reverend John Lathrop. Since all indications are that Phillis was a steady Patriot, the Wheatley household during the mid-1770s must have been a somewhat troubling establishment.
2. Edward D. Seeber, in *Anti-Slavery Opinion in France during the Second Half of the Eighteenth Century*, observes of Voltaire's attitude toward Africans in general that "His opinion of them, it must be admitted, was not very high. He considered them as different from the white race in intelligence as they were in outward appearance" (57). Here Voltaire predicts Jefferson's position in *Notes on the State of Virginia*.
3. See Mason (1966) xxxv–xlvii for a discussion of reviews of Wheatley's 1773 and 1834/1835/1838 editions of her poetry, and for additional comments upon her work made during the late eighteenth and the entire nineteenth centuries. Mason's discussion complements my own.
4. I have in mind especially Wheatley's crucially significant letter to Samuel Occom, the Mohegan evangelist of late-eighteenth-century, revolutionary America, written in February 1774 and printed in a dozen colonial American newspapers, not known to Wheatley's nineteenth- or twentieth-century readers (before 1975). This letter, first published in 1975 by Charles W. Akers in "Our Modern Egyptians': Phillis Wheatley and the Whig Campaign against Slavery in Revolutionary Boston" (*Journal of Negro History* 60.3: 397–410), clearly states her provocative attitude toward the issue of freedom for her Black brothers and sisters. For it is in this letter that Wheatley trumpets such eloquent freedom declarations as "in every human Breast God has implanted a Principle, which we call Love of Freedom; it is impatient of Oppression, and pants for Deliverance" (177).

Chapter 3. Wheatley Intellectually Gifted—Maybe

1. Vendler performs a similar but elaborate practice on William Wordsworth's "I wandered Lonely as a Cloud." She traces the Latin, Greek, Old English, and Middle English roots of several words used by Wordsworth. She,

nevertheless, chooses to ignore the fact that this zion of British Romanticism pilfered his sister's (Dorothy's) commonplace/diary for the best imagery that occurs in this poem.
2. For this insight regarding the contrast between Wheatley's interiorization and the largely public positioning of Milton and Pope, I am indebted to my good friend and colleague, Professor Russell Rutter.
3. Dana D. Nelson's *The Word in Black and White: Reading "Race" in American Literature, 1638–1876* (New York: Oxford UP, 1992) promises to present a thorough analysis of "the dynamics of Anglo-American attitudes about race" (taken from the book's jacket) during the years indicated. Nelson's discussion (16–20) of Jefferson's *Notes*, particularly its infamous chap. 14, "Laws," however, makes no mention of Phillis Wheatley or of Jefferson's attack upon her. I, for one, cannot take seriously any discussion that pretends to investigate Jefferson's impact on racism in Early American literature which totally ignores Jefferson's assault on Wheatley, America's best poet before 1800.

Chapter 4. African Origins

1. For a thorough discussion of the conditions under which Wheatley first arrived in Boston, consult William H. Robinson, *Phillis Wheatley and Her Writings* (New York: Garland, 1984) 2–8. The quotations are both from Margaretta Oddell's "Memoir," which first appeared in print as a preface to the 1834 Boston edition of Wheatley's *Poems*. This sketch has long been considered the most authoritative biographical portrait and is reprinted (430–50) in Robinson's edition of the *Writings*: the quotation may be found on 430–31.
2. The phrase "the inertia of Wheatley's African heritage" is adapted from the similar phrase "the inertia of African heritage" used by Gold Refined Wilson in the early article, "The Religion of the American Negro Slave: His Attitude Toward Life and Death," appearing in *Journal of Negro History* 8.1 (1923): 44. Although this piece is largely based on research which has now become superseded by more recent and accurate data, Wilson does draw some valuable conclusions, e.g., that "what was religion in Africa was generally regarded by the American slaves themselves to be mere superstition" (45).
3. Robinson, *Writings* 286n. In addition, Robinson is careful to note, "Whether she is being poetically extravagant or defensive or indeed autobiographical in this poem, Phillis is the first Black American poet to rhapsodize about Black Africa."
4. The climate of Gambia has been described as essentially humid the year round in the regions closest to the Gambia, the most navigable river in West Africa. The average temperature for the year is between 77 and 82 degrees F. The vegetation resembles closely that of savannah or grassland. These grasslands provide some of the richest arable soil in Africa; farming

has long been the principal source of Gambian economy. The swamps and shrubs that line the banks of the river give way to parklands and tall grasses on the higher slopes, creating ideal conditions for cattle. It should be added that Gambia, the country, is surrounded by Senegal on all sides except where its great river enters the Atlantic. In fact, the country is no more than a thin, ribbonlike strip some 40 miles wide running along the Gambia River approximately 210 miles into Senegal. See Evid Forde, "Gambia, The" and "Gambia River," in *The New Encyclopedia Britannica: Macropedia*, 1974 ed., and R. J. Harrison Church, *West Africa: A Study of the Environment and Man's Use of It* (London: Longman, 1974) 224–32.

5. Daniel P. Mannix and Malcolm Cowley, *Black Cargoes: A History of the Atlantic Slave Trade, 1518–1865* (New York: Viking, 1962) 14, 21. In her treatment of Wheatley and George Moses Horton, *Bid the Vassal Soar* (Washington, DC: Harvard UP, 1974), Merle A. Richmond reaches a similar conclusion regarding the African peoples from which Wheatley came; see the interesting discussion on 12.

6. Quinn maintains in *Mandingo Kingdoms* that, even as late as the nineteenth century, "some Fula were thoroughly Islamized; . . . others were in the process of conversion; . . . and others were still firmly animist" (21). Trimingham discusses at length the slow process of conversion to Islam among the West African peoples. For a long period of time the conversion process merely accommodated itself to the animistic and fetishistic elements already present among the various cultures in West Africa. In fact, the Muslims first began to penetrate the Sudan during the eleventh century, and as observed hardly all of the Fulani of West Africa had been totally converted to Islam some eight hundred years later. See especially 21–46 of Trimingham's *Islam in West Africa* for a thorough description of this slow conversion process. Also see Colin McEvedy, *The Penguin Atlas of African History* (London: Penguin, 1980) 76, 84.

7. In the classic work of anthropology *Religion in Primitive Culture* (New York: Harper and Row, 1958), E. B. Tylor defines animism as "the belief in [expired] souls and in the future state, in controlling deities and subordinate spirits, these doctrines practically resulting in some kind of active worship," and fetishism as "that subordinate department [dependent on animism] which it properly belongs to, namely, the doctrine of spirits embodied in, or attached to, or conveying influence through, certain material objects" (11, 230).

8. See Ruth Finnegan's discussion of early literacy among the peoples of West Africa in *Oral Literature in Africa* (London: Oxford UP, 1970), esp. 49–51. But for a modified view, see Albert S. Gérard's *African Language Literatures: An Introduction to the Literary History of Sub-Saharan Africa* (Washington, DC: Three Continents, 1981) 48. Gérard maintains that the claim for a long tradition of *ajami* literatures, that is, literary expressions of various African language groups, especially of the Fulani, recorded in Arabic script, is a plausible and an attractive one. The truth of the matter

is, however, "there is no firm evidence . . . that the Fulani language, or any other West African vernacular, was written down before the lifetime of Usman dan Fodio [1754–1817], who thus may claim to be not only the main agent of the Arabic renascence, but also one of the founders of the *ajami* tradition." So, since Wheatley is thought to have been born within a year of Usman, it would have been unlikely she would have been introduced to any tradition founded by him before her departure from Africa. Nevertheless, there would have been opportunity for Wheatley to have acquired a measure of knowledge of Arabic and Arabic script.

My colleague Eric D. Lamore has informed me that the Quaker Philadelphian Anthony Benezet published in 1771 *Some Historical Account of Guinea . . . With An Inquiry into the Rise and Progress of the Slave Trade,* in which the author quotes extensively from Adanson's *Voyage to Senegal* (12–14); this long passage contains the very one in which Adanson has pointed out the "Negroes's" (Fula's) extensive knowledge of astronomy.

Of the "Fulis" (or Fula) Benezet, prompted by another text, observes as well that: "They are good farmers, and make harvest of corn, cotton, tobacco, etc. and breed great numbers of cattle of all kinds" (8). If Wheatley was aware of this tract from the famous abolitionist Benezet, surely it would have underscored her memory of her African homeland.

9. The majority of the proceedings which marked this momentous event, sponsored and hosted by the Jackson State University during November 1973, have been printed in the *Jackson State Review* 6.1 (Summer 1974). Alice Walker's essay is entitled, "In Search of Our Mothers' Garden: Honoring the Creativity of the Black Woman," 44–53; I quote from 48–49.

10. Finnegan 4. In *The Black Mind,* Dathorne (63) takes the importance of music to African poetry a step further to include dance. In his words, "it is difficult to separate poetry, music, and dance; indeed they cannot be said to exist separately. This applies to all African oral verse."

11. I do not dismiss poetry written in couplets as somehow automatically ineligible to be considered lyric, though I do find Hugh Holman and William Harmon's definition of the genre most helpful: "A brief subjective poem strongly marked by imagination, melody, and emotion, and creating for the reader a single, unified impression"—from *A Handbook to Literature,* 8th ed. (Upper Saddle River, NJ: Prentice Hall, 2000) 299. As one of Wheatley's most subjectively passionate poems, I think "On Being Brought . . ." is a fine contribution to the genre. In the original 1773 *Poems,* Mason's "Negroes" is spelled "Negros."

12. Such "glances" have even sparked the writing of an entire doctoral dissertation, Kenneth R. Holder's "Some Linguistic Aspects of the Heroic Couplet in the Poetry of Phillis Wheatley" (Diss., North Texas State Univ., 1973). This 288-page study, regrettably, concludes a great deal about Holder's method of investigation but offers practically nothing about

how we should read Wheatley's poetry. Quite simply it is an exercise in linguistic analysis, not a piece of literary criticism.

13. I came across this passage from Pope by accident while sampling selections in the delightful anthology, *A Book of English Pastoral Verse*, ed. John Barrell and John Bull (New York: Oxford UP, 1975) 282–83.

14. The first appearance in print of this poem was in an article by Mukhtar Ali Isani, "'On the Death of General Wooster': An Unpublished Poem by Phillis Wheatley," *Modern Philology* 77.3 (February 1980): 206–309.

15. Joseph Malof, "The Native Rhythm of English Meters," *Texas Studies in Literature and Language* 5 (1964): 586. Also see, for example, Northrop Frye, *Anatomy of Criticism* (Princeton, NJ: Princeton UP, 1957) 251, and Paul Fussell, *Poetic Meter and Poetic Form*, 2nd ed. (New York: Random House, 1979) 64–65. But Fussell cautions that those espousing this theory "tend to neglect the fact that in the Old English line, structural alliteration and strong medial caesura are characteristics that are as strong as its four stresses: Modern English has had no difficulty in casting off these and other equally powerful characteristics of Old English verse" (65).

16. Actually there were several versions of Wheatley's elegy printed on both sides of the Atlantic ranging in length from forty-seven to sixty-four lines. The forty-seven-line version appears in the 1773 *Poems*. For additional details regarding variants of this poem, see *The Collected Works of Phillis Wheatley*, ed. John C. Shields (New York: Oxford UP, 1988) 206–11.

17. For a fuller discussion of the Puritan elegy, see Robert Henson "Form and Content of the Puritan Funeral Elegy," *American Literature* 32.1 (1960): 11–27. Although Henson restricts this form of the elegy to the productions of colonial American writers, it should be noted that many Christian elegists of the eighteenth century, whether Puritan or not, adopted this basic structure. Hence my qualifier, "so-called," in the above discussion.

18. Finnegan 109. However, Finnegan does go on to conclude, "But in general terms and apart from Islamic influences, epic seems to be of remarkably little significance in African oral literature, and the *a priori* assumption that epic is the natural form for many non-literate peoples turns out to have little support" (110). Isidore Okpewho's *The Epic in Africa: Toward a Poetics of the Oral Performance* (New York: Columbia UP, 1979), nevertheless, demonstrates convincingly that an oral epic tradition did (and in some areas still does) exist in Africa: according to Okpewho, the examples of African epic that he explicates share many of the characteristics of the Homeric epics, of *Gilgamesh*, of *Beowulf*, and of *The Song of Igor's Campaign*. More recently Stephen Belcher, *Epic Traditions of Africa* (Bloomington: Indiana UP, 1999) 142–63, greatly extends Okpewho's groundbreaking work; indeed, he devotes an entire chapter to Fulani epic "Traditions of the Fula." Daniel P. Biebuyck's article on African poetry, entitled "African Poetry: In the Indigenous Epic," in *The New Princeton Encyclopedia Poetry and Poetics*, ed. Alex Preminger and Terry V. F. Brogan (Princeton, NJ: Princeton UP, 1993) 12–15, barely mentions praise poetry and names the

Fulani only once; rather Biebuyck concentrates his attention on a broad description of the epic in Africa. While Biebuyck's article is helpful for the epic, Lyndon Harries's "African Poetry," appearing in the earlier 1974 edition of the *Princeton Encyclopedia*, gives abundant detail about the praise poem

19. Dathorne 19. Okpewho (cited in n18) even observes that the African audiences of oral epics "believe that the gods are responsible for evil as well as good" (9).

20. Dathorne 57. It should be observed here that another possible source for her focus in the elegies on the living is her literary mentor, the renowned poet and minister of colonial Boston, Mather Byles. Details of Wheatley's literary association with Byles, along with specific information regarding his recommended structure of the elegy, will be explored in the next chapter.

Chapter 5. Post-African Religious Development

1. For a more thorough delineation of the Christian praxis of the often complex meditative process, consult the following texts. Augustine's analytical description of the process may be found in his *De Trinitate* (On the Trinity), particularly books 10 through 15. Help toward understanding how philosophical meditation undergoes the transition to mystical meditation (and union with the Deity), see Pierre Pourrat's *Christian Spirituality*, vol. 1 (London: Burns, Oats, and Washborne, 1922), passim—as concerns the movement from philosophic theology to mystical theology. The first volume of the more recent *Christian Spirituality*, ed. Bernard McGinn and John Meyendorff (New York: Crossroad, 1983), esp. 276–86, is also helpful. As for the mystical process in general, consult Evelyn Underhill's widely known (and reliable) *Mysticism: A Study in the Nature and Development of Man's Spiritual Consciousness* (New York: E. P. Dutton, 1961) and the more recent (but not necessarily better) *Understanding Mysticism*, ed. Richard Woods (Garden City, NY: Doubleday, 1980). Of course, Jean Leclercq, *The Love of Learning and the Desire for God*, 2nd ed. (New York: Fordham UP, 1974) 16–21, 27, 89–91, 230 (all for *meditatio*), presents the best discussion of the contemplative life within the Catholic faith. For a detailed review of Augustinian thought, the place to begin is Allan P. Fitzgerald, gen. ed., *Augustine through the Ages: A Encyclopedia* (Grand Rapids; Eerdmans, 1999).

2. I should point out that renowned Milton scholar James Holly Hanford has held that there is scarcely a line in *Paradise Lost* that does not echo some line from Vergil's *Aeneid*. The difference here between the two poets' handling of classicism is that Wheatley is obvious whereas Milton is subtle.

3. The other elegies by Wheatley whose action resides in the world of the chthonic include "On the Death of a Young Gentleman" (27), "To a Lady on the Death of Her Husband" (29), "To a Lady on the Death of Her Children, on the Death of Her Son and Their Brothers" (82), "To a

Gentleman and Lady on the Death of the Lady's Brother and Sister, and a Child of the Name of *Avis,* Aged One Year" (84), and "To the Honourable T.H. Esq.; on the Death of His Daughter" (98).

Chapter 6. Intellectual Development

1. It occurs to me that some may wish to see the pattern in "On Imagination" in terms of the Pindaric ode, with its strophes and antistrophes and epodes—i.e., a triadic structure. The first three stanzas, each a quatrain rhyming aa bb, would appear to match this triadic structure. Arguably stanza 1, which extols the power of imagination, followed by a second stanza devoted to the invocation to the muse (certainly an arresting variation on the conventional and expected initial [opening lines] invocation) and concluded by a third stanza which switches to an analysis of how the fancy serves the imagination as locator of "some lov'd object" for the purpose of focusing the operation of imagination, appears to imitate strophic motion answered by the antistrophic movement, both of which lead into a "wind-up" epode.

    Examination of the content of these first stanzas, however, exposes a different pattern. While here all three stanzas repeat the same pattern, hence departing from the Pindaric's odes similar pattern for the strophe and antistrophe and different scheme for the epode, the content of each stanza moves from one subject, to another and thence to a third (subordinate to the first) consequently more closely resembling the more relaxed Horatian ode.

    As for the remainder of "On Imagination," the first three quatrains are succeeded by two ten-line stanzas, then by one of eight lines and then by a concluding stanza of thirteen lines; surely this pattern falls far afield of that obtaining for the formal Pindaric ode. Furthermore, Wheatley's consistent iambic pentameter couplets do not follow the irregular stanzaic pattern of variations in number of lines, in lengths of lines, and in rhyme scheme which characterizes the irregular Pindaric ode.

2. See, for example, the article by Warren W. Wiersbe, "Imagination: The Preacher's Neglected Ally," *Leadership* 4.2 (Spring 1983): 22–27. Although the title sounds seductively positive, Wiersbe insists that the imagination he extols be a "sanctified imagination," just as had Jonathan Edwards in his *Religious Affections*.

3. Engell blunders badly when he calls Freneau's "Power of Fancy" "a singularly early claim [in America] for the imaginative faculty" (194). The truth is that before 1770, poets as diverse as Edward Taylor, Thomas Godfrey, Mather Byles, Samuel Cooper, and of course Phillis Wheatley had a great deal to say regarding the poet's faculty. The importance of imagination to Taylor and Godfrey, whose theoretics did not instruct Wheatley, deserve a brief survey here.

    In his now published large body of poetry, Edward Taylor names the fancy (opting for this disyllabic synonym rather than the often more awkward pentasyllabic imagination) almost fifty times—warrant enough to provoke examination. Yet a full analysis of Taylor's use of this faculty is yet to be accomplished. By the early 1680s, if not before, we find Taylor putting into verse his passionate devotion to God by a precise use of the meditative faculties of memory (fancy), understanding, and will, effecting the construction of an Augustinian image of God the Father (memory), the Son (understanding/reason), and the Holy Ghost (will or resolve). In his "Prologue," which prefaces both the First and Second Series of meditations, Taylor as poet, calling himself a "Crumb of Dust," laments his "dull Fancy" which he "would gladly grinde / Unto an Edge on Zions Pretious Stone" (1). Entirely appropriate to the process of meditation, though at the same time humbling himself before his God, Taylor here solicits the faculty of fancy as that power which enables the movement of his poetic process.

At some points in his *Preparatory Meditations* Series one and two (all composed as exercises leading to the composition of his sermons), Taylor names fancy internally, that is, not at the beginning of the poem. He usually does so within the context of how this faculty enables his act of poésis. In a late meditation of the Second Series, for example, the poet asserts that his "Muses Hermitage is grown so old / Her Spirits shiver doe, her Phancy's Laws / Are much transgresst. She sits so Crampt with cold." Later in this poem he calls upon inspiration from his God to animate his "frozen Phancy" (305). Though the "heate of Phancy" appears to have abandoned the seventy-five-year-old poet, his assertion that fancy has laws is an arresting one.

In a much earlier meditation from the First Series, dating from 1686, when Taylor was forty-four, the poet exclaims: "My Phancys in a Maze, my thoughts agast, / Word in an Extasy" (30). The notion that the fancy could become lost in a labyrinth (a recurring image pattern in Taylor) implies that this faculty cares not for chaos but seeks order. Whereas in his prose sermons, imagination seems lawless, a fictive purveyor of untruth as in the *Christographia* sermons wherein "Fictitious imaginations . . . are the Efficacy of Errours" (*Christographia* 354), to the poet (not the minister) imagination is not merely essential to set in motion the act of creativity, but even carries with it the rules of rhetoric. Fancy then becomes in Taylor an early articulation of the poet's reason.

Another illustration from Taylor's poetry corroborates this interpretation. In an elegy on the death of Samuel Hooker, son of the famous Puritan patriarch, Thomas Hooker, Taylor praises Samuel for his "Wisdom rich, / With Spirits fand from foggy Vapors which / Do Reason cloud: a Fine spun Fancy, Quick, / Producing Notions brave, and Rhetorick" (Taylor 477–78). The words here would have us understand an unclouded reason in terms of a finely wrought imagination whose bold creations become manifest in the products of skilled rhetoric. Herein Taylor has recognized that the reason which resides within the restrictions of dogma and the reason dwelling in the mind of the poet may well not be equivalent.

Thomas Godfrey, another Early American poet who believed imagination to be necessary to poésis and who wrote about thirty years later than Taylor, composed the wholly secular five-hundred-line "The Court of Fancy," printed in Philadelphia in 1762; this work presented a view of fancy closely resembling Mark Akenside's moral but also secular perspective in his 1744 *Pleasures of Imagination*. His close friend Nathaniel Evans, who eventually edited a collection of Godfrey's work, wrote an elegy on Godfrey's death in the following year in which he praised the fire of his departed friend's imagination. Evans claims that Godfrey's poetry constituted "The emanation of a soul divine"; and that the fire of his fancy ("fancy's fire") "with judgment had combin'd / To guide each effort of th' enraptur'd mind" (Silverman 405). Note the close parallels here between the American Godfrey and the British Duff; both require the management (recall Shaftsbury) of imagination by "judgment."

Other poets who participated in the phenomenon of America's investigation of imagination include John Adams (the poet, not the president), Richard Lewis (an especially fine poet), and William Dawson. Dawson, from Virginia, and Lewis, from Maryland, ascertain that the South had poets who contributed to the evolution of Early America's aesthetic theoretics of the imagination.

4. For this suggestion that the "heaven-born maid" could be Minerva, I am indebted to my colleague and fellow student in literary studies, Sanford Freedman; I was fortunate enough to meet Professor Freedman in Frances Ferguson's 1984 National Endowment for the Humanities Summer Seminar on "The Aesthetics and Politics of the Sublime."

5. Curiously the Apocrypha does use similar phrasing but in a wholly inappropriate context. Fourth Maccabees has the phrases "fan the fire" (5:32) and "fanning the flames" (9:19); but rather than bearing any association with inspiration, each occurrence marks an instance of torture! So I find these cases inapposite sources for either Cooper or Wheatley.

6. As might be expected, both poets display in their elegies several characteristics of the personal elegy of the English Renaissance. But curiously Byles's elegies do not come within what Robert Henson distinguishes as the Puritan funeral elegy, but a few of Wheatley's do. See Henson, "Form and Content of the Puritan Funeral Elegy," *American Literature* 32 1 (1970): 11–27; A. L. Bennett, "The Puritan Rhetorical Conventions in the Renaissance Personal Elegy," *Studies in Philology* 51.2 (1954): 107–26; Gregory Rigsby, "Form and Content in Phillis Wheatley's Elegies," *College Language Association Journal* 19.2 (1975): 248–57; and my discussion of this subject in my unpublished dissertation, "Phillis Wheatley's Poetics of Ascent" (University of Tennessee, 1978) 100–105.

7. See Samuel Holt Monk's *The Sublime* (Ann Arbor: U of Michigan P, 1960) 31–32, for a discussion of how Boileau deduced that this suggestion from Longinus's treatise—that God's creation of light is an

example of sublimity—is actually the epitome and the zenith of the sublime image in literature.

8. It should be observed that both Pope and James Thomson, authors whose works were easily available to Wheatley, also make concrete references to the sublime. In Pope's preface to his famous translation of the *Iliad*, written early in his career, Wheatley possibly sensed a kindred spirit in the youthful poet who spoke unreservedly of such subjects as sublimity and imagination; both subjects offered a sickly Black slave girl (Wheatley was chronically asthmatic) and a deformed, Roman Catholic alienate means of momentary escape. But while Pope later satirized the excesses of the sublime in *Peri Bathous* and spoke of the unbridled imagination as a "dangr'ous art" in the *Essay on Man* (ii, 1. 143), Wheatley wrote her most ambitious poems specifically about the imagination and the sublime. Thomson is well known for his emphasis upon the sublime in *The Seasons*. Even though an American edition of Thomson's work did not appear until 1777, four years after the publication of Wheatley's *Poems*, it is reasonable to posit Wheatley saw a copy of a British edition. The word "sublime" or some form of this word appears ten times in *The Seasons*, usually as an adjective. But once Thomson uses the adverb "sublimely" (p. 110, 1. 1562 of "Summer" in J. Logie Robertson's edition of 1908), and three times he makes a past participle of the word thus, "sublimed" (p. 34, 1. 827 of "Spring"; p. 37, 1. 900 of "Spring"; and p. 85, 1. 912 of "Summer"). Neither Wheatley nor Byles ever uses these derivatives of sublime. Hence Wheatley's use of "sublime" more closely resembles Byles's use of this word than it does either Pope's or Thomson's.

9. Another poet of the eighteenth century for whom one may expect Wheatley to display an affinity in her use of sun imagery is James Thomson, particularly in his "Summer." But perhaps surprisingly their treatment of solar imagery varies markedly. In the early portion of "Summer," Thomson presents an apostrophe to the sun: "O Sun! / Soul of surrounding worlds! in whom best seen / Shines out thy Maker!" (p. 56, 11. 94–96 in J. Logie Robertson's 1908 edition). This image parallels Wheatley's use of the sun, but later Thomson speaks of God's "servant-sun" (p. 66, 1. 341). The sun is never a servant in Wheatley; rather she always refers to the sun as the most exalted symbol of God's majesty over the world. Thomson does, however, refer to Apollo, like Wheatley is so given to do; but such a reference only appears once in "Summer" ("his weary chariot," p. 113, 1. 1625) and then only once more in "Winter" ("Apollo's animating fire," p. 210, 1. 660). Wheatley names Apollo seven times; Phoebus, twelve; and Sol twice in the body of her extant work. So pronounced is her use of sun imagery in connection with her understanding of God (once she even calls George Whitefield, the renowned voice of the Great Awakening in Colonial America, "the setting sun" [22]) that what Wheatley constructs in her application of this imagery is a conscious syncretism of her African

religious consciousness, her New England Congregationalism, and her knowledge of classicism.

10. This quote by Byles may be found in Early American Imprints under the title, *God Glorious in the Scenes of the Winter* (Boston: Green for Gookin, 1744) 15.

11. Actually this "Young Gentleman" Byles refers to has been identified by C. Lennart Carlson, editor of *Poems*, to be Byles himself (xiii–xiv). Byles was notorious as an incorrigible prankster and a biting wit, and he was fond of perpetrating such hoaxes. Nonetheless, this particular hoax gave him opportunity to expound upon his own theory of poetry.

12. Byles may very likely have thought he should give up, at least publicly, an avocation which during this period in Colonial American history was especially looked down upon in a man of the cloth. In the eighth chapter of *Manuductio ad Ministerium* (1726), for example, Byles's uncle, Cotton Mather, had cautioned young ministers not to be seduced by a too frequent indulgence of the muses: "Be not so set upon Poetry, to be always poring on the Passionate and Measured Pages. . . . But especially preserve the Chastity of your Soul from the Dangers you may incur, by a Conversation with Muses that are no better than Harlots" (in *Colonial and Federalist American Writing*, ed. George F. Homer and Robert A. Bain [New York: Odyssey, 1966] 242).

13. For other examples of embedded sonnets see pages 10, 15, 30, 40–41, 43–44, 46–47, 52, 73, 98, 106, 138, 144–45, and 153. Curiously, the number of embedded sonnets in her extant verse totals fourteen. Someone needs to investigate Wheatley's penchant for this somewhat unique and frequent application.

14. For Wheatley's other sources in the poetry of Mark Akenside and Edward Young, see notes to *The Collected Works of Phillis Wheatley*.

Works Cited and Consulted

Abrams, M. H. *A Glossary of Literary Terms*. 8th ed. Boston: Thomas Wadsworth, 2005.

———. *The Mirror and the Lamp: Romantic Theory and the Critical Tradition*. New York: Norton, 1953.

Adams, Abigail. "Letter to Mercy Otis Warren, April 27, 1776." *Early American Writings*. Gen ed., Carla Mulford. New York: Oxford UP, 2002.

Adams, Percy G. *Graces of Harmony: Alliteration, Assonance, and Consonance in Eighteenth-Century British Poetry*. Athens: U of Georgia P, 1977.

Adanson, Michel. *A Voyage to Senegal, the Isle of Goree, and the River Gambia*. London: Sir Richard Phillips, 1759.

Addison, Joseph. *The Spectator*. Ed. Donald F. Bond. 4 vols. London: Oxford UP, 1965.

Adler, Mortimer J. *The Idea of Freedom: A Dialectical Examination of the Conceptions of Freedom*. 2 vols. Garden City, NY: Doubleday, 1958–61.

Akenside, Mark. *The Poetical Works of Mark Akenside*. London: George Bell, 1894.

Akers, Charles W. *The Divine Politician: Samuel Cooper and the American Revolution in Boston*. Boston: Northeastern UP, 1982.

———. "'Our Modern Egyptians': Phillis Wheatley and the Whig Campaign against Slavery in Revolutionary Boston." *Journal of Negro History* 60.3 (1975): 397–410.

Allen, Walter, Jr. "The Epyllion: A Chapter in the History of Literary Criticism." *Transactions of the American Philological Association* 71 (1940): 1–26.

———. "The Non-Existent Classical Epyllion." *Studies in Philology* 55 (1950): 515–18.

Allen, William G. *Wheatley, Banneker and Horton*. Boston: Press of Daniel Losing Jr., 1849.

Amory, Hugh, and David D. Hall, eds. *A History of the Book in America*. Vol. 1 of *The Colonial Book in the Atlantic World*. New York: Cambridge UP, 2000.

Anderson, William S., ed. *Ovid's Metamorphoses: Books 6–10*. Norman: U of Oklahoma P, 1972.

Andrews, William L. *To Tell a Free Story: The First Century of Afro-America Autobiography, 1760–1865*. Chicago: U of Illinois P, 1988.

Andrews, William L., Frances Smith Forster, and Trudier Harris, eds. *The Oxford Companion to African American Literature*. New York, Oxford UP, 1997.

Applegate, Ann. "Phillis Wheatley: Her Critics and Her Contribution." *Negro American Literature Forum* 9.4 (1975): 123–26.

Augustine (Saint). *On the Holy Trinity; Doctrinal Treatises; Moral Treatises.* In Vol. 3 of *Nicene and Post-Nicene Fathers.* Ed. Philip Schaff. Peabody, MA: Hendrickson, 1994.

Bacon, Francis. "Advancement of Learning." *Critical Essays of the Seventeenth Century.* Ed. J. E. Spingarn. Vol. 1. 1908. Honolulu: UP of the Pacific, 2005.

Bacon, Martha. *Puritan Promenade.* Boston: Houghton Mifflin, 1964.

Baker, Houston A., Jr. *The Journey Back: Issues in Black Literature and Culture.* Chicago: U of Chicago P, 1980.

———. *Workings of the Spirit: The Poetics of Afro-American Women's Writing.* Chicago: U of Chicago P, 1991.

Baldwin, James. "Religious Elements in Black Literature." Knoxville: Committee on U of Tennessee Cultural Attractions, 18 May 1978.

Balkun, Mary McAleer. "Phillis Wheatley's Construction of Otherness and the Rhetoric of Performed Ideology." *African American Review* 36.1 (Spring 2002): 121–36.

Barrell, John, and John Bull, eds. *A Book of English Pastoral Verse.* New York: Oxford UP, 1975.

Barzun, Jacques. *From Dawn to Decadence: 500 Years of Western Cultural Life, 1500 to the Present.* New York: Harper Collins, 2000.

Bassard, Katherine C. *Spiritual Interrogations: Culture, Gender, and Community in Early African American Women's Writing.* Princeton, NJ: Princeton UP, 1999.

Bate, Walton Jackson. *From Classic to Romantic: Premises of Taste in Eighteenth-Century England.* Cambridge, MA: Harvard UP, 1946.

Bayly, Anselm. *The Alliance of Musick, Poetry, and Oratory.* 1789. New York: Garland, 1972.

Belcher, Stephen. *Epic Traditions of Africa.* Bloomington: Indiana UP, 1999.

Bennett, A. L. "The Principal Rhetorical Conventions in the Renaissance Personal Elegy." *Studies in Philology* 51.2 (1954): 95–126.

Bennett, Paula. "Phillis Wheatley's Vocation and the Paradox of the 'Afric Muse.'" Spec. issue of *PMLA* 113.1 (January 1998): 64–76.

Berlin, Ira. *Many Thousands Gone: The First Two Centuries of Slavery in North America.* Cambridge, MA: Belknap P of Harvard UP, 1998.

Berman, Eleanor Davidson. *Thomas Jefferson among the Arts: An Essay in Early American Esthetics.* New York: Philosophical Library, 1947.

Biebuyck, Daniel P. "African Poetry: In the Indigenous Epic Tradition." *The New Princeton Encyclopedia of Poetry and Poetics.* 3rd Ed. Alex Preminger and Terry V. F. Brogan. Princeton: Princeton UP, 1993.

Bigsby, C. W. E., ed. *Poetry and Drama.* Vol. 2 in *The Black American Writer.* Baltimore: Penguin, 1971.

Billings, William. *The New England Psalm Singer* (1770). Ed. Karl Kroeger. Vol. 1 of *The Complete Works of William Billings.* Boston: American Musicological Society and Colonial Society of Massachusetts, 1981.

Birkle, Carmen. "Border Crossings and Identity Creation in Phillis Wheatley's Poetry." In *The Construction and Contestation of African Cultures and Identities on the Early National Period.* Ed. Ydo J. Hebel. Universitätsverlag C. Heidelberg Winter, 1999.

Bloom, Harold, ed. *African-American Poets: Phillis Wheatley through Melvin B. Tolson.* Philadelphia: Chelsea House, 2003. (Reprints Mason's 1989 "Introduction" and O'Neal's "Subtle War")

Blumenbach, Johann F. *The Anthropological Treatises on Johann Friedrich Blumenbach.* 1865. Boston: Milford House, 1973.

Blyden, Edward Wilmot. *Christianity, Islam, and the Negro Race.* London: W. B. Whittington, 1887.

Boas, George. "Macrocosm and Microcosm." In *The Dictionary of the History of Ideas.* New York: Scribner, 1973–74.

Bond, Donald F. "'Distrust' of Imagination in English Neo-Classicism." *Philological Quarterly* 14.4 (1935): 54–69.

———. "The Neo-Classical Psychology of the Imagination." *Journal of English Literary History* 4.4 (1937): 245–64.

Bontemps, Arna and Langston Hughes, eds. *The Poetry of the Negro, 1746–1970.* Garden City, NY: Anchor P, 1970.

Boulton, Alexander O. "The American Paradox: Jeffersonian Equality and Racial Science." *American Quarterly* 47.3 (September 1995): 467–93.

Bradley, Sculley, gen. ed. *The American Tradition in Literature.* 4th ed. Vol. 1. New York: Grosset and Dunlap, 1974.

Brandon, S. G. F. "Henotheism." In *A Dictionary of Comparative Religion.* New York: Charles Scribner's Sons, 1970.

Brawley, Benjamin. *Early Negro American Writers.* Chapel Hill: U of North Carolina P, 1935.

———. *Negro Builders and Heroes.* Chapel Hill: U of North Carolina P, 1937.

———. *The Negro Genius: A New Appraisal of the Achievement of the American Negro in Literature and the Fine Arts.* New York, NY: Dodd Mead, 1937.

———. *The Negro in Literature and Art in the United States.* 1929. New York: AMS P, 1971.

Brindenbaugh, Carl. "The First Published Poems of Phillis Wheatley." *New England Quarterly* 42 (December 1969): 583–84.

Brooks, Joanna. *American Lazarus: Religion and the Rise of African-American and Native American Literature.* New York: Oxford UP, 2003.

Brown, Gillian. *The Consent of the Governed: The Lockean Legacy in Early American Culture.* Cambridge, MA: Harvard UP, 2001.

Brown, Hallie Quinn. *Homespun Heroines and Other Women of Distinction.* New York, NY: Oxford UP, 1988.

Brown, John. *A Dissertation on the Rise, Union, and Power, the Progression, Separations, and Corruptions of Poetry and Music.* 1763. New York: Garland Publishing, 1971.

Brown, Marshall. *Preromanticism.* Stanford, CA: Stanford UP, 1991.

Brown, Sterling, gen. ed. *The Negro Caravan.* 1941. New York: Arno, 1969.

———. *Negro Poetry and Drama*. 1937. New York: Atheneum, 1969.
Bruce, Dickson D., Jr. *The Origins of African American Literature, 1680–1865*. Charlottesville: U of Virginia P, 2001.
Burke, Edmund. *Philosophical Enquiry into the Origin of Our Ideas of the Sublime and Beautiful*. Ed. J. T. Boulton. New York: Columbia UP, 1958.
Burke, Helen. "Problematizing American Dissent: The Subject of Phillis Wheatley." In *Cohesion and Dissent in America*. Eds. Carol Colatrella and Joseph Alkana. Albany: State U of New York P, 1994. 193–209.
Burke, Kenneth. *The Philosophy of Literary Form: Studies in Symbolic Action*. 3rd ed. Berkeley: U of California P, 1973.
Burnet, Thomas. *The Sacred Theory of the Earth*. London, 1690–91. Carbondale: Southern Illinois UP, 1965.
Burroughs, Margaret G. "Do Birds of a Feather Flock Together?" *Jackson State Review* 6.1 (1974): 61–73.
Buttrick, George A., gen. ed. *The Interpreter's Bible*. Vol. 5. Nashville: Abingdon, 1956.
Bly, Antonio T. "Wheatley's 'On the Affray in King Street." *Explicator* 56.4 (1998): 177–80.
———. "Wheatley's 'On the Death of a Young Lady of Five Years of Age." *Explicator* 58.1 (1999): 10–13.
———. "Wheatley's 'To the University of Cambridge in New-England." *Explicator* 55.4 (1997): 205–8.
Byles, Mather. *God Glorious in the Scenes of the Winter*. Boston: Green for Gookin, 1744.
———. *Poems on Several Occasions*. Boston: 1744.
———. *Poems on Several Occasions*. Introduction by C. Lennart Carlson. New York: Columbia UP, 1942.
Carretta, Vincent. "Phillis Wheatley, the Mansfield Decision of 1772, and the Choice of Identity." *Early America Re-Explored: New Readings in Colonial, Early National, and Antebellum Culture*. Ed. and introduction by Klaus H. Schmidt and Fritz Fleischmann. New York: Peter Lang, 2000. 201–23.
———, ed. *Complete Writings: Phillis Wheatley*. 4th ed. Penguin, 2001.
Carretta, Vincent, and Philip Gould, eds. *Genius in Bondage: Literature of the Early Black Atlantic*. Lexington: UP of Kentucky, 2001.
Carroll, Frances Laverne, and Mary Meacham. *The Library at Mount Vernon*. Pittsburgh: Beta Phi Mu, 1977.
Carruth, Hayden, and George Perkins. "Poetry: Before 1960." *Benét's Reader's Encyclopedia of American Literature*. Ed. George Perkins et al. New York: Harper Collins, 1991.
Cavell, Anthony J. *Jackson State Review* 6 (Summer 1974). (Special issue reporting on the proceedings and presentations of papers delivered at the Phillis Wheatley Poetry Festival, November 6, 1973)
Charron, Pierre. *Of Wisdom: Three Books Written in French*. Trans. Samson Lennard. London: Blount and Aspley, 1625.

———. *Of Wisdom: Three Books Written Originally in French by the Sieur de Charron.* Trans. George Stanhope. 2nd ed. London: R. Bonwick, 1707.

Chauncy, Charles. *Enthusiasm Described and Caution'd Against.* Boston, 1742.

Church, R. J. Harrison. *West Africa: A Study of the Environment and Man's Use of It.* London: Longman, 1974.

Cima, Gay Gibson. "Black and Unmarked: Phillis Wheatley, Mercy Otis Warren, and the Limits of Strategic Anonymity." *Theatre Journal* 52.4 (2000): 465–95.

Clarke, Mary T. "The Trinity in Latin Christianity." In *Christian Spirituality: Origins to the Twelfth Century.* Ed. Bernard McGinn and John Meyendorff. New York: Crossroad, 1985.

Clarke, Peter B. *West Africa and Islam: A Study of Religious Development from the Eighth to the Twentieth Century.* London: Edward Arnold, 1982.

Clarkson, Thomas. *An Essay on the Slavery and Commerce of the Human Species, Particularly the African.* 1785. Miami, FL: Mnemosyne, 1969.

Coleridge, Samuel Taylor. *The Portable Coleridge.* Ed. I. A. Richards. New York: Viking, 1950.

Collins, Terence. "Phillis Wheatley: The Dark Side of Poetry." *Phylon* 36.1 (1975): 78–88.

Conner, Kimberly Rae. *Conversions and Vision in the Writings of African-American Women.* Knoxville: U of Tennessee P, 1994.

Cook, Elizabeth C. *Literary Influences in Colonial [American] Newspapers, 1704–1750.* 1912. Port Washington, NY: Kennikat, 1966.

Cooper, Anthony Ashley, Third Earl of Shaftsbury. *Characteristicks of Men, Manners, Opinions, Times.* 6th ed. 3 vols. London: J. Purser, 1737–38.

Cooper, David, ed. *A Companion to Aesthetics.* Oxford: Blackwell, 1992.

Copleston, Frederick. *Kant.* Part 1 of *Modern Philosophy.* Vol. 6 of *A History of Philosophy.* Garden City, NY: Doubleday, 1960.

Countryman, Edward, ed. *How Did American Slavery Begin?* New York: Bedford/St. Martin's, 1999.

Coviello, Peter. "Agonizing Affection: Affect and Nation in Early America." *Early American Literature* 37.3 (Fall 2002): 439–68.

Cowell, Pattie, ed. *Women Poets in Pre-Revolutionary America, 1650–1775: An Anthology.* Troy, NY: Whitston Publishing, 1981.

Cunliffe, Marcus. "Thomas Jefferson and the Dangers of the Past." *Wilson Quarterly* 6.1 (Winter 1982): 107.

Daly, Robert. "Powers of Humility and the Presence of Readers in Anne Bradstreet and Phillis Wheatley." In *Puritanism in America: The Seventeenth through the Nineteenth Centuries.* Ed. Michael Schuldiner. Lewiston, NY: Mellen, 1993. 1–24.

Dathorne, O. R. *The Black Mind: A History of African Literature.* Minneapolis: U of Minnesota P, 1972.

Davis, Arthur P. "Personal Elements in the Poetry of Phillis Wheatley." *Phylon* 14 (1953): 191–98.

Davis, David Brion. *The Problem of Slavery in Western Culture*. Ithaca, NY: Cornell UP, 1966.

Deane, Charles, ed. *Letters of Phillis Wheatly [sic], the Negro-Slave Poet of Boston*. Boston: J. Wilson and Son, 1864.

de Bruijn, Mirjan, and Han van Dijk. "State Formation and the Decline of Pastoralism: The Fulani in Central Mali." In *Conflict and the Decline of Pastoralism in the Horn of Africa*. Ed. John Markakis. London: Macmillan, 1993.

Delany, Martin R. *The Condition, Elevation, Emigration, and Destiny of the Colored People of the United States*. Rpt. ed. Intro. Benjamin Quarles. Salem, NH: Ayer Company, 1988.

Dennis, John. *The Critical Works of John Dennis*. Ed. Edward N. Hooker. Vol. 1. Baltimore: Johns Hopkins UP, 1939.

Dewey, Edward H. "Prince, Thomas." *Dictionary of American Biography*. 1935.

Draper, John. *The Funeral Elegy and the Rise of English Romanticism*. 1929. New York: Phaeton, 1967.

Duff, William. *Critical Observations on the Writings of the Most Celebrated Original Geniuses in Poetry*. 1770.

———. *An Essay on Original Genius and Its Various Modes of Exertion in Philosophy and the Fine Arts, Particularly Poetry*. London, 1767.

Dunlap, Jane. *Poems on Several Sermons Preached by the Rev'd . . . George Whitefield*. Boston: 1771.

Dyson, Michael Eric. *Reflecting Black: African-American Cultural Criticism*. Minneapolis: U of Minnesota P, 1993.

Edwards, Jonathan. *Treatise Concerning the Religious Affections*. 1746. Ed. John E. Smith. New Haven, CT: Yale UP, 1959.

Eliade, Mircea. *Patterns in Comparative Religion*. Trans. Rosemary Sheed. New York: World, 1958.

———, gen. ed. *The Encyclopedia of Religion*. 8 vols. New York: Macmillan, 1987.

Elliott, Emory. *Power in the Pulpit in Puritan New England*. Princeton, NJ: Princeton UP, 1975.

———. *Revolutionary Writers: Literature and Authority in the New Republic, 1725–1810*. New York: Oxford UP, 1982.

Elliot, Emory, et al., eds. *Aesthetics in a Multicultural Age*. New York: Oxford UP, 2002.

Ellison, Julie. *Cato's Tears and the Making of Anglo-American Emotion*. Chicago: U of Chicago P, 1999.

———. "The Politics of Fancy in the Age of Sensibility." In *Re-Visioning Romanticism: British Women Writers, 1776–1837*. Ed. Carol S. Wilson and Joel Haefner. Philadelphia: U of Pennsylvania P, 1994. 228–55. (Includes several pages on Wheatley)

Emerson, Everett, ed. *American Literature, 1764–1789: The Revolutionary Years*. Madison: U of Wisconsin P, 1977.

Engell, James. *The Creative Imagination: Enlightenment to Romanticism*. Cambridge, MA: Harvard UP, 1981.

Ennis, Daniel J. "Poetry and American Revolutionary Identity: The Case of Phillis Wheatley and John Paul Jones." *Studies in Eighteenth–Century Culture* 31 (2002): 85–98.

Erickson, Erik H. *Childhood and Society*. 2nd ed. New York: Norton, 1964.

———. "Life Cycle." *International Encyclopedia of the Social Sciences*. 1968 ed.

Erkkila, Betsy. "Phillis Wheatley and the Black American Revolution." *A Mixed Race: Ethnicity in Early America*. Ed. Frank Shuffelton. New York: Oxford UP, 1993. 225–40.

Farah, Caesar E. *Islam: Beliefs and Observances*. Woodbury, NY: Barron's Educational Series, 1970.

Felker, Christopher D. "'The tongues of the learned are insufficient': Phillis Wheatley, Publishing Objectives, and Personal Liberty." *Resources for American Literary Study* 20.2 (1994): 149–79.

Ferguson, Margaret, Mary Jo Salter, and Jon Stallworthy, eds. *The Norton Anthology of Poetry*. 5th ed. New York: Norton, 2005.

Ferguson, Robert A. "The American Enlightenment, 1750–1820." In *The Cambridge History of American Literature, 1590–1820*. Ed. Sacvan Bercovitch. Cambridge: Cambridge UP, 1994. 345–537.

Finkelman, Paul. *Slavery and the Founders: Race and Liberty in the Age of Jefferson*. New York: Sharpe, 1996.

Finnegan, Ruth. *Oral Literature in Africa*. Nairobi: Oxford UP, 1970.

Finney, Gretchen L. "Harmony or Rapture in Music." *Dictionary of the History of Ideas*. New York: Charles Scribner's Sons, 1973–74. Vol. 2:388–95.

Fitzgerald, Allan D, gen. ed. *Augustine through the Ages: An Encyclopedia*. Grand Rapids: Eerdmans, 1999.

Flanzbaum, Hilene. "Unprecedented Liberties: Re-reading Phillis Wheatley." *MELUS* 18.3 (Fall 1993): 71–80.

Fleischmann, W. B., and John K. Newman. "Classicism." *Princeton Encyclopedia of Poetry and Poetics*. Ed. Alex Preminger. 3rd ed. Princeton, NJ: Princeton UP, 1993.

Flexner, James T. *George Washington: Anguish and Farewell (1793–1799)*. Vol. 4. Boston: Little, Brown, 1972.

Fogle, Stephen F. "Ode." *Princeton Encyclopedia of Poetry and Poetics*, 2nd ed. Princeton, NJ: Princeton UP, 1974.

Forde, Evid. "Gambia, The." *The New Encyclopedia Britannica: Macropedia* 1974 ed.

———."Gambia River." *The New Encyclopedia Britannica: Macropedia* 1974 ed.

Foster, Frances Smith. *Written by Herself: Literary Production by African American Women, 1746–1892*. Bloomington: Indiana UP, 1993. (Pages 30–43 discuss Wheatley)

Franklin, Benjamin. *The Writings of Benjamin Franklin*. Ed. Albert H. Smyth. Vol. 6. New York: Macmillan, 1907.

Franklin, John Hope. *From Slavery to Freedom: A History of Negro Americans*. 5th ed. New York: Knopf, 1980.

Frye, Northrop. *Anatomy of Criticism*. Princeton, NJ: Princeton UP, 1957.
———. *The Educated Imagination*. Bloomington: Indiana UP, 1964.
Fussell, Paul. *Poetic Meter and Poetic Form*. 2nd ed. New York: Random House, 1979.
Gallaway, Francis. *Reason, Rule, and Revolt in English Classicism*. Lexington: U of Kentucky P, 1966.
Gardner, Howard. *Developmental Psychology: An Introduction*. Boston: Little Brown, 1978.
Garrisen, William Lloyd. "To Maecenas" to the thirty-eighth poem from the 1773 *Poems*. *Liberator*. February 11–December 22, 1832.
Gates, Henry Louis, Jr. *Figures in Black: Words, Signs, and the Racial Self*. New York: Oxford UP, 1987.
———. "Phillis Wheatley and the Nature of the Negro." *Critical Essays on Phillis Wheatley*. Ed. William H. Robinson. Boston: Hall, 1982.
Gelles, Edith B. *Portia: The World of Abigail Adams*. Bloomington: Indiana UP, 1992.
Gérard, Albert S. *African Language Literatures: An Introduction to the Literary History of Sub-Saharan Africa*. Washington, DC: Three Continents, 1981.
Gibson, Donald B. "Literature: Poetry." *Encyclopedia of Black America*. Ed. W. Augustus Low and Virgil A. Clift. New York: McGraw-Hill, 1981.
Giddings, Paula. "Critical Evaluation of Phillis Wheatley." *Jackson State Review* 6.1 (1974): 74–81.
Gifford, Terry. *Pastoral*. New York: Routledge, 1999.
Giles, Paul. *Transatlantic Insurrections: British Culture and the Formation of American Literature, 1750–1860*. Philadelphia: U of Pennsylvania P, 2001.
———. *Virtual Americas: Transatlantic Imaginary*. Durham, NC: Duke UP, 2002.
Gilles, John. "The Awakening of American Negro Literature 1619–1900." In *Poetry and Drama*. Vol. 2 of *The Black American Writer*. Ed. C. W. E. Bigsby. Baltimore: Penguin, 1969.
Gillies, John. , ed. *Memoirs of George Whitefield*. Middletown, CT: Hunt and Noyes, 1834.
Gilroy, Paul. *The Black Atlantic: Modernity and Double-Consciousness*. Cambridge, MA: Harvard UP, 1993.
Goldberg, David Theo. *Racist Culture: Philosophy and the Politics of Meaning*. Oxford: Blackwell, 1993.
Gould, Nathaniel D. *Church Music in America*. Boston: A.N. Johnson, 1853; rpt. New York: AMS P, 1972.
Graham, Shirley. *The Story of Phillis Wheatley: Poetess of the American Revolution*. New York: Messner, 1949.
Gray, Richard, ed. *The Cambridge History of Africa, from c1600 to c1790*. Cambridge: Cambridge UP, 1975.
Greene, Jack P. *The Intellectual Construction of America: Exceptionalism and Identity from 1492 to 1800*. Chapel Hill: U of North Carolina P, 1993.

Greene, Jack P., and J. R. Pole, eds. *The Blackwell Encyclopedia of the American Revolution.* Cambridge, MA: Basil Blackwell, 1991.

Greene, Lorenzo. *The Negro in Colonial New England.* New York: Columbia UP, 1942.

Grégoire, Henri. *An Enquiry Concerning the Intellectual and Moral Faculties and Literature of Negroes.* Trans. P. B. Warden. 1810. College Park, MD: McGrath, 1967.

Grimsted, David. "Anglo-American Racism and Phillis Wheatley's Sable Veil, 'Lenth'nd Chain" and "Knitted Heart." *Women in the Age of the American Revolution.* Ed. Ronald Hoffman and Peter Albert. Charlottesville: UP of Virginia, 1989.

Hamilton, Edith. *Mythology.* Boston: Little, Brown, 1940.

Hanfmann, George M., and John R. Pollard. "Muses." *The Oxford Classical Dictionary.* Ed. N. G. Hammond and H. H. Scullard. 3rd ed. New York: Oxford UP, 1996.

Harmon, William, and C. Hugh Holman. *A Handbook to Literature.* 10th ed. Upper Saddle River, NJ: Prentice-Hall, 2006.

Harries, Lyndon. "African Poetry." *Princeton Encyclopedia of Poetry and Poetics,* 2nd ed. Alex Preminger, ed. Princeton, NJ: Princeton UP, 1974–. 909–11.

Harris, Sharon M., ed. *American Women Writers to 1800.* New York: Oxford UP, 1996.

Haslam, Gerald. "The Awakening of American Negro Literature 1619–1900." In *Poetry and Drama.* Vol. 2 of *The Black American Writer.* Ed. C. W. E. Bigsby. Baltimore: Penguin, 1969.

Hayden, Lucy K. "Classical Tidings from the Afric Muse: Phillis Wheatley's Use of Greek and Roman Mythology." *College Language Association Journal* 35.4 (June 1992): 432–47.

Heartman, Charles F. *Phillis Wheatley: A Critical Attempt and a Bibliography of Her Writings.* New York: Printed for the author, 1915.

Henry, Lauren. "Sunshine and Shady Groves: What Blake's 'Little Black Boy' Learned from African Writers." *Blake/An Illustrated Quarterly* 29.1 (Summer 1995): 4–11.

Henson, Robert. "Form and Content of the Puritan Funeral Elegy." *American Literature* 32.1 (1960): 11–27.

Herron, Carolivia. "Early African American Poetry." In *The Columbia History of American Poetry.* Ed. Jay Parini and Brett C. Miller. New York: Columbia UP, 1993. 16–32.

———. "Milton and Afro-American Literature." In *Re-membering Milton: Essays on the Texts and Traditions.* Ed. Mary Nyquist and Margaret W. Ferguson, New York: Methuen, 1988. 278–300.

Hirschfeld, Fritz. *George Washington and Slavery: A Documentary Portrayal.* Columbia: U of Missouri P, 1997.

Hobbes, Thomas. "Answer to Davenant's Preface to *Gondibert.*" In *Critical Essays of the Seventeenth Century.* Ed. J. E. Spingarn. Vol. 2. 1908. Honolulu: UP of the Pacific, 2005.

———. *Leviathan*. 1688. Indianapolis: Hackett, 1994.
Hodges, Norman E. W. *Black History*. New York: Monarch, 1971.
Hoffman, Ronald, and Peter J. Albert, eds. *Women in the Age of the American Revolution*. Charlottesville: U of Virginia P, 1989.
Hoffmeister, Gerhart, ed. *European Romanticism: Literary Cross-Currents, Modes, and Models*. Detroit: Wayne State UP, 1990.
Holder, Kenneth R. "Some Linguistic Aspects of the Heroic Couplet in the Poetry of Phillis Wheatley." Diss., North Texas State U, 1973.
Hornblower, Simon, and Anthony Spawforth, eds. *The Oxford Classical Dictionary*. 3rd ed. New York: Oxford UP, 1996.
Horner, George F., and Robert A. Bain, eds. *Colonial and Federalist American Writing*. New York: Odyssey, 1966.
Horton, James O., and Lois E. Horton. *In Hope of Liberty: Culture, Community, and Protest among Northern Free Blacks, 1700–1860*. New York: Oxford UP, 1997.
Howatson, M. C., ed. *The Oxford Companion to Classical Literature*. 2nd ed. New York: Oxford UP, 1989.
Huddleson, Eugene L. "Matilda's 'On Reading the Poems of Phillis Wheatley, the African Poetess.'" *Early American Literature* 5.3 (1970–71): 57–67.
Hughes, Langston. *Famous American Negroes*. New York: Dodd, Mead, 1954.
Hume, David. "Of National Characters." In *The Philosophical Works of David Hume*. Vol. 3. Boston: Little, Brown, 1854. 217–36.
Hutner, Gordon, ed. *American Literature, American Culture*. New York: Oxford UP, 1999.
Hyatt, Vera Lawrence, and Rex Nettleford, eds. *Race, Discourse, and the Origin of the Americas: A New World View*. Washington, DC: Smithsonian Institution, 1995.
Hyneman, Charles S., and Donald S. Lutz, eds. *American Political Writing during the Founding Era, 1760–1805*. 2 vols. Indianapolis: Liberty Press, 1983.
Imlay, Gilbert. *A Topographical Description of the Western Territory of North America*. 3rd ed. London: Debrett, 1797.
Interpreter's Bible (1952).
Isani, Mukhtar Ali. "The British Reception of Wheatley's *Poems on Various Subjects*." *Journal of Negro History* 66.2 (Summer 1981): 144–49.
———. "The First Proposed Edition of *Poems on Various Subjects* and the Phillis Wheatley Canon." *American Literature* 49.1 (March 1977): 97–103.
———. "'Gambia on My Soul': Africa and the Africans in the Writings of Phillis Wheatley." *MELUS* 6.1 (1979): 64–72.
———. "The Methodist Connection: New Variants of Some Phillis Wheatley Poems." *Early American Literature* 22 (Spring 1987): 108–13.
———. "'On the Death of General Wooster': An Unpublished Poem by Phillis Wheatley." *Modern Philology* 77.3 (February 1980): 206–9.
———. "The Original Version of Wheatley's 'On the Death of Dr. Samuel Marshall.'" *Studies in Black Literature* 7.3 (1976): 20.

---. "Phillis Wheatley and the Elegiac Mode." In *Critical Essays on Phillis Wheatley.* Ed. William H. Robinson. Boston: Hall, 1982.

---. "Wheatley's Departure for London and Her 'Farewell to America.'" *South Atlantic Bulletin* 42.4 (1977): 123–29.

Jackson, Sara Dunlap. "Letters of Phillis Wheatley and Susanna Wheatley." *Journal of Negro History* 57.2 (1972): 211–15.

Jacobson, Edith. *The Self and the Object World.* New York: International Universities, 1964.

Jamison, Angelene. "Analysis of Selected Poetry of Phillis Wheatley." *Journal of Negro Education* 43.3 (1974): 408–16.

Janak, Mindy, and Maurice Duke. "Martha Wadsworth Brewster (fl. 1725–1757)." In *American Writers before 1800: A Biographical and Critical Dictionary.* Ed. James A. Levernier and Douglas R. Wilmes. Westport, CT.: Greenwood, 1983.

Jefferson, Thomas. *Notes on the State of Virginia.* Ed. and intro. Frank Shuffelton. New York: Penguin, 1999.

Jennings, Regina. "African Sun Imagery in the Poetry of Phillis Wheatley." *Pennsylvania English* 22.1–2 (Fall–Spring 2000): 68–76.

Johnson, Charles, and Patricia Smith. *Africans in America: America's Journey through Slavery.* New York: Harcourt Brace, 1998.

Johnson, James Weldon. *The Book of American Poetry.* 2nd ed. New York: Harcourt Brace, 1931.

Jordan, June. "The Difficult Miracle of Black Poetry in America; Or, Something Like a Sonnet for Phillis Wheatley." *Massachusetts Review* 27.2 (Summer 1986): 252–62.

Jordan, Winthrop. *White over Black: American Attitudes toward the Negro, 1550–1812.* Chapel Hill: U of North Carolina P, 1967.

Jung, Carl G. *Aion: Researches Into the Collective Unconscious.* Trans. R. F. C. Hull. Princeton, NJ: Princeton UP, 1968.

---. *Archetypes and the Collective Unconscious.* Trans. R. F. C. Hull. New York: Pantheon, 1959.

---. "On the Relation of Analytical Psychology to Poetry." In *The Portable Jung.* Ed. Joseph Campbell. New York: Viking, 1971.

---. "Psychology and Literature." *The Spirit in Man, Art and Literature.* Trans. R. F. C. Hull. New York: Random House, 1966.

---. *Psychology and Religion: West and East.* Trans. R. F. C. Hull. Princeton, NJ: Princeton UP, 1969.

Kames, Lord, Henry Home. *Elements of Criticism.* 2 Vols. 6th ed. 1785. New York: Garland, 1972.

Kant, Immanuel. *Critique of Aesthetic Judgment.* Trans. James C. Meredith. Oxford: Clarendon, 1911.

---. *Observations on the Feeling of the Beautiful and the Sublime.* Trans. T. Goldthwait. Berkeley: U of California P, 1981.

Kaplan, Sidney. *The Black Presence in the Era of the American Revolution: 1777–1800.* Greenwich, CT: New York Graphic Society, 1973.

Kay, Dennis. *Melodious Tears: The English Funeral Elegy from Spenser to Milton.* Oxford: Clarendon, 1990.
Keats, John. *Complete Poems and Selected Letters.* Ed. Clarence P. Thorpe. New York: Odyssey, 1935.
Kelly, Michael, ed. *Encyclopedia of Aesthetics.* 4 vols. New York: Oxford UP, 1999.
Kendrick, Robert L. "Other Questions: Phillis Wheatley and the Ethics of Interpretation." *Cultural Critique* 38 (Winter 1997–98): 39–64.
———. "Re-Membering America: Phillis Wheatley's Intertextual Epic." *African American Review* 30.1 (1996): 71–88.
Kerber, Linda K. *Women of the Republic.* Chapel Hill: U of North Carolina P, 1980.
King, William. *An Historical Account of the Heathen Gods and Heroes.* London, 1710.
Klinkowitz, Jerome. "Early Writers: Jupiter Hammon, Phillis Wheatley, and Benjamin Banneker." *Black American Writers: Bibliographical Essays.* Ed. M. Thomas Inge, Maurice Duke, Jackson R. Bryer. 2 vols. New York: St. Martins, 1978. 1–20.
Kogel, Renée. *Pierre Charron.* Geneva: Librairie Droz, 1972.
Kors, Alan C., ed. *Encyclopedia of the Enlightenment.* 4 vols. New York: Oxford UP, 2003.
Kovel, Joel. *White Racism: A Psychohistory.* New York: Random House, 1970.
Kuncio, Robert C. "Some Unpublished Poems of Phillis Wheatley." *New England Quarterly* 43 (1970): 287–97.
Lambert, Frank. *Pedlar in Divinity: George Whitefield and the Transatlantic Revivals.* Princeton, NJ: Princeton UP, 1994.
Lan, E. W. *The Manners and Customs of the Modern Egyptians.* London: Everyman's Library, 1954.
Landry, Donna. *The Muses of Resistance: Laboring-Class Women's Poetry in Britain, 1739–1796.* Cambridge: Cambridge UP, 1990.
Lauter, Paul. "Society and the Profession, 1958–83." *PMLA* 99.3 (May 1984): 420.
Leclercq, Jean. *The Love of Learning and the Desire for God.* 2nd ed. New York: Fordham UP, 1974.
Lee, A. Robert. "Selves Subscribed: Early Afro-America and the Signifying of Phillis Wheatley, Jupiter Hammon, Olaudah Equiano and David Walker." In *Making America/Making American Literature.* Ed. A. Robert Lee and W. M. Verhoeven. Amsterdam: Rodopi, 1996. 275–95.
Lehman, David, ed. *The Oxford Book of American Poetry.* New York: Oxford UP, 2006.
Lester, Neal A. "'Not My Mother, Not My Sister, But It's Me, O Lord, Standing . . .': Alice Walker's 'The Child Who Favored Daughter' as Neo-Slave Narrative." *Studies in Short Fiction* 34.3 (Summer 1997): 289–306.
Levernier, James A. "Legacy Profile: Phillis Wheatley." *Legacy* 13.1 (1996): 65–75.

———. "Style as Protest in the Poetry of Phillis Wheatley." *Style* 27.2 (Summer 1993): 172–93.

———. "Wheatley's ON BEING BROUGHT FROM AFRICA TO AMERICA." *Explicator* 40 (Fall 1981): 25–26.

Levernier, James A., and Douglas R. Wilmes, eds. *American Writers before 1800: A Biographical and Critical Dictionary*. 3 vols. Westport, CT: Greenwood, 1983.

Locke, John. *An Essay Concerning Human Understanding*. 4th ed. 2 vols. 1696.

———. *Some Thoughts Concerning Education*. 1693. Menston, Eng.: Scolar, 1970.

———. *Two Treatises of Government*. Ed. Peter Laslett. 2nd ed. Cambridge: Cambridge UP, 1988.

Locke, Mary S. *Anti-Slavery in America: From the Introduction of African Slaves to the Prohibition of the Slave Trade, 1619–1808*. 1901. New York: Peter Smith, 1965.

Logan, Rayford W., and Michael R. Winston, eds. *Dictionary of the American Negro Biography*. New York: Norton, 1982.

Loggins, Vernon. *The Negro Author: His Development in America*. New York: Columbia UP, 1931.

Long, William J. *American Literature*. Boston: Ginn, 1913.

Lossing, Benson. *The Pictorial Field Book of the Revolution*. 2 vols. New York: Harper's, 1855.

Lucas, Paul. *American Odyssey, 1607–1789*. Englewood Cliffs, NJ: Prentice-Hall, 1984.

Makouta-Mboukou, Jean-Pierre. *Black African Literature: An Introduction*. Trans. Alexander Mboukou. Washington, DC: Black Orpheus, 1973.

Malof, Joseph. "The Native Rhythm of English Meters." *Texas Studies in Literature and Language* 5 (1964): 580–94.

Mannix, Daniel P., and Malcolm Cowley. *Black Cargoes: A History of the Atlantic Slave Trade, 1518–1865*. New York: Viking, 1962.

Mason, Julian. "'Ocean': A New Poem by Phillis Wheatley." *Early American Literature* 34 (1999): 78–83.

Mason, Julian, ed. *The Poems of Phillis Wheatley*. Chapel Hill: U of North Carolina P, 1966.

———. *The Poems of Phillis Wheatley*. 2nd ed. Chapel Hill: U of North Carolina P, 1989.

Mather, Cotton. *The Christian Philosopher*. Ed. Winton Solberg. Chicago: U of Chicago P, 2000.

Matson, R. Lynn. "Phillis Wheatley—Soul Sister?" *Phylon* 33.3 (1972): 222–30.

May, Henry F. *The Enlightenment in America*. New York: Oxford UP, 1976.

Mays, Benjamin E. *The Negro's God as Reflected in His Literature*. New York: Russell and Russell, 1938.

McBride, Dwight A. *Impossible Witnesses: Truth, Abolitionism, and Slave Testimony*. New York: New York UP, 2001.

McCalman, Iain, gen. ed. *An Oxford Companion to the Romantic Age, British Culture 1776–1832*. New York: Oxford UP, 1999.

McEvedy, Colin. *The Penguin Atlas of African History*. New York: Penguin, 1980.

McKay, David, and Richard Crawford. *William Billings of Boston: Eighteenth-Century Composer*. Princeton, NJ: Princeton UP, 1975.

McKay, Michelle, and William J. Scheick. "The Other Song in Phillis Wheatley's 'On Imagination.'" *Studies in the Literary Imagination* 27.1 (1994): 71–84.

McKay, Nellie. "Naming the Problem That Led to the Question 'Who Shall Teach African American Literature?'; or, Are We Ready to Disband the Wheatley Court?" *PMLA* 113.3 (May 1998): 359–69.

McMichael, George, gen. ed. *Anthology of American Literature*. Vol. 1. New York: Macmillan, 1974.

McWhorter, John H. *Losing the Race: Self-Sabotage in Black America*. New York: Free Press, 2000.

Meltzer, Milton. *Slavery: A World History*. 2 vols. in one. New York: Da Capo, 1993.

Miller, Perry. *The New England Mind: From Colony to Province*. Boston: Beacon, 1953.

Miller, Perry, and Thomas H. Johnson, eds. *The Puritans: A Source Book of Their Writings*. Rev. ed. 2 vols. New York: Harper and Row, 1963.

Mintz, Steven, ed. *African American Voices: The Life Cycle of Slavery*. Rev. ed. New York: Brandywine, 1996.

Mollien, G. *Travels in Africa To the Sources of the Senegal and Gambia*. London: Sir Richard Phillips, 1825.

Molho, Anthony and Gordon S. Wood, eds. *Imagined Histories: American Historians Interpret the Past*. Princeton, NJ: Princeton UP, 1998.

Monk, Samuel Holt. "'A Grace Beyond the Reach of Art.'" *Journal of the History of Ideas* 5.2 (1944): 131–50.

———. *The Sublime: A Study of Critical Theories in XVIII-Century England*. 2nd ed. Ann Arbor: U of Michigan P, 1960.

Montesquieu, Baron de. *The Spirit of the Laws*. Trans. Thomas Nugent. New York: Hafner, 1949.

Morris, David B. *The Religious Sublime: Christian Poetry and Critical Tradition in Eighteenth-Century England*. Lexington: U of Kentucky P, 1972.

Morrison, Toni. *Playing in the Dark: Whiteness and the Literary Imagination*. Cambridge: Harvard UP, 1992.

Mossell, N. F. *The Work of the Afro-American Woman*. Joanne Braxton, "Introduction." New York: Oxford UP, 1988.

Mulford, Carla, General Ed. *Early American Writings*. New York: Oxford UP, 2002.

Munsinger, Harry. *Fundamentals of Child Development*. 2nd ed. New York: Holt, Reinhart, and Winston, 1975.

Munzing, Helen. "Phillis Wheatley's Textual Hybridity." In *Multiculturalism and the American Self*. Ed. William Boelhower and Alfred Horning. Heidelberg: Universitätsverlag C. Winter, 2000. 51–78.

Murdock, Kenneth B. "Byles, Mather." *DAB* (1927).

Nelson, Dana D. *The Word in Black and White: Reading "Race" in American Literature, 1638–1876.* New York: Oxford UP, 1992.

New Interpreter's Bible (1994).

Nielsen, A. L. "Patterns of Subversion in the Works of Phillis Wheatley and Jupiter Hammon." *The Western Journal of Black Studies.* 6.4 (Winter 1982): 212–19.

Nott, Walt. "From 'uncultivated Barbarian' to 'Poetic Genius': The Public Presence of Phillis Wheatley." *MELUS* 18.3 (Fall 1993): 21–32.

Nygren, Anders. *Agape and Eros.* London: S.P.C.K., 1953.

———. "Eros and Agape." In *A Handbook of Christian Theology.* Ed. Marvin Halverson and Arthur A. Cohen. New York: World, 1958.

Oddell, Margaretta M. "Memoir." In *Memoir and Poems of Phillis Wheatley: A Native African and a Slave. Also, Poems by a Slave.* 3rd ed. 1838. Boston: Mnemosyne, 1969.

Ogude, S.E. *Genius in Bondage: A Study of the Origins of African Literature in English.* Ile–Ife, Nigeria: U of Ife P, 1983.

———. "Slavery and the African Imagination: A Critical Perspective." *World Literature Today: A Literary Quarterly of the University of Oklahoma* 55.1 (1981): 21–25.

Ogunyemi, Chikweyne Okonjo. "Phillis Wheatley: The Modest Beginning." *Studies in Black Literature* 7.3 (1976): 16–19.

Okpewho, Isidore. *The Epic of Africa: Toward a Poetics of Oral Performance.* New York: Columbia UP, 1979.

O'Neale, Sondra. *Jupiter Hammon and the Biblical Beginnings of African-American Literature.* Metuchen, NJ: Scarecrow, 1993.

———. "Phillis Wheatley." *American Colonial Writers, 1735–1781.* Ed. Emory Elliot. Gale Research, 1984.

———. "A Slave's Subtle War: Phillis Wheatley's Use of Biblical Myth and Symbol." *Early American Literature* 21.2 (Fall 1986): 144–65.

Orban, Katalin. "Dominant and Submerged Discourses in *The Life of Olandah Equiano* (or Gustavus Vassa?)." *African American Review* 27.4 (1993): 655–64.

Parks, Carole A. "Phillis Wheatley Comes Home." *Black World* 23.4 (1974): 92–97.

Perkins, William. *A Treatise of Mans Imaginations, Shewing His Naturall Euill Thoughts: His Want of Good Thoughts: The Way to Reforme Them.* Cambridge, England: John Legat, 1607.

Peterson, Merrill D. "Jefferson, Thomas." *American National Biography.* Ed. John A. Garraty and Mark C. Carnes. Vol. 11. New York: Oxford UP, 1999.

Piersen, William D. *Black Yankees: The Development of an Afro-American Subculture in Eighteenth-Century New England.* Amherst: U of Massachusetts P, 1988.

Pietas et Gratulatio (anonymous). Boston: J. Green and J. Russell, 1761.

Pope, Alexander. *The Poetry and Prose of Alexander Pope.* Ed. Aubrey Williams. New York: Houghton Mifflin, 1969.

Porter, Dorothy. "Historical and Bibliographical Data of Phillis Wheatley's Publications." *Jackson State Review* 6.1 (1974): 54–60.

———. *North American Negro Poets*. Hattiesburg, MS: Brook Farm, 1945.

Porter, Dorothy Burnett, ed. *Early Negro Writing, 1760–1837*. Baltimore: Black Classic, 1997.

Potts, Abbie F. *The Elegiac Mode: Poetic Form in Wordsworth and Other Elegists*. Ithaca, NY: Cornell UP, 1967.

Pourrat, Pierre. *Christian Spirituality*. Vol. 1. London: Burns, Oats, and Washborne, 1922.

Price, Martin. *To the Palace of Wisdom: Studies in Order and Energy from Dryden to Blake*. Carbondale: Southern Illinois UP, 1964.

Prince, Dorothy Mains. "Phillis Wheatley: The Duplicity of Freedom." *Maryland Humanities* 78 (Summer 2001): 21–24.

Quarles, Benjamin. "A Phillis Wheatley Letter." *Journal of Negro History* 34 (October 1949): 462–66.

Quinn, Charles A. *Mandingo Kingdoms: Traditionalism, Islam, and European Expansion*. Evanston, IN: Northwestern UP, 1972.

Rampersad, Arnold. *The Oxford Anthology of African-American Poetry*. New York: Oxford UP, 2000.

Rankine, Patrice. *Ulysses in Black: Ralph Ellison, Classicism, and African American Literature*. Madison, WI: U of Wisconsin P, 2006.

Redding, J. Saunders. *To Make a Poet Black*. Chapel Hill: U of North Carolina P, 1939.

———. "Wheatley, Phillis." *Dictionary of the American Negro Biography*. Ed. Rayford W. Logan and Michael R. Winston. New York: Norton, 1982.

Reinhold, Meyer. *Classica Americana: The Greek and Roman Heritage in the United States*. Detroit: Wayne State UP, 1984.

Reising, Russell J. *Loose Ends: Closure and Crisis in the American Social Text*. Duke UP, 1996.

———. "Trafficking in White: Phillis Wheatley's Semiotics of Radical Representation." *Genre* 22.3 (Fall 1989): 231–61.

Renfro, G. Herbert, ed. *Life and Works of Phillis Wheatley*. 1916.Miami, FL: Mnemosyne , 1969.

Reuben, Paul P. "Chapter 2: Early American Literature: 1700–1800—Phillis Wheatley (1753–1784)." *PAL: Perspectives in American Literature—A Research and Reference Guide*. August 26, 2002 < http://www.csustan.edu/english/reuben/pal/chap2/wheatley.html>.

Reynolds, Sir Joshua. *Discourses on Art*. Ed. Robert R. Wark. San Marino, CA: Huntington Library, 1959.

Rice, Eugene F., Jr. *The Renaissance Idea of Wisdom*. Cambridge, MA: Harvard UP, 1958.

Rice, Grantland S. *The Transformation of Authorship in America*. Chicago: U of Chicago P, 1997.

Richard, Carl J. *The Founders and the Classics: Greece, Rome and the American Enlightenment*. Cambridge, MA: Harvard UP, 1994.

Richards, Phillip M. "Phillis Wheatley and Literary Americanization." *American Quarterly* 44.2 (June 1992): 163–91.

———. "Phillis Wheatley, Americanization, the Sublime, and the Romance of America." *Style* 27.2 (Summer 1993): 194–221.

———. "Phillis Wheatley's Craft as Reflected in Her Revised Elegies." *Journal of Negro Education* 47 (Fall 1978): 402–13.

Richmond, Merle A. *Bid the Vassal Soar: Interpretive Essays on the Life and Poetry of Phillis Wheatley and George Moses Horton.* Washington, DC: Howard UP, 1974.

Riesman, Paul. *Freedom in Fulani Social Life: An Introspective Ethnography.* Chicago: U of Chicago P, 1977.

Rigsby, Gregory. "From and Content in Phillis Wheatley's Elegies." *College Language Association Journal* 19.2 (1975): 248–57.

Rinaldi, Ann. *Hang a Thousand Trees with Ribbons: The Story of Phillis Wheatley.* San Diego: Harcourt, 1996.

Robinson, William H. *Black New England Letters: The Uses of Writing in Black New England.* Boston: Trustees of the Public Library of the City of Boston, 1977.

———. *Early Black American Poets: Selections with Biographical and Critical Introductions.* Dubuque, IA: Wm. C. Brown, 1969.

———. *Phillis Wheatley: A Bio-Bibliography.* Boston: Hall, 1981.

———. "Phillis Wheatley: Colonial Quandary." *College Language Association Journal* 9.1 (1965): 25–38.

———. *Phillis Wheatley in the Black American Beginnings.* Detroit: Broadside, 1975.

———. *Phillis Wheatley and Her Writings.* New York: Garland, 1984.

Robinson, William, ed. *Critical Essays on Phillis Wheatley.* Boston: Hall, 1982.

Rogal, Samuel. "Phillis Wheatley's Methodist Connection." *Black American Literature Forum* 21 (Spring–Summer 1987): 85–95.

Rohrbach, Augusta. "Violence and the Visual: The Phenomenology of Vision and Racial Stereotyping." *International Studies in Philosophy* 23 (1994): 71–82.

Ruland, Richard, ed. *The Native Muse: Theories of American Literature from Bradford to Whitman.* New York: Dutton, 1972.

Rush, Benjamin. "An Address . . . Upon Slave-Keeping." *From the Puritans to Abraham Lincoln.* Vol. 1 of *Racial Thought in America.* Louis Ruchames. Amherst: U of Massachusetts P, 1969.

Sabin, Joseph, gen. ed. *A Dictionary of Books Relating to America from Its Discovery to the Present Time.* New York: Bibliographical Society of America, 1936.

Sacks, Peter M. *The English Elegy: Studies in the Genre from Spenser to Yeats.* Baltimore: Johns Hopkins UP, 1985.

Salzman, Jack, David L. Smith, and Cornel West, eds. *Encyclopedia of African-American Culture and History.* 5 vols. New York: Macmillan, 1996.

Samkutty, E. C. "The Promised Land in Afro-American Poetic Vision." *CLA Journal* 35.4 (June 1992): 422–31. (Includes discussion of Wheatley)

Scheick, William J. *Authority and Female Authorship in Colonial America.* Lexington: UP of Kentucky, 1998.
———. "Phillis Wheatley and Oliver Goldsmith: A Fugitive Satire." *Early American Literature* 19.1 (1984): 82–84.
———. "Phillis Wheatley's Appropriation of Isaiah." *Early American Literature* 27.2 (1992): 135–40.
———. "Subjection and Prophecy in Phillis Wheatley's Verse Paraphrases of Scripture." *College Literature* 22 (1995): 122–31.
Schomburg, Arthur H. "Introduction." *Phillis Wheatley: Poems and Letters.* Ed. Charles F. Heartman. 1915. Miami, FL: Mnemosyne, 1969.
Scruggs, Charles. "Phillis Wheatley, the Aesthetic, and the Form of Life." *Studies in Eighteenth-Century Culture* 26. Ed. Syndy M. Conger and Julie C. Hayes. Baltimore: Johns Hopkins UP, 1998.
———. "Phillis Wheatley and the Poetical Legacy of Eighteenth Century England." *Studies in Eighteenth-Century Culture* 10 (1981): 279–95.
Scully, Malcome G. "Endowment Chief Assails State of Humanities on College Campuses." *Chronicle of Higher Education* 29.11 (November 28, 1984): 16, col. 2.
Seccombe, Joseph. "Business and Diversion Inoffensive to God; and Necessary for the Comfort and Support of Human Society . . . in the Fishing Season." Boston: Kneeland, 1743.
———. *A Specimen of the Harmony of Wisdom and Felicity.* Boston, 1743.
———. *Some Occasional Thoughts on the Influence of the Spirit with Seasonable Cautions against Mistakes and Abuses.* Boston, 1742.
Seeber, Edward Derbyshire. *Anti-Slavery Opinion in France during the Second Half of the Eighteenth Century.* Baltimore: Johns Hopkins UP, 1937; New York: Greenwood, 1969.
Selinger, Eric M. "'Too Pathetic, Too Pitiable': Emerson's Lessons in Love's Philosophy." *ESQ (Emerson Society Quarterly)* 40.2 (1994): 139–82.
Shields, John C. *The American Aeneas: Classical Origins of the American Self.* Knoxville, TN: U of Tennessee P, 2001.
———. "Phillis Wheatley." In *African American Writers.* Ed. Valerie Smith, Lea Baechler, and A. Walton Litz. New York: Charles Scribner's Sons, 1991. 472–91.
———. "Phillis Wheatley." *Black Women in America: An Historical Encyclopedia.* Ed. Darlene Clark Hine. Vol. 2. Brooklyn, NY: Carlson, 1993. 1251–55.
———. "Phillis Wheatley." In *Notable Black American Women.* Ed. Jessie Carney Smith. Detroit: Gale Research, 1243–48. Reprinted in *Epic Lives: 100 Black Women Who Made a Difference.* Ed. Jessie Carney Smith. Detroit: Visible Ink, 1993. 587–94, 632.
———. "Phillis Wheatley and Mather Byles: A Study in Literary Relationship." *College Literature* 23 (June 1980): 377–90.
———. "Phillis Wheatley's Subversive Pastoral." *Eighteenth-Century Studies* 27.4 (Summer 1994): 631–47.
Shields, John C, ed. *The Collected Works of Phillis Wheatley.* New York: Oxford UP, 1988.

Shields, John C., guest ed. Spec issue of *African-American Poetics, Style* 27.2 (Summer 1993). Contains four essays on Phillis Wheatley as follows:
> Kendrick, Robert L. "Snatching a Laurel, Wearing a Mask: Phillis Wheatley's Literary Nationalism and the Problem of Style." 222–51.
> Levernier, James A., Jr. "Style as Protest in the Poetry of Phillis Wheatley." 172–93.
> Richards, Phillip M. "Phillis Wheatley, Americanization, the Sublime, and the Romance of America." 194–221.
> Shields, John C. "Phillis Wheatley's Subversion of Classical Stylistics." 252–70.

Shiner, Carol, and Joel Haefner, eds. *Re-Visioning Romanticism*. Philadelphia: U of Pennsylvania P, 1994.

Shipton, Clifford. *Sibley's Biographical Sketches of Those Who Attended Harvard College*. Vol. 11. *1741–1745*. Cambridge, MA: Charles William Sever, University Bookstore, 1960.

Shuffelton, Frank. "Four Letters by Phillis Wheatley." *Early American Literature* 8.3 (Winter 1974): 257–71.

———. "On Her Own Footing: Phillis Wheatley in Freedom." In *Genius in Bondage: Literature of the Early Black Atlantic*. Ed. Vincent Carretta and Philip Gould. Lexington: UP of Kentucky, 2001.

———. "Phillis Wheatley, the Aesthetic, and the Form of Life." *Studies in Eighteenth-Century Culture* 26 (1998): 73–85.

Sibley, Agnes M. *Alexander Pope's Prestige in America 1785–1835*. New York: Columbia UP, 1949.

Silverman, Kenneth, ed. *Colonial American Poetry*. New York: Hafner, 1968.

———. *A Cultural History of the American Revolution*. New York: Crowell, 1976.

———. "Four New Letters by Phillis Wheatley." *Early American Literature* 8.3 (1974): 255–71.

———. *The Life and Times of Cotton Mather*. New York: Columbia UP, 1984.

Silvers, Anita. "Pure Historicism and the Heritage of Hero(in)es: Who Grows In Phillis Wheatley's Garden?" *Journal of Aesthetics and Art Criticism* 51 (1993): 475–82.

Smith, Cynthia J. "'To Maecenas': Phillis Wheatley's Invocation of an Idealized Reader." *Black American Literature Forum* 23.3 (Fall 1989): 579–92.

Smith, Eleanor. "Phillis Wheatley: A Black Perspective." *Journal of Negro Education* 43.3 (1974): 401–7.

Smith, Valerie, ed. *African American Writers*. 2nd ed. New York: Gale, 2001.

Spiller, Robert E., gen. ed. *Literary History of the United States: Bibliography*. 4th ed. New York: Macmillan, 1974.

Stedman, John C. *A Narrative of a Five Years' Expedition against the Revolted Negroes of Surinam*. 2 vols. London: J. J. Johnson, 1796.

Steele, Thomas J., S.J. "The Figure of Columbia: Phillis Wheatley Plus George Washington." *New England Quarterly* 54.2 (June 1981): 264–66.

Taylor, Edward. *The Poems of Edward Taylor*. Ed. Donald E. Stanford. New Haven, CT: Yale UP, 1960.

Thomas, Hugh. *The Slave Trade: The Story of the Atlantic Slave Trade, 1440–1870*. New York: Simon and Schuster, 1997.

Thomson, James. *James Thomson: Poetical Works.* Ed. J. Logie Robertson. London: Oxford UP, 1908.
Trimingham, J. Spencer. *Islam in West Africa.* London: Oxford UP, 1959.
Turner, Richard Brent. *Islam in the African-American Experience.* Bloomington: Indiana UP, 1997.
Tuveson, Ernest. *The Imagination as a Means of Grace: Locke and the Aesthetics of Romanticism.* Berkeley: U of California P, 1960.
Tyler, Moses Coit. *History of American Literature During the Colonial Time, 1607–1765.* 2 vols. 1878. Reprinted as one volume. Ithaca, NY: Cornell UP, 1950.
———. *Literary History of the American Revolution.* 2 vols. 1897. Reprinted as one volume. New York: Burt Franklin, 1970.
Tylor, Sir Edward B. *Religion in Primitive Culture.* New York: Harper and Row, 1958.
Underhill, Evelyn. *Mysticism: A Study in the Nature and Development of Man's Spiritual Consciousness.* New York: Dutton, 1961.
Vendler, Helen. *Poems, Poets, Poetry: An Introduction and Anthology.* 2nd ed. New York: Bedford/St. Martin's, 2002.
von Franz, M.-L. "The Process of Individuation." In *Man and His Symbols.* Ed. Carl G. Jung. Garden City, NY: Doubleday, 1964.
Walker, Alice. "In Search of Our Mother's Gardens: Honoring the Creativity of the Black Woman." *Jackson State Review* 6.1 (1974): 44–53.
Walker, Cheryl. *The Nightingale's Burden: Women Poets and American Culture before 1900.* Bloomington: Indiana UP, 1982.
Walker, Jeffrey B. *The Devil Undone: The Life of Benjamin Church (1734–1778) to Which Is Added, an Edition of His Complete Poetry.* Diss., Auburn University, 1977.
Warren, Kenneth W. "Phillis Wheatley's Vision." *The New Yorker.* 17–24 Feb. 2003: 18.
Watson, Marsha. "A Classic Case: Phillis Wheatley and Her Poetry." *Early American Literature* 31.2 (1996): 103–33.
Wellek, Rene. "Classicism in Literature." *Dictionary of the History of Ideas.* Ed. Philip P. Wiener. New York: Charles Scribner's Sons, 1973.
Whitlow, Roger. *Black American Literature: A Critical History.* Totowa, NJ: Littlefield, Adams, 1973.
Wiersbe, Warren W. "Imagination: The Preacher's Neglected Ally." *Leadership* 4.2 (Spring 1983): 22–27.
Wilcox, Kirstin. "The Body into Print: Marketing Phillis Wheatley." *American Literature* 71.1 (March 1999): 1–29.
Willcox, William B., ed. *The Papers of Benjamin Franklin.* 20: 291–93.
Wilson, Gold Refined. "The Religion of the American Negro Slave: How Attitude toward Life and Death." *Journal of Negro History* 8.1 (1923): 41–71.
Winterer, Caroline. *The Culture of Classicism: Ancient Greece and Rome in American Intellectual Life, 1780–1910.* Baltimore: Johns Hopkins UP, 2002.

Witham, W. Tasker. *Living American Literature*. Book 1: *Panorama of American Literature*. New York: Stephen Daye, 1947.
Wood, Marcus. *The Poetry of Slavery: An Anglo-American Anthology, 1764–1865*. New York: Oxford UP, 2003.
Woods, Richard, ed. *Understanding Mysticism*. Garden City, NY: Doubleday, 1980.
Woodson, Carter G., and Charles H. Wesley. *The Negro in Our History*. 10th ed. Washington, DC: Associated, 1962.
Wright, Richard. "Negro Literature in the United States." *White Man, Listen!* New York: Harper Perennial, 1995. 71–110.
Wright, Ruth. *The Poems of Phillis Wheatley*. Philadelphia: Wrights, 1930.
Yellin, Jean Fagan. *The Intricate Knot: Black Figures in American Literature, 1776–1863*. New York: New York UP, 1972.
Yolton, John W., ed. *The Blackwell Companion to the Enlightenment*. Oxford: Blackwell, 1991.
Young, Melissa. *The Fulani Peoples of Burkina Faso and the Republic of Niger*. 1999. <http://www.byhisgrace.com/Fulani/profile.htm> 1/21/2001.
Zafar, Rafia. *We Wear the Mask: African Americans Write American Literature, 1760–1870*. New York: Columbia UP, 1997.

Index

Abrams, M. H., 22, 194n2
Adamic myth, 93–94
Adams, Abigail, 33
Adams, John (poet), 205n3
Adams, John (president), 33
Adanson, Michel, 102–3, 200
Addison, Joseph, 151, 155, 157–58, 160, 189
"Address to the Atheist, An," 79, 129–32, 186
"Address to the Deist, An," 79, 129, 132, 186
Adler, Mortimer J., 27, 30, 32, 35, 39, 40, 187–88, 195n8–9, 195n12
Aeneid, Vergil, 93, 202n2
aestheticism, 148, 151, 156, 161–63
African Americans: Afro-British, 91,92; Black Aesthetic, 9, 12; civil rights; 62–63; enslavement of (*see* African American enslavement); prejudices against, 1–4, 6, 44, 47–48, 50, 54–55, 108, 147, 180–81
African American enslavement, 2–4, 16–17, 22–23, 26–28, 31–36, 38–39, 41, 43–48, 50, 52–54, 66, 72, 81, 83, 94, 99, 104, 107, 130, 181, 187
African literature and the arts, 7, 19, 30, 46–47, 49, 58–62, 102–3, 106, 109–10, 112–13, 119, 121, 150, 185; elegy, 122; epics, 118, 120, 122, 136–37
Akenside, Mark, 22, 74, 86, 126, 205n3, 207n14
Akers, Charles W., 164, 197n4

Allen, William G., 54
American Aeneas, The, John C. Shields, 5, 12, 18, 93, 142, 179
Andrews, John, 7, 67
Animism, 77, 85, 100–101, 125, 130, 132, 148, 180, 189, 199n7
Applegate, Ann, 66
Ariosto, Ludovico, 161
Aristotle, 155–56
Ars Poetica, Horace, 125, 150
atheism, 24, 130
Attucks, Crispus, 34, 65, 95–96
Augustine, 133–34, 143, 145, 148, 155, 175, 189, 202n1. *See also meditatio*

Bacon, Francis, 156
Baker, Houston, 31, 39, 44, 195n17, 196n30
Banneker, Benjamin, 3, 54
Barzun, Jacques, 5
Belcher, Stephen, 118–19, 201n18
Bellum Civile, Lucan, 169
Bennett, A. L., 205n6
Berlin, Ira, 41
Biebuyck, Daniel P., 118, 120, 201n18
Billings, William, 126, 155, 162, 166–69, 182, 190; *New-England Psalm-Singer*, 126–27, 166
Bloom, Harold, 82–83
Blumenbach, Johann F., 20, 51–52
Bontemps, Arna, 61
Bowdoin, James, 30
Bradstreet, Anne, 5, 15, 133
Brawley, Benjamin, 59
breath-groups, 110

Brewster, Martha, 7, 15
Brown, Hallie Quinn, 58
Brown, Marshall, 19
Brown, Sterling, 59, 61
Burke, Edmund, 126, 128, 151, 155, 157–59
Burnet, Thomas, 126, 140–41, 189
Burroughs, Margaret G., 65
Byles, Mather, 13, 19, 30, 62, 74, 82, 127–28, 141, 146, 149, 154–56, 162, 182, 190, 202n20, 202n3, 205n6, 206n8, 207n10–12; and Wheatley, 168–80; "The Almighty Conqueror," 177; "Bombastic and Grubstreet Style: A Satire," 176; "The Conflagration," 141; "Eternity," 172; "Goliath's Defeat," 169; "An Hymn to Christ," 175; "Hymn at Sea," 170; "New England Hymn," 169, 172; *Poems on Several Occasions*, 82, 128, 169, 172, 175, 177–78, 180; "To a Friend on the Death of a Relative," 171; "To an Ingenious Young Gentleman," 170, 174, 202n3, 207n11; "To Pictorio, On the Sight of His Pictures," 170, 172, 176; "Written in Milton's *Paradise Lost*," 170, 177

caesura, 110, 112, 201n15
Callimachus, 170
Calvinism, 140, 153, 173
Carretta, Vincent, 74, 91

Characteristics, Earl of
   Shaftsbury, 125
Charron, Pierre, 138–41,
   143–45, 155–58, 162, 176,
   182, 189
Chauncy, Charles, 22, 30,
   155, 162–63
Christian Philosopher, Cotton
   Mather, 140
Christianity, 10–13, 15–16,
   23, 34–37, 40, 50, 77–79,
   92–95, 101, 106–9, 114,
   119, 125, 129–32, 134–38,
   140, 142–43, 145–48,
   153–54, 170, 175, 178,
   180–82, 189, 194n10,
   201n17, 202n1; Congre-
   gationalism, 2, 4, 11, 15,
   17, 21, 24, 35, 82, 127, 129,
   132, 189, 207n9, 205n6
Church, Benjamin, 114–16,
   122, 126
Church, R. J. Harrison,
   198–99n4
Clarke, Mary T., 133
Clarkson, Thomas, 20, 51–52, 63
Classicism, American, 12–13,
   15, 18–19, 93, 142
Classicism, ancient, 12, 18,
   36–37, 48, 91, 93, 98,
   119–20, 133, 136–37, 191,
   157, 172, 177–78, 194n2
Coleridge, Samuel Taylor,
   20, 52
Collins, Terence, 22, 64
Collins, William, 22, 125
Colonial America, 4–5,
   12–13, 22–23, 28, 30, 33,
   38, 49, 60, 65, 74, 88, 96,
   104, 114–15, 126, 128,
   162, 187–88, 201n17,
   202n20, 206n9, 207n12
Common Sense, Thomas
   Paine, 73
Cooper, Samuel, 8, 11, 92,
   121–22, 126, 129, 140–41,
   147, 154–55, 162–67, 182,
   190, 203n3, 205n5
Coriello, Peter, 89, 92–94
Cunliffe, Marcus, 193n1

Dante, 174
Dathorne, O. R., 104, 105–6,
   110, 112, 118, 122,
   200n10, 202n19–20
Davis, Arthur P., 10, 61–62,
   64, 96

De Trinitate, Augustine, 133,
   145, 202n1
de Vattel, Emmerick, 126
Dennis, John, 126, 151,
   155–58, 189
Divine Transubstantiation,
   42, 92
Donne, John, 133
Douglass, Fredrick, 38, 53
Dryden, John, 18, 155–57
DuBois, W. E. B., 43–44,
   61, 88
Duff, William, 126, 155,
   161–62, 205n3
Dunbar, Paul Lawrence,
   46–47
Dunlap, Jane, 6, 15, 194n5–6

eclogues, 91, 150, 179
Eclogues, Vergil, 150, 179
echo device, 120
ecphonesis, 47
Edwards, Jonathan, 21–22,
   139–40, 152–53, 161–62,
   180, 182, 203n2
elegiac form, 13, 19, 20–21,
   24, 29, 31, 37, 67, 100,
   114–17, 121, 169, 188,
   201n17, 202n20
elegiac mode, 18, 20–21,
   85, 165
elegiac praxis, 13, 21
elegy(ies), 6, 8, 10–11, 13,
   16, 19, 21, 24, 29, 31,
   37, 56, 67, 74, 81–83,
   94–95, 100, 104, 114–17,
   120–23, 128–29, 139,
   146–47, 164–65, 167,
   169–72, 188, 201n10,
   202n20, 202n3, 204n3,
   205n3, 205n6
"Elegy to . . . the Learned Dr.
   Samuel Cooper," 8, 11,
   147, 166–67
"Elegy on Leaving——,
   An," 147
Eliade, Mircea, 101
Elliott, Emory, 23, 38, 185,
   190, 195n6
Emerson, Ralph Waldo, 162
encomium(ia), 49–50, 115,
Engell, James, 156, 161,
   162–63, 203n3
Enlightenment, 17, 22–23, 38,
   81, 102, 142, 186,
enlightenment, moderate,
   18, 22–23

Ennis, Daniel J., 89–91
epic, 19, 36, 45, 80, 88, 104,
   117–20, 122, 136–37,
   149–50,
   169–70, 179, 188,
   201n18, 202n19
epic simile, 50
epitaph, 128, 171
"Epithalamium to
   Mrs. H——," 29
epyllion(ia), 36, 88, 104, 118–
   20, 136, 142, 170, 179–80
Equiano, Olaudah, 9, 65, 92
Erkkila, Betsy, 89–90, 94
*Essay Concerning Human
   Understanding*, John
   Locke, 126, 152
Essay on Man, Alexander
   Pope, 155

fancy, 21, 52, 58, 80, 85–88,
   144, 150, 152–53,
   155–57, 159, 162, 168,
   174, 176, 182, 203n1,
   203–5n3
"Farewell to America, A," 25
Ferguson, Robert A., 16
Finnegan, Ruth, 104, 106,
   110, 112, 114, 115,
   117–18, 121, 199n8,
   200n10, 201n18
Fitch, Timothy, 98
Flexner, James T., 4
Foster, Frances Smith, 73
Franklin, Benjamin, 49, 57,
   90, 92, 142
Franklin, John Hope, 26, 32,
   34, 195n7, 196n19
freedom. *See* liberation
   poetics
Freneau, Philip, 5, 162, 203n3
Frye, Northrop, 112, 201n15
Fulani or Fula, 100–103,
   119, 121, 182–83, 199n6,
   199–200n8, 201–2n18
"Funeral Poem on the Death
   of C.E. an Infant of
   Twelve Months, An,"
   165
Fussell, Paul, 112, 201n15

Gambia, 20, 31, 82, 85,
   97–100, 102–4, 198–99n4
Garrison, William Lloyd, 53
Gates, Henry Louis, Jr., 2, 8,
   71, 81

Genesis, 143, 151; 1:3, 173; 6:5, 153–54; 8:21, 153–54
Geneva Bible, 93, 153–54
George II, 163–64
George III, 55, 163–64, 166
Gérard, Albert S., 199n8
Gibson, Donald B., 10–12
Giddings, Paula, 66
Gilroy, Paul, 7–8, 31, 41, 84, 100
Goethe, Johann Wolfgang von, 20
"Goliath of Gath," 36–37, 73, 80, 88, 117–19, 142, 160, 169–70, 179
Graham, Shirley, 61
Great Awakening, 6, 94, 114, 139, 162, 206n9
Greene, Lorenzo, 32, 35–36, 38, 196n19–21, 196n24, 196n28
Grégoire, Henri, 52–53

Hamilton, Edith, 86
Hammon, Jupiter, 47, 50, 72, 76, 81, 108, 134, 137, 148, 189; "An Address to Miss Phillis Wheatley, Ethiopian Poetess," 50, 131
Hancock, John, 30, 90, 126
Harlem Renaissance, 58, 62–63
Harmon, William, 5, 194n2, 200n11
Harper, Francis, 47
Harries, Lyndon, 109, 117, 118, 201n18
Harvard University, 82, 127–28, 139
Haslam, Gerald, 63
Hastings, Selina, Countess of Huntingdon, 29, 67, 116–17, 139, 146–47, 180
Heartman, Charles F., 57
henotheism(stic), 118, 132, 136
Henson, Robert, 201n17, 205n6
Herbert, George, 133
Hesiod, 137
heterocosm, 20, 52, 80–81, 87, 137, 158, 161, 187
Hobbes, Thomas, 88, 151–52, 155–56
Hoffmeister, Gerhart, 20

Holy Sonnets, John Donne, 133
Holder, Kenneth R., 66, 200n12
Holman, C. Hugh, 5, 194n2, 200n11
Homer, 54, 83, 150, 179
Horace, 53, 149, 151, 154
Horatian ode, 45, 150, 177, 203n1,
Horton, George Moses, 47, 53–54, 63, 75, 81, 199n5
Hughes, Langston, 61
Hume, David, 48, 81
Hutchinson, Thomas, 30, 127–28
Hutner, Gordon, 81
hymn, 19, 25, 51–52, 109–10, 113–14, 166, 169–72, 175, 177
"Hymn to the Evening," 25, 51, 109, 171
"Hymn to Humanity," 25, 113
"Hymn to the Morning," 25, 51–52, 109, 166, 171
hymn stanza, 169, 171

Iliad, 125, 149, 169, 178
imagination, 1, 3, 9–10, 17–19, 21–23, 38–40, 52, 80, 85–87, 93, 118, 127, 133–34, 138, 139–40, 142, 150, 152–65, 168–69, 175–77, 180, 182, 188, 190, 200n11, 203n1–3, 206n8
Imlay, Gilbert, 20, 51–52, 63
Isaiah, 88, 136–37; 25:6, 88; 63, 132
"Isaiah lxiii. 1–8," 25, 135–37, 150, 173
Isani, Mukhtar Ali, 6, 10, 48, 73, 193n2, 195n14, 201n14
Islam, 77, 85, 100–102, 125, 130, 132, 138, 148, 180–81, 189, 195n16, 199n6, 201n18

Jefferson, Thomas, 1–4, 7, 9, 26, 41, 48–52, 54–56, 60, 62, 81, 83, 92–94, 191, 193n1, 197n2, 198n3
Jerome, 154
Johnson, James Weldon, 46–47, 60, 66–67

Jones, John Paul, 49, 89–90
Jordan, June, 30–31, 58, 195n16
Jordan, Winthrop, 27, 195n11, 196n21

Kames, Henry Home, Lord, 21–22, 88, 126, 151, 155, 157, 160, 165, 189
Kant, Immanuel, 81, 151, 158–60
Kaplan, Sidney, 65
Keats, John, 159
Kerber, Linda, 24
King James Version (of the Bible), 82, 98, 125, 135–36, 153–54, 172–73
King, William, 137–38, 146

Landry, Donna, 30–31, 58, 195n16
Lauter, Paul, 8
Law of Nations, The, Emmerick de Vattel, 126
Leclercq Jean, 202n1
Levernier, James A., 73, 107, 194n8
Leviathan, Thomas Hobbes, 126, 151–12,
liberation poetics, 3, 5, 9–11, 13, 15, 18–23, 25–28, 32–33, 38–41, 44, 79, 83, 87, 89–90, 94, 101, 108, 126, 134–35, 137, 144, 148–49, 151, 157, 159, 164, 168, 175–76, 179, 181, 185–88, 190
"Liberty and Peace," 33, 96, 105, 113, 164
Locke, John, 21, 141, 151–53, 156, 164, 182
Loggins, Vernon, 59
Long, William J., 56–57, 58, 60
Longinus, 157, 205n7
Lucan, 169
Lucas, Paul, 28, 195n13
lyric, 19–20, 106–7, 109–10, 150, 166, 168, 200n11,

Makouta-Mboukou, Jean-Pierre, 106, 118
Malof, Joseph, 112, 201n15
Marshal, Samuel, 120, 146
Marvel, Andrew, 133

Mason, Julian, 54, 62, 74, 82–83, 87, 98, 197n3, 200n11
Mather, Cotton, 19, 82, 127, 141–42, 207n12
Matson, R. Lynn, 64, 66–67
May, Henry F., 16, 23
McBride, Dwight A., 73, 74, 94
McKay, Michelle, 83, 85–87, 96
McKay, Nellie, 7
meditatio, 133–34, 142–43, 145, 148, 157, 175, 189, 202n1, 203–5n3
Melville, Herman, 26, 53
Metamorphoses, Ovid, 149
Meyhew, Jonathan, 126
Middle Passage, 31, 130
Miller, Perry, 93
Milton, John, 74, 80–81, 83, 125, 132, 136–37, 166, 169, 172–73, 198n2, 202n2; "L'Allegro," 109; "Il Penseroso," 109
Mollien, G., 103–4
Monk, Samuel Holt, 151, 158, 159, 205n7
Morris, David B., 22, 135, 157
Morrison, Toni, 186, 190–91
Mossell, Gertrude E. H. Bustill (N. F. Mossell), 55
Mossell, N. F. *See* Mossell, Gertrude E. H. Bustill
Mulford, Carla, 87–88
Munzing, Helen, 73
muse(s), 8–9, 36–37, 49, 53, 57, 68, 72, 80, 86, 89–90, 103, 109–10, 131, 136, 142, 147, 166, 168–73, 175, 177–79, 196n26, 203n1, 204n3, 207n12
music in poetry, 19, 37, 67, 83, 103–4, 106, 109–12, 168, 200n10

Native Americans, 103, 138, 147, 180–81
Nelson, Dana D., 198n3
neoclassicism, 11, 12, 18, 45, 59–60, 69, 87, 89
Nielsen, A. L., 72
Night Thoughts, Edward Young, 125

"Niobe in Distress . . ." 25, 36, 39–40, 80, 110, 117–20, 136–37, 142, 160, 170, 179

Occom, Samson, 35, 72, 81, 187
"Ocean," 25, 74
Oddell, Margaretta M., 31, 53–55, 58, 72, 97, 99, 101, 103, 127–28, 182, 194n7, 198n1
Odyssey, 125, 149
"Ode to Neptune," 25, 170
"Ode to a Nightingale," John Keats, 80, 176
Ogude, S. E., 9–10, 72
Ogunyemi, Chikweyne Okonjo, 64
Okpewho, Isidore, 110, 112, 118–20, 201n18, 202n19
"On Being Brought from Africa to America," 59, 62, 74–79, 88, 106–8, 116, 128, 148, 200n11
"On the Death of Dr. Samuel Marshall," 77, 120, 146
"On the Death of General Wooster," 16, 33, 81, 96, 111–13, 201n14
"On the Death of J.C. an Infant," 52, 56
"On the Death of Mr. Snyder Murder'd by Richardson," 33, 95, 104–5
"On the Death of the Rev. Dr. Sewell, 1789," 128–29
"On the Death of the Rev. Mr. George Whitefield," 6, 29, 62, 77, 114–17
"On the Death of a Young Gentleman," 202–3n3
"On Imagination," 1, 3, 20–21, 25–26, 36, 39–40, 51–52, 56, 61–62, 71, 77, 79–80, 83–84, 86–88, 96, 110, 134, 137, 144, 150, 152, 157–60, 165, 168, 170, 175–76, 186–87, 203n1
"On Messrs. Hussey and Coffin," 34, 195n17
"On Recollection," 8, 25–26, 36, 40, 62, 73, 84, 144, 150, 155, 170, 172, 186

"On Virtue," 138, 170, 173
O'Neale, Sondra, 72–73, 82
orality, 119–20
Orlando Furioso, Ludovico Ariosto, 161
Ovid, 118–20, 170

paean, 109
Pain, Philip, 133
Paine, Thomas, 49, 89, 130
painting and poetics, 150–51, 156
panegyrics, 24, 53, 89, 103–4, 112–14, 117–18, 121–23, 188
Paradise Lost, John Milton, 36, 79–80, 173, 177
Paradiso, Dante, 174
Pascal, Blaise, 132–35, 175–76
pastoral, 19, 45, 91, 99, 147, 150, 166, 178–79
pastoral elegy, 19, 147
Peri Hupsous, Longinus, 125, 151, 173
Perkins, William, 153, 161, 182
Peters, John, 31, 58–59
Peterson, Merrill D., 2
Philosophical Enquiry into the Origin of Our Ideas of the Sublime and Beautiful, A, Edmund Burke, 126
Phillips, John, 125
"Phillis's Reply," 97, 99
Piersen, William D., 36
pietas, 19, 93
Pietas et Gratulatio, 92, 147, 155, 162, 163–66
Pindaric ode, 150, 203n1
Plato, 156
Plato, Ann, 47
Pleasures of Imagination, Mark Akenside, 86, 125
Poe, Edgar Allan, 162, 191
Poems on Various Subjects, Religious and Moral, 1, 3, 5–7, 21, 26–27, 29, 33, 40, 48–53, 65, 67–68, 73, 75–77, 81–83, 88, 93, 95–96, 106, 108, 113, 117, 127–28, 131–32, 146, 149, 162, 165, 169, 177, 180–81, 189, 193n2–3, 195n14, 198n1, 200n11, 201n16, 206n8

INDEX

political liberty. *See* liberation poetics
political poems or poetry, 32, 33, 34, 35, 89, 94–96, 105, 113, 126, 151–52, 163–64, 181
politic(s), 13, 15–17, 22, 27–29, 32–35, 63, 75, 89–91, 93–96, 105, 112–13, 121, 126, 151, 163–64, 167, 181, 186–87, 194n10, 197n1, 205n
Pope, Alexander, 4–5, 9, 11–13, 18, 21, 22, 54, 59, 66, 74, 79, 81, 83, 88, 111, 125–26, 136, 149, 166, 169–70, 172–73, 178, 198n2, 201n13, 206n8
Porter, Dorothy, 65
Potts, Abbie F., 20, 195n4
Prepatory Meditations, Edward Taylor, 195–96n17
preromanticism, 18–20
Price, Martin, 134–35, 175
Prince, Thomas, 127–28
Proposal, first (1772), 6–7, 25, 29–30, 67, 77, 96, 108, 193n2
Proposal, second (1779), 29, 90
Proverbs 1:7, 138
Puritanism, 10, 23, 153–54, 182, 201n17, 203–5n3

Quarrels, Francis, 133
Quinn, Charles A., 199n6

racism. *See* African Americans
Rape of the Lock, The, Alexander Pope, 36
Redding, J. Saunders, 59–60, 64, 68, 74, 81, 89, 194n10
Reed, Joseph, 49
Renfro, G. Herbert, 45, 57–58
Rice, Eugene F., Jr., 139, 143–45
Richards, Phillip M., 73
Richmond, Merle A., 63, 101, 199n5
Riesman, Paul, 103, 121, 182–83
Rigsby, Gregory, 67, 205n6
Robinson, William, H., 1, 6, 30–31, 62–63, 66–67,
71–72, 74, 98–99, 103, 130, 193n1–2, 194n7, 195n14, 197n1, 198n1, 198n3
Romanticism, 4–5, 19–20, 23, 25, 42, 52, 54, 57, 158, 162, 177, 190, 197–98n2
Rush, Benjamin, 12, 50, 63

Sacred Theory of the Earth, Thomas Burnet, 141
Sacks, Peter M., 21
Sagesse, de la, Pierre Charron, 139–40, 144–45, 162
Sancho, Ignatius, 9
Scheick, William J., 83, 87–89, 96
Schomburg, Arthur H., 57–58, 66, 74
Seccombe, Joseph, 126, 138–42, 145, 155, 162–63, 182
secularization, 18, 22, 125, 135, 137, 141–42, 145, 180, 182
Seeber, Edward Derbyshire, 197n2
Sewall, Joseph, 11, 24, 121–22, 127–32, 137–39, 141, 147, 154–55, 167, 182
sexism. *See* women, prejudices against
Shaftsbury, Earl of, 155, 157–58, 189, 203–5n3
Shakespeare, William, 125, 166, 172–73
Shenstone, William, 125
solar worship, 77, 85, 100–102, 109, 125, 130, 137–38, 143, 148, 174, 180–81, 188–89, 195n16, 206n9
Souls of Black Folk, W. E. B. DuBois, 84
Spectator, Joseph Addison, 158
Stedman, John G., 20, 52
sublime, 18–9, 21–22, 40, 73, 125, 134–35, 137, 151, 155, 157–61, 163, 165, 173, 178, 205n4, 205n7, 206n8

Tanner, Obour, 31, 130
Taylor, Edward, 5, 133, 195–96n17, 203–5n3
Terence, 10, 47, 179
Terry, Lucy, 47
Thomson, James, 22, 126, 169, 172–73, 206n8–9; *The Seasons*, 125
Thornton, John, 34, 146–47, 180–81
"Thoughts on the Works of Providence," 19, 25–26, 34, 40, 62, 102, 113, 133–34, 138, 140, 142, 150–51, 160, 172, 174–75, 186
"To a Clergyman on the Death of his Lady," 171–72
"To a Gentleman and Lady on the Death of the Lady's . . ." 202–3n3
"To a Gentleman of the Navy," 25
"To His Excellency General Washington," 3, 33, 49, 91, 96, 104–5, 113–14, 164
"To the Honorable T.H. Esq.; on the Death of His Daughter," 202–3n3
"To the King's Most Excellent Majesty," 33, 95–96, 112–14
"To a Lady on the Death of Her Children . . ." 202–3n3
"To Maecenas," 10, 25–26, 40, 47–48, 53, 78, 80, 149–50, 177–78, 186
"To Mrs. Leonard on the Death of Her Husband," 146
"To the Right Honorable William, Earl of Dartmouth," 33, 52, 55, 73, 75, 97–98, 113
"To Samuel Quincy, Esq; a Panegyrick," 95, 112
"To S.M. a Young African Painter, On Seeing His Works," 3, 25, 62, 113, 170
"To the University of Cambridge in New England," 72, 138, 170
Treatise on the Religious Affections, Jonathan Edwards, 93, 163
Turell, Jane, 15

Two Treaties on Government, John Locke, 126
Tyler, Moses Coit, 56–57, 58, 68
Tyndale, William, 153–55, 161

Vendler, Helen, 76, 78, 197n1
Vergil, 19, 91, 125, 136, 147, 149–50, 154, 178–79
Voltaire, 20, 49, 197n2
Vulgate (Latin version of Bible), Jerome, 154

Walcott, Roger, 133
Walker, Alice, 65, 106, 200n9
Walker, Cheryl, 6, 194n4
Walker v. Jennison, 32
Warren, Mercy Otis, 33
Warren, Joseph, 126
Washington, George, 1, 3–4, 49–50, 89–91, 104, 142
Watts, Isaac, 171
Webster, Noah, 12
Wellek, Rene, 18–19, 194n2
Wesley, Charles, 114–17, 122; "An Elegy on the Late Reverend George Whitefield," 114
Wesley, John, 115
Wheatley, John, 7, 30, 79, 82, 97, 127–28, 149, 188–89, 197n1
Wheatley, Mary, 82, 87, 89, 97, 127, 197n1
Wheatley, Nathaniel, 82, 89, 97, 197n1
Wheatley, Phillis, 1–13, 15–69, 71–123, 125–183, 185–191, 193n1–3, 194n7, 194n9–10, 195n14, 195n16–17, 197n3–4, 198n1–3, 199n5, 200n8, 200n11–12, 201n14, 201n16, 202n20, 202n2–3, 203n1, 203n3, 205n5–6, 206n8–9, 207n13–14; African heritage, 4, 8–10, 13, 15, 17, 23–25, 30–31, 33, 36, 40, 42, 62, 72, 78, 85, 97–104, 106–9, 117–18, 120–23, 131, 137–38, 145–46, 148, 171, 180, 182–83, 185, 188–90 (*see also* Gambia); classicism in work, 5, 11, 12, 35–37, 45, 80, 101, 109, 118, 120, 131–32, 136, 142, 145–46, 148–51, 170–71, 174, 179–82, 185, 189–91, 202n2, 206–7n9; education, 30, 35–36, 38, 52, 54, 77, 82, 87–88, 97, 102–4, 108, 125–28, 138, 149, 165, 182; origins, chapter four; and politics (*see* politic(s); on racism, 1–3, 6, 7, 45, 47–48, 67–68, 167, 180, 186, 198n3; and slavery, 15–17, 17, 22–23, 25–26, 28–30, 40–41, 51–53, 55, 57, 59, 64, 73–76, 81, 83–86, 94–95, 97, 99, 103, 106, 108, 113, 128, 130, 144, 165, 175, 177, 179, 181, 186–87, 193–94n3, 206n8; subversion in, 15, 21, 25–26, 45, 64, 72, 77–78, 81, 83, 91–92, 95, 107–8, 178, 181–82, 186–87
Wheatley, Susannah, 53, 67, 82, 97, 103, 116, 127–28, 146, 149, 167, 188–89, 197n1
Whitefield, George, 6, 29, 94, 114–17, 122, 139, 162, 206n9
Whitlow, Roger, 63
wisdom, 7, 24, 26, 28, 34, 37, 41, 75, 77, 80, 83–84, 88, 94, 121, 125, 131, 134, 138–47, 151, 158–59, 162, 165, 174, 179, 182, 185, 187, 189, 204n3
Wilson, Gold Refined, 130, 198n2
Witham, W. Tasker, 61
Wollstonecraft, Mary, 20, 51
women, prejudices against, 4–8, 17, 21, 24, 33, 43–44, 47, 58, 82, 103, 121, 182–83
Wood, Marcus, 75–76
Woodson, Carter G., 99
Wooster, David, 16, 81, 90
Wordsworth, William, 21, 51, 79, 178, 197n1
Work and Days, Hesiod, 137
Wright, Richard, 61

Young, Edward, 22, 74, 126, 207n14

Zafar, Rafia, 73